AF445423

EXPLORING MICHIGAN'S SUNRISE COASTS

LAKE ERIE
DETROIT RIVER
LAKE ST. CLAIR
ST. CLAIR RIVER
LAKE HURON

LUNA PIER TO MACKINAC ISLAND

Copyright 2022 Julie Albrecht Royce
LENKK PRESS
Editor: Violet Moore
Cover Design: Bob Royce
Cover Photo *Edwin H. Gott* crossing under the Mackinac Bridge, Courtesy of Gary Martin, coastalbeacons.com
ISBN 979-8-9855037-0-8

For Courtney and Jes

You may have caused a few of my gray hairs, but you are also my gift to the world and my greatest source of pride. I couldn't love you more.

No matter where you go or how often you return, your roots are pure Michigan.

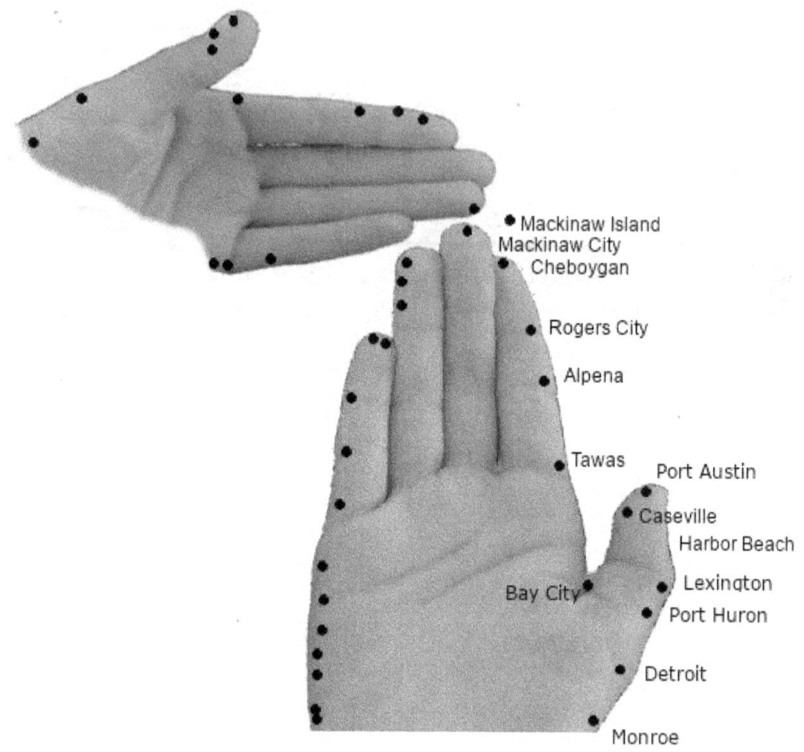

Hand Map of Michigan
with Cities Along the Sunrise Coasts

Why is Michigan a great state? There are numerous reasons, but somewhere on that list is one claim that no other place in the country can match. Michiganders carry their state map at the end of their wrists.

"Where are you from?" is the standard opening question, whether you meet someone on a cruise ship, at a party, or on a Florida beach where snowbirds fly in the winter. You hold up your right hand and with the index finger of your left, indicate the spot near the knuckle of your thumb, and say, "Lexington."

TABLE OF CONTENTS

BOOK ONE
EXPLORING MICHIGAN'S SUNRISE COASTS

Welcome to Michigan. Courtesy of Bob Royce.

FOUR OUT OF FIVE GREAT LAKES PREFER MICHIGAN

Largest Cities Along the Sunrise Coasts

The nine largest cities along Michigan's Sunrise Coastlines from worldpopulationreview.com 2019 Census are:

Detroit 713,898

Dearborn 93,587

St. Clair Shores 60,104

Grosse Pointe 46,000 (total for the five Pointes)

Bay City 32,661

Port Huron 29,762

Monroe 19,439

New Baltimore 12,449

Alpena 10,483

INTRODUCTION AND OVERVIEW

In an earlier life, Julie Royce was a Michigan First Assistant Attorney General and worked for then-Attorney General, Jennifer Granholm. The year 2003 brought changes for both Ms. Granholm and Ms. Royce. Granholm became the 47th Governor of Michigan. Royce took a state-offered early out and retired. Her husband, Bob, and she moved to the little beach town of Lexington in Michigan's Thumb. They bought a condominium overlooking the harbor just steps from the home where she was born.

During the Royces' first summer in Lexington, Governor Granholm visited a local restaurant and gave a pro-Michigan speech. She exhorted her audience to spread the word about what an amazing place Michigan was to live and visit. Royce, a would-be-author, caught the fever.

That evening, she and six of her friends sat around a table with a view of Lake Huron's shoreline. Spurred by the governor's passion, Royce announced, "I am going to write a travel book about Michigan's Thumb."

One of the guests stared her straight in the eyes and asked, "And what will you put on page two?"

Her enthusiasm undaunted, and possibly aided by the fact that attorneys are verbose, she managed a 269-page travel book that was carried in local gift shops. The first half of the book included lodging, restaurants, and shops. However, it missed much of what was important—the history and local lore. Royce believed that travelers wanted a better understanding of the places to which they traveled and some interesting background reading.

She created a second half to the book called, *A Bit of History and a Bit of Fun*. It provided the background about the area. Royce enjoyed researching and writing the Thumb book so much that she authored a guide to Michigan's Sunset Coast. She had plans to write a third book focusing on the Upper Peninsula coastlines. Before she achieved that goal, life transplanted her to California. But she never lost her love for Michigan. After several years, and significant change in the travel industry, she returned her attention to her home state. She wanted to follow the St. Lawrence Seaway as it defined Michigan's borders.

How we obtain information had changed since Thunder Bay Press published *Traveling Michigan's Thumb* and *Traveling Michigan's Sunset Coast* more than a decade earlier. Today's travelers turn to the internet for information about hotels, motels, and eateries. When they want hours, prices, or maps, they go online. There are cellphone apps for every travel function.

The upside of these changes is immediacy. By the time the earlier books were published, several places had closed. New businesses had sprouted. However, the information included in the second half of the previous guides still offered background and interesting local stories.

Thus, was born the idea of a traveler's companion to Michigan's Great Lakes waterways and coastal towns and villages. It envisioned a trip starting on I-75 in Michigan's southeast corner, travel along Lake Erie, the Detroit River, Lake St. Clair, St. Clair River, Lake Huron, St. Mary's River, Lake Superior's southern coast, and Lake Michigan's northern and sunset coasts. The route ended at Michigan's most southwestern point. What started as a one-book project ended up filling three volumes.

Exploring Michigan's Sunrise Coasts includes city histories, museums, parks, beaches, lighthouses, ghost stories, shipwrecks, stories about the famous or infamous with ties to the lakeshores, disasters that shaped the state, and movies and books set along the many Sunrise Coasts of Michigan. (Elmore Leonard planted *The Big Bounce* in Michigan's Thumb.) The reader could turn to the internet for specific details, and the web could provide the latest updates. What Royce visualized was a traveler's companion to add flavor.

This book doesn't include the types of shops most susceptible to frequent turnover. The few art galleries mentioned are only a sampling, and they have a long business history. They were open as these travel books were researched. With COVID-19 and fluctuations in business climate, it is wise to call if a gallery or museum is your reason for a trip. Otherwise, walk the small town, and you'll likely find that if one gallery has closed, another has sprung up to replace it.

Royce did not add a bibliography. Much of what is included in these guides is stories—no way to prove the truth. While she has enjoyed the research, these are not meant to be historical reference books.

The Mackinac Bridge. Courtesy of Gary Martin.

The Mackinac Bridge connects the lower peninsula to the upper peninsula and Lake Huron to Lake Michigan. It is a widely recognized iconic symbol of the Great Lakes State.

Legends. The following categories have been included, as applicable, for each city or stop:

- MUSEUMS
- BEACHES, PARKS, AND TRAILS
- OTHER STOPS TO CONSIDER
- LIGHTHOUSES
- SHIPWRECKS
- THE FAMOUS OR INFAMOUS WITH TIES TO THE CITY
- BOOKS AND MOVIES WITH TIES TO THE CITY
- GHOST STORIES

From Lake Erie Shipwreck Exhibit. Courtesy of Pixabay Free Images.

Note about Shipwrecks. Some wrecks will be included with information about the lake that cradles their bones, as in the case of Lake Erie's Marquette & Bessemer #2 or the G.P. Griffith because it is often impossible to know exactly where the ship went down. Some wrecks, however, are covered in the discussion of a specific city since the ill-fated ship sank in nearby waters. In a few cases, you can dive and explore her remains.

LAKE ERIE

Three billion years ago the underlying structure for the Great Lakes Basin was created during the Precambrian Era, a time marked by major volcanic activity and glaciers. The volcanoes formed great mountains, and the melting of the glaciers formed huge glacial lakes. The original lakes, left behind by these retreating glaciers, were much larger than the Great Lakes as we know them today. Evidence of their original size can be seen in the beach ridges and eroded bluffs hundreds of feet above and beyond the current shore.

Lake Erie claims only a few miles of the Southeast Michigan coastline. Erie also borders parts of Ohio, Pennsylvania, New York, and Ontario, Canada. The lake is 569 feet above sea level and is the shallowest of the Great Lakes with an average depth of 62 feet and a maximum depth of 210 feet. Erie is the smallest of the five by volume at 116 cubic miles of water. Erie's name came from the Iroquois word *erielhonan*, which translates as long tail. If you enter Michigan on I-75 from the South, just past Toledo, you'll travel roughly parallel to Lake Erie alongside the cities of Luna Pier and Monroe before Erie gives way to the Detroit River.

No matter where you travel in Michigan, you are never more than 85 miles from the shore of one of the state's fabulous Great Lakes. Forty of Michigan's eighty-three counties border a Great Lake. If that's not enough water to satisfy you, Michigan has more than 11,000 inland lakes. They, however, will remain the subject of other travel guides.

Walking the Beach

How better to greet the morning? Michiganders are blessed with over 3,000 miles of shoreline, compared to Florida's approximate 2,000, and California's meager 1,000.

There cannot be a person alive, at least not in Michigan, who hasn't enjoyed the simple, relaxing pleasure of walking a beach. It frees us to indulge that overwhelming urge to shed sandals and feel the sand massage our toes or the shallow water cool our bare feet.

Your Right to Walk the Beach

There has been an ongoing debate in Michigan over what exactly are your rights to walk the beach. Property owners on occasion post signs declaring the beach in front of their cottages "Private," or warn you to "Keep Out." Beach walkers have worried that they have no right to walk along the shore. Sometimes, seduced by the great lake's majesty, they ignored their guilt and simply did it anyway, suffering the fear that someone would burst out a front door, scream at them, or shoo them away.

In 2005 the Michigan Supreme Court heard the issue of who owns the beaches, or at least that narrow strip at the water's edge. One side argued that citizens did not have a right to walk on land they did not own. The other side retorted that the beach at the water's edge is held in public trust, and everyone can enjoy the delight of walking along it.

The Supreme Court's ruling, although not providing complete clarification, declared that the land up to the "ordinary high-water mark" is not owned by individual land owners, and anyone can walk on it. Of course, the question begging additional elucidation was how you determine the ordinary high-water mark. It is not always as easily distinguished as the high court would suggest. Regardless, you are probably safe walking the water's edge without fear of being chastised—at least not —by anyone.

Searching for Treasure along the Shore

Every child, or the child in every one, thrills not just to walking the beach, but to finding treasures in the midst of such splendor.

It is easy to spot limestone, shale, slate, granite, and quartzite along the lakeshores. You can also find driftwood along the Great Lakes. Each lake, however, offers its own unique prize: Lake Erie, sea glass; Lake Huron, Pudding Stones; Lake Superior, Agates; and Lake Michigan, Petoskey Stones.

Shale, Slate, and Skipping Stones

Shale is a sedimentary rock formed by deposits of successive layers of clay or volcanic ash. Slate is a fine-grained, homogeneous, sedimentary rock which has been metamorphosed from shale to the harder and more permanent slate. Neither is very pretty, and both are common along lakeshores.

Shale appears to crumble in layers. The value of this stone to a beach walker is its worthiness as a perfect skipping stone. The ancient amusement of skipping stones is quite possibly as old as the relationship between man and lakes. Different countries call it by different names, but everywhere there is a lake, there is the pastime of skipping stones over its surface. The British call it stone skimming. The Irish reference it as stone skiffing. To the Danes, it is smutting, and to the French it is ricochet. Guinness listed 38 jumps, or skips, as a record.

If you can throw a stone at (not into) the water so it hits at the correct angle to make it touch the surface and jump up from the water at least once, you have skipped a stone.

The point, of course, is to make it skip as many times as possible.

Driftwood

Pieces of wood fall into the lake, are subjected to long periods of tossing and tumbling in the waves and sand, and are transformed into driftwood. Chunks often look contorted. Because the wood is dead, once dried it is very light. Large specimens are interesting adornments to gardens and lawns. Smaller pieces can be added to floral arrangements, centerpieces, or set on a shelf as a natural sculpture.

Beach Glass

Beach glass is formed when broken pieces of glass are worn smooth by years of waves pitching them about in the sand and rocks. They are shaped naturally, and no two pieces are ever alike. Sea glass is used to make jewelry and for a variety of hobby and decorative purposes.

Clear glass turns into a milky white piece of sea glass through the polishing process. You will also discover brown and green pieces. The rarest and most difficult pieces to find are blue.

Picking up sea glass is a redemptive process. It allows you to take something that has been discarded and declared useless and celebrate its transformation. You carry the tiny bits home, for whatever purpose you have declared their destiny, hoping to preserve a memory.

Some may snub their nose and declare, "It's just broken glass." The proper retort is, "Yes, but in the same way a diamond is just a lump of coal."

● BOOKS WITH TIES TO THE GREAT LAKES

Dan Egan, ***The Death and Life of the Great Lakes*** (2017). A chilling, compelling, and cautiously optimistic nonfictional account of how we have abused the Great

Lakes. The five lakes hold at least 20 percent of the world's freshwater supply. They are the source of drinking water for forty million people. Yet we have allowed manufacturers to pollute them, and ocean vessels coming through the St. Lawrence Seaway to dump ballast water and introduce invading predator species like the sea lamprey, alewives, and zebra mussel, all of which could spell environmental disaster for the freshwater seas. Asian carp remain a threat. Scientists strive to prevent these invaders from making their way from rivers into the lakes where their presence could ring another death knell for those lesser bodies of water.

This is not a beach read. In spite of its serious and exhausting narrative, the author fashions an absorbing account of human arrogance, carelessness, and well-intentioned mistakes that have threatened the lakes' ecosystem. Egan's highly-acclaimed book is a must-read for anyone who loves the Great Lakes and cares about their survival.

<<>>

Author Herman Melville in his classic, **Moby Dick**, describes Great Lakes sailors in chapter 53, The Town-Ho. Of course, Town-Ho meant something different in 1851 when Melville's book was published! The protagonist, Ishmael, is recounting a story he passed on previously—and swears to the truth of—about Steelkilt, a lakeman. "This lakeman," the author writes, "in the landlocked heart of our America had yet been nurtured by all those agrarian freebooting impressions popularly connected with the open ocean. For in their interflowing aggregate, those grand freshwater seas of ours—Erie, and Ontario, and Huron, and Superior, and Michigan—possess an ocean-like expansiveness, with many of the ocean's noblest traits; with many of its rimmed varieties of races and climes . . . they float alike the full-rigged merchant ship, the armed cruiser of the State, the steamer, and the beech canoe; they are swept by Borean and dismasting blasts as direful as any that lash the salted wave; they know what shipwrecks are, for out of sight of land, however inland, they have drowned full many a midnight ship with all its shrieking crew. Thus, gentlemen, though an inlander, Steelkilt was wild-ocean born, and wild-ocean nurtured."

• SHIPWRECKS OF LAKE ERIE

Marquette & Bessemer #2. It is estimated that the Great Lakes are the graveyard for 8,000 ill-fated ships. Lake Erie claimed about a quarter of them. Of the 2,000 or so that sunk to her murky, shallow bottom, fewer than 400 have been found. One of the most mysterious is the steamship *Marquette & Bessemer #2,* a train-car ferry.

President Franklin Roosevelt declared December 7, 1941, a day that would live on in infamy. Thirty-two years prior to that pronouncement, on December 7, 1909, Lake Erie suffered her own lesser-known tragedy—one that claimed the lives of the thirty crew members and the one passenger aboard the *Marquette & Bessemer #2.*

The ship set sail from Conneaut, Ohio, for Port Stanley, Ontario, Canada. Shortly after her departure, a massive storm bore down on the great lake, blowing winds to 70 knots and forcing temperatures from 40°F to 10°F in less than twenty-four hours. Five days later, a lifeboat containing the frozen bodies of nine of the steamer's crew was found.

With the body of Steward George R. Smith were two large knives and a meat cleaver from the ship's galley. It is believed the lifeboat originally held ten men because the clothes of a tenth person were found aboard. Rumors persisted that the tenth person went mad and jumped overboard. Only five other bodies from the *Marquette & Bessemer No. 2* were ever found. One of them, the corpse of the ship's Captain Robert McLeod, washed ashore nearly a year later. It had sustained severe slash wounds. The source of the captain's injuries, combined with the knives found on Steward Smith's body, fueled speculation about what might have happened during the final moments of this disaster. Those questions, along with the final resting place of the ship, remain a mystery. With no survivors who witnessed the horror, the *Marquette & Bessemer #2* holds tight to her secrets.

After the wreck, the general manager of the Marquette and Bessemer Company said, "It is my opinion that the heavy seas broke the key which held the cars in place and weighted heavily with coal, they raced to the stern of the boat.

"She probably turned turtle and sank without a minute's warning. This is borne out by the fact that the men were splendidly drilled, and only a short time would have sufficed for them to launch the boats, which with proper handling, would ride almost any storm."

<<>>

Marquette and Bessemer #2.
Courtesy of Wikipedia, Public Domain.

G. P. Griffith. The Great Lakes waterways carried millions of immigrants to their piece of the promised land. A few thousand of those travelers never made it. On June 18, 1850, the paddlewheel steamer, *S.S. G.P. Griffith* earned the dubious honor of Lake Erie's greatest nautical disaster. The previous night, the *Griffith* had departed Buffalo with 326 passengers, mostly German immigrants, headed for Cleveland to join relatives who had settled there.

Fire erupted in the cargo hold. The ship beelined toward land but struck a sandbar a half mile from shore. En masse, passengers leaped into the water. Some were churned under by the paddle wheels. Some were knocked unconscious by those who landed on top of them. The next day, a few lucky ones—thirty men and one woman—made it to shore and were rescued.

Estimates placed the dead at between 241 and 289. The ship's manifest was never found so it was impossible to know for sure. It was the largest Great Lakes tragedy up to that point, and even today remains the third most deadly disaster on the lakes, after the *S.S. Eastland* and the *Lady Elgin* both of which went down in Lake Michigan.

The *G.P. Griffith.*
Courtesy of Wikipedia. Public Domain.

As the bodies of the *Griffith's* dead washed up over the next few days, most were interred in a mass grave. In a ghoulish postscript, visitors to the site saw that the grave had been plundered, leaving the corpses exposed. It was common knowledge that immigrants sailed to their new country carrying with them the entire sum of their wealth. Ten days after the wreck, additional bodies began to wash ashore. These later corpses had been weighted down by gold-filled money belts. As the remains bloated, they rose to the surface. Any bodies that could be identified were taken to Cleveland.

1. Luna Pier

Six miles into your sojourn around Michigan's Coastline, you can take Exit 6 from I-75 and find yourself with one of your first views of Lake Erie. Sunrise can be spectacular. Established in the early years of the twentieth century and originally known as Lakewood, Luna Pier is a small city (2020 population 1,503) in Monroe County.

Welcome to Luna Pier. Courtesy of Bob Royce.

Luna Pier was a resort for residents of Toledo and Detroit, offering an 800-foot crescent-shaped pier made of concrete and flanked by a sandy beach with a manmade rock embankment. For today's traveler, entering Michigan from the southeast, it provides your first chance to pay homage to Michigan's sand and water.

● Ghost Stories and a Sea Monster

Camp Lady of the Lake comes in several versions. People have a hard time agreeing which haunting of Camp Lady of the Lake—if any—bears a semblance to truth. These are the main versions passed around. You can decide for yourself.

Story one. In the early 1900s, in the area which became Camp Lady of the Lake in Monroe County, there was a fifteen-or-sixteen-year-old girl named Florence who fell in love. She and her sweetheart were separated when World War I broke out. The young man enlisted and shipped out to fight for his country. He died on a blood-soaked battlefield.

This was too much for Florence. Her mind couldn't cope with the tragedy. Her depression, delusions, or other mental deterioration caused neighbors to describe her as feebleminded. Florence embraced a single-minded goal in life—to be reunited with her lost lover. She wandered into the woods on a bright sunny day that seemed to encourage life. She sat with her back to a large maple and closed her eyes. She saw him. He waited . . . encouraged her. From the oversized-pocket of her dress, she extracted her father's pistol. She aimed the muzzle upward from beneath her chin and pulled the trigger.

To this day, some people believe that Florence's ghost haunts the nearby woods, roaming about, and standing by the lakeshore looking for her young suitor. Some folks say they have seen her. Locals have dubbed her the Lady of the Lake.

Various witnesses claim to have captured electronic voice recordings of her laughter, while others insist they have snapped pictures including one of a young girl dressed in radiating white. The pictures of her ghost included in various publications, however, often appear to be out-of-focus shots of fog.

Story two suggests there was a camp (Camp Lady of the Lake) in Luna Pier that was opened as a place to send orphans. It burned down sometime in the late 60s or early 70s when the woman in charge of the camp left after dark to take a walk. While she was gone, fire broke out, and the children were burned alive. The camp is haunted by the ghosts of these unfortunate youngsters.

A third story alleges the area is the haunt of young girls killed by construction workers employed to build more cabins. The girls' ghosts seem to favor proximity to a rusted-out swing set.

Despite attempts to verify the background of Camp Lady of the Lake, a Catholic camp, through church records, nothing useful was found. Some locals call all three stories pure horse pucky while others endeavor to make you a believer.

<<>>

Bessie is a prehistoric-appearing monster that has long and often been reported to live in a watery haunt of Lake Erie. You can stand on the shore in Luna Pier, Monroe, or any other of Lake Erie's shore towns and, if you are lucky, you may spot her.

The description of this sea behemoth paints a doppelganger of the famous Scottish Loch Ness monster. The earliest reports of an odd creature lurking in Lake Erie are traced back centuries to the Native Americans who told tales of a giant water spirit they called Oniare. They described Oniare as a horned water serpent with poisonous breath. The beast capsized canoes and then devoured the vessels' occupants. However, Oniare was partial to offerings and spared those who presented sufficient gifts. Sometimes the Thunder God, Hinon, stepped in to protect hapless victims.

In one ancient story, Rain Old Man transformed two elderly Seneca into young, strong men and then bid them destroy his enemy, a great horned snake. He said, "There is a wide opening extending from one end of the world to the other. In this opening, there is a great rock and in the rock is a person with enormous horns. He is our enemy, and we have tried to kill him, but failed. I have made you young and strong, and now you must crush the rock and destroy this evil foe." The newly transformed, young men did as they were bid. They struck the rock with all their strength. The rock splintered, and a man stepped forward. From his back sprouted the head of an enormous horned serpent, and the men were able to kill the man-snake.

Perhaps the first recorded encounter of the sea monster occurred in 1793. The captain of the sloop *Felicity* was hunting ducks when he spotted a snake-like creature more than 16 feet long undulating through the water.

Numerous additional reports have surfaced since 1793. In July 1817, a ship's crew sighted the animal and described it as 40 feet long with a body a foot in diameter, covered with grayish scales. It was no ordinary reptile or fish and resembled a Brontosaurus or Plesiosaurus. About that same time, or only months removed, another crew claimed to observe a copper-colored creature 60 feet long. Either the animal was growing or the imaginations were. The second crew fired at the beast with muskets which were ineffectual.

A third incident that same year involved the Dusseau brothers, who reported coming upon a huge, beached monster they described as looking like a 30-foot-long sturgeon with arms. When the brothers returned with help, all that remained were silver dollar-sized scales.

Time and the stories moved forward. On May 5, 1896, four eyewitnesses claim to have watched for forty-five minutes while a 30-foot serpent churned up the water as it swam about before disappearing shortly before nightfall. They described what they saw as possessing a dog-shaped head and pointy tail.

By July 1892, newspapers grew curious after a sighting reported by the crew of a ship bound for Toledo. The ship's course took it a half mile from an area of foaming and swirling water. The sailors moved closer and saw the thing "wrestling about in the waters as if fighting with an unseen foe." They watched the creature relax and stretch out full length—estimated at 50 feet long and four feet thick—with its head sticking up above the water an additional four feet. The crew described the animal's eyes as "viciously sparkling."

Sightings continued over the years. In September 1990, there were at least two more noteworthy reports. The first, on September 4, involved the Harold Bricker family. The Brickers spotted the creature, by then named Bessie, as it swam about a fifth of a mile away. A few days later, September 11, 1990, Jim Johnson and Steve Dircks reported seeing the long-rumored beast from a third story building where they claimed it lay motionless in the water for several minutes.

With reports coming nearly every year, folks grew to believe there had to be some truth to the many stories. *The Daily Register* of Sandusky, Ohio, carried the story that the monster was able to live both on land and in water, and called it a "fierce, ugly, coiling thing." Rewards were offered to anyone who captured Bessie alive.

By the 1990s, with expanded interest, locals figured out how to capitalize on their prehistoric-like monster. The *Wall Street Journal* ran an article on July 29, 1993, that took a skeptical approach to the tales dubbing them a shrewd marketing ploy aimed at drawing tourists.

From the early Native American tales that warned the monster ate humans to the early 2000s, the animal seemed to shun or at least cause no harm to humans. Its peaceful nature took a sharp about-face on August 13, 2001, when something weird and unknown began attacking swimmers. These assaults, reported in the *Ottawa Citizen*, started an investigation into what might be hiding beneath the waters with its sights set on hapless humans.

The natural suspects—lamprey eels, invading round gobies, muskellunge, and turtles—were ruled out. Bowfin, a stalking, ambush predator, was not excluded. Bowfins are prehistoric fish relics that continue to lurk in reedy, shallow, inland waters and prey at night. Bessie wasn't officially considered a possible culprit. One thing is certain. If a swimmer was bitten by a 60-foot-long, snake-like predator, that swimmer would remember it.

Lake Sturgeon. Pixabay Free Images.

David Davies, a fisheries biologist familiar with the Great Lakes, spent considerable hours on the inland sea, Erie. Asked to speculate on what the monster might be, he quipped, "It looks like a brontosaurus, don't you think?" In his more serious moments, he opined the animal might be a large specimen of the lake sturgeon which can live 150 years, weigh more than 300 pounds, and grow longer than seven feet. In many ways the sturgeon seems caught in a prehistoric time warp. Although Davies was joking when he suggested it might be a dinosaur, he wasn't far from the truth since his more serious answer, a sturgeon, suggests a fish that co-existed during the time of dinosaurs. Once abundant in all five lakes, the sturgeon was overfished for its eggs which were dubbed the poor man's caviar.

In the summer of 1998, a Lake Erie fisherman caught a 7-foot, 4-inch, 250-pound sturgeon. You come across this guy or his bigger brother and mix that sighting with a couple of beers and a bit of imagination . . .? That's one theory of how Bessie came to be.

From all of the hubbub, we can state several facts:

1. Bessie has captured our imaginations. She has had a minor league hockey team named after her, a rock band called itself South Bay Bessie, and maybe most flattering of all is a seasonal beer called Lake Erie Monster showing a picture of Bessie.

Lake Erie Monster Beer.
Pixabay Free Images.

2. While no one knows for certain what inspired the legend of Bessie, when these many stories swim through the waves, it is likely that something unusual is out there.

3. Many folks won't go boating, fishing, or swimming in Lake Erie after the sun sets.

2. THE MONROE WELCOME CENTER

Exit at the 10-mile marker off 1-75 to the Monroe Welcome Center. If you have entered Michigan from the southeast, this will be your first opportunity to gather the specific time-sensitive or current information you will want for your trip. The Gateway Center is worth the time. The building is new, spacious, and chock full of travel offerings for the entire state. Racks and racks of brochures provide information about local festivals, campsites, maps, and other relevant information—all free of charge and dispensed by knowledgeable and friendly staff. They will even help you make motel or campground reservations and warn you of highway construction. In Michigan there is a saying that you will enjoy four seasons: Fall, Winter, Spring, and Highway Construction.

Sign identifies Michigan Rocks.
Courtesy of Bob Royce.

This is an especially interesting stop for geology enthusiasts because a walkway through rock gardens showcases 38 rock samples gathered from throughout Michigan. Each is identified with history about its formation and where it came from.

3. MONROE

Fourteen miles into Michigan as you travel north on 1-75, you will come to Monroe, a city of 19,599 as of the 2020 census. Located on the western shore of Lake Erie, Monroe is the largest city and the county seat of Monroe County.

The area was first settled by Native Americans, predominantly the Potawatomie or Bodawatomie, a tribe of Algonquin origin known as one of the Three Brothers which included Ojibwe and Odawa who lived around Monroe hundreds of years before Europeans arrived in the late seventeenth century. In 1679 Robert de LaSalle, during his exploration on *Le Griffon*, claimed the area for New France.

In 1784 after the American Revolutionary War, the Potawatomie allowed a Canadian named Francis Navarre to settle around the River Raisin. The area became known as Frenchtown, later renamed Monroe during president James Monroe's term in office. In 1837 Michigan became a state, and Monroe was incorporated as a city.

Monroe has a strong military history. During the War of 1812 with Great Britain, it was the site of the Battle of Frenchtown and is remembered for the battle cry, *Remember the Raisin.* Monroe was also the adopted hometown of General George Armstrong Custer who was born in New Rumley, Ohio.

Monroe was the home of La-Z-Boy, the recliner made famous for its popularity in living rooms across the country.

Downtown Monroe. Courtesy of Bob Royce.

Monroe County Historical Museum. Located at 126 South Monroe Street, the museum is the perfect place to pass an afternoon. It houses a large General George Armstrong Custer exhibit. Custer moved to Monroe where he went to school and then married the beautiful Elizabeth Bacon. Bacon's family owned the land on which the museum now sits.

The Original People exhibit has artifacts from early Native American culture and an exhibit devoted to the early French settlers of southeastern Michigan. The museum's extensive Victorian exhibit provides examples of Victorian furniture, glass, decorative arts, and clothing. Archivists and helpful staff provide answers to your questions.

George and Libby Custer. Courtesy of Pixabay Free Images.

An interesting fact from Monroe history was that it was almost the site of a civil war during the Toledo War of 1835. The conflict, also known as the Michigan-Ohio War, was a bloodless dispute that was resolved when Michigan gave up Toledo in exchange for the Upper Peninsula.

● BEACHES, PARKS, AND TRAILS

Sterling State Park, 2800 State Park Drive, provides one of the scarce sandy swimming beaches in the area. It has a boat launch, nature trails (it connects with the Heritage Trail), campgrounds, picnic pavilions, and restrooms. The Lake Erie shoreline in Michigan doesn't boast the state's most favored beaches, so this is a rare gem. If the afternoon is hot, and a day playing in the water is on your agenda, this might be your place. There is a variable entrance fee depending upon whether you want an annual or daily pass and whether you are a Michigan resident.

The **River Raisin Heritage Trail**. If you are looking to get away from it all and commune with nature, this is the spot to check out. The trail connects Sterling State Park, the Ford Marsh located within the Detroit River International Wildlife Refuge, the River Raisin National Battlefield Park, and downtown Monroe. There are eight miles of paved trails for walking and biking. Along the way, you will spot wildlife including bald eagles, migrating birds, ducks, egrets, sandhill cranes, chipmunks, muskrats, and deer. You may even see an occasional shy fox out for a morning stroll. The path starts at East Elm Avenue and North Dixie Highway. The entry to the state park is marked by a metal sign sculpted with an eagle, egret, and other birds.

• OTHER STOPS TO CONSIDER

River Raisin National Battlefield Park.
Courtesy of Bob Royce.

River Raisin National Battlefield Park, 1403 East Elm Avenue. Because of its proximity to Detroit, the area around Monroe was of major importance during the War of 1812. After Fort Detroit surrendered to the British in August 1812, American forces attempted to retake the city. They camped along the River Raisin. A force of 200 Native Americans and 63 Canadian militia were driven to retreat north away from the River Raisin by 600 Kentucky militiamen and 100 French soldiers. This skirmish on January 18, 1813, is referred to as the First Battle of the River Raisin. Days later, on January 22, a force of 800 Native Americans and nearly 600 British fighters surprised the Americans and captured Frenchtown. The American militia were inexperienced, ill-trained, and poorly equipped. They endured horrific losses: 397 killed and 547 captured. It was the largest battle that ever took place on Michigan soil. The British and their allies suffered only minimal losses.

When the British departed for Detroit with their captives, they left the wounded Americans under the guard of a small British detachment fortified by Native American allies. The morning after the battle, other Native Americans descended on Frenchtown, plundered and burned homes, and killed many of the American captives. Those acts gave rise to the battle cry *Remember the Raisin!* which inspired other American troops to victories that ended the War of 1812.

<<>>

The **Battlefield Park Visitor Center** offers a museum with artifacts, exhibits, a 15-minute movie which details the conflict, and a collection of original military firearms.

<<>>

The **Woodland Cemetery**, 438 Jerome Street. Depending on your taste, this may be the perfect afternoon outing. Traipsing around headstones, taking etchings, and making notes may be a reasonable afternoon pursuits for those researching family history. If that's not a pastime of your choosing, you'll be happy to find there are very few graveyards included in this travel guide. But Monroe's Woodland Cemetery provides the final resting places of some of Michigan's most interesting citizens.

One of the state's oldest public cemeteries, it has graves of state pioneers, politicians, and veterans of every U.S. military conflict from the Revolutionary War to Vietnam. It is fascinating (perhaps morbidly so) to stand in front of headstones and imagine the deceased's story. An infant dead at six months. Cholera? An elderly couple dying on the same day. A tragic accident? Suicide? Murder-suicide? Another plague?

Woodland site 26 is the Custer Burial Plot. Interred there are General George Armstrong Custer's parents, Emanuel and Marie, as well as his brother Boston, and nephew Harry Reed, both of whom died with George in the Battle of Little Big Horn. George Armstrong Custer is buried at West Point, NY.

• THE FAMOUS OR INFAMOUS WITH TIES TO MONROE

General George Armstrong Custer is the most famous native son of Monroe. His wife, author Elizabeth Bacon Custer, is well-known in her own right. As a couple, they retain a major place in the history of Monroe.

Statue of George Armstrong Custer.
Courtesy of Bob Royce.

George moved to Monroe in early childhood, attended school there, married Elizabeth "Libbie" Bacon, daughter of a local judge from Monroe, and adopted the city as his hometown. In 1910 the city unveiled a statue in his honor.

The Equestrian statue of General George Armstrong Custer by Edward Clark Potter is located at the corner of

Elm Avenue and North Monroe Street. It was listed on the Register of Historic Places on December 9, 1994.

Custer graduated from West Point in 1861, bottom of his class and known as the cadet who tested boundaries. He garnered 726 demerits while attending the academy, and his record remains one of the worst in the school's history. Although a troublemaker, Custer was also bold, brave, and arrogant. He earned respect in the Civil War and was brevetted brigadier general of volunteers at age 23. At Gettysburg, he commanded the Michigan Cavalry Brigade—the Wolverines. Although greatly outnumbered, he defeated Jeb Stuart at Cemetery Ridge.

History remembers him best for the Battle of the Little Bighorn in Montana Territory, where his 7th Cavalry fought a coalition of Native American tribes led by Crazy Horse. Custer and his entire detachment died in the battle known as *Custer's Last Stand*. With Custer that day, were his youngest brother, Boston Custer, and his nephew, Harry "Autie" Reed.

After her husband's death, Libbie Bacon Custer, who was both beautiful and intelligent, never remarried. She devoted the remainder of her life to George's legacy. Her books and lectures did much to paint her husband as a hero. In retrospect, history has been less kind—especially regarding Little Big Horn.

<<>>

Christie Brinkley, born Christie Lee Hudson, in Monroe in 1954, was the small-town, girl-next-door who became one of the most famous models of all time. Her net worth in 2019 was estimated at $80 million. Brinkley appeared on more than 500 magazine covers.

She later worked as an actress, illustrator, television personality, photographer, writer, designer, and activist for human rights, animal rights, and the environment.

<<>>

Valerie Harper, actress and star of sitcoms *The Mary Tyler Moore Show, Rhoda,* and *Valerie*, grew up in Monroe.

<<>>

Mary Harris Jones, known as Mother Jones, was born in Cork, Ireland, and grew to fame as an activist in the United States. Mary's family first emigrated to Canada where she received enough training to secure a teaching position at a convent in Monroe, Michigan, on August 31, 1859, at the age of 23. She described the school as a "depressing place." Tiring of her profession, Jones moved first to Chicago and then to Memphis.

Mary's life was mired in tragedy. She lost her husband and their four children to a yellow fever epidemic in Memphis. She returned to Chicago and opened a dress shop. She lost her shop and everything she owned in the Great Chicago Fire of 1871. She helped rebuild the city, but during the rebuilding joined the Knights of Labor and began organizing. Among her famous quotes, "I asked a man in prison once how he happened to be there, and he said he had stolen a pair of shoes. I told him if he had stolen a railroad, he would be a United States Senator" and another of her well-known lines, "Mourn the dead, but fight like hell for the living."

<<>>

Kaye Lani Rae Rafko Wilson, crowned Miss America in 1988, was born in Monroe, where a street is now named in her honor. Rafko was the first registered nurse to become Miss America. She was a cohost of *Only in Monroe*, a monthly public-access television program. A July 2015 episode of the show was taken over by Late Show host Stephen Colbert because of the importance of the guest, rapper Eminem. Rafko was in the 1989 film documentary *Roger & Me*.

<<>>

Vernon J. Sneider, a novelist, is best known for *Teahouse of the August Moon,* a Pulitzer Prize drama winner in 1954. The book was adapted as a Broadway play and later a motion picture. Sneider was born (1916) and died (1981) in Monroe.

• BOOKS AND MOVIES WITH TIES TO MONROE

General George Armstrong Custer has been portrayed in more than seventy films and TV movies. In the 1940 movie, ***Santa Fe Trail,*** his character was played by Ronald Reagan. In the 1941 movie, ***They Died with Their Boots On,*** Errol Flynn landed the role of Custer, and Olivia de Havilland was his Libbie.

<<>>

Stephen Ambrose weaves known facts into a story that reads like a novel in ***Crazy Horse and Custer: The Parallel Lives of Two American Warriors***.

<<>>

Elliot J. Gorn, ***Mother Jones: The Most Dangerous Woman in America***, April 15, 2002, and ***Mother Jones: Raising Cain and Consciousness*** (Women's Biography Series) by Simon Cordery, March 31, 2010, tell the story of Mary Harris Jones, who lived for a short while in Monroe.

<<>>

Vernon Sneider's ***Teahouse of the August Moon,*** is a comedy-drama that was made into a movie starring Marlon Brando. (See The Famous or Infamous with Ties to Monroe.)

• GHOST STORIES

Dog Lady. The good people of Monroe have conflicting— and often strong—feelings about the urban legend or ghost story of the Dog Lady.

A young woman at the Monroe Historical Museum's front desk first mentioned the ghost story to this travel writer. A staff member in the archives on the second floor was friendly, helpful, and quite accommodating. However, on the topic of the Dog Lady, he was emphatic. "It's pure hogwash, and I wish folks would stop perpetuating it."

Alternately called the Dog Lady Island ghost, this legend, like many others of dubious origin, has evolved with added detail as it passed down the generations—growing more elaborate with the repeated telling.

Dog Lady. Courtesy of Pixabay Free Images.

Fifteen miles north of the Ohio border on I-75 is Dixie Highway/Dunbar Road. If you drive East, before you reach Lake Erie, you will pass Plum Creek. From there you can see an unimpressive, rubbish-adorned island attached to the mainland by a causeway. Originally called Fox Island, later Kausler Island, and now often referred to as Dog Lady Island, it isn't likely to be one of your favorite travel stops. Still, you might find the sad story interesting.

The owners, back when it was Fox Island, built a grand mansion on the little piece of land and intended it as a women's religious retreat. After they sold the property, the next owners, the Kauslers, occupied the home until they decided to move closer to the center of town. The property has since housed communes, a pig farm, and the ultimate disgrace—a garbage pit. In the early 1960s, the house burned. The charred remains passed to an old woman who had lived there with her husband. After her spouse's death, she remained on the island and was isolated except for the company of her Doberman Pinschers.

During the old woman's tenancy on the property, it became a place for teenagers to flee the restraints of authority—their party hangout. Because of the old lady's dogs, the young people called the place dog island.

The reclusive old woman grew stranger and stranger. The best guess for her deterioration was the ravages of senility piled atop her seclusion.

The teenagers, who trespassed on her property, insisted they saw her glowing eyes peering out from the bushes. She dressed in rags and was always accompanied by her pack of growling, vicious dogs with whom she seemed more at ease than with humans. She began to emulate dog ways, running about on all fours and eating off the ground, even devouring small animal prey—although she always left the head untouched. Some of the kids who repeated these tales swore that she attacked them, or at least rushed at them the same as her canine friends did.

And at some point, the legend continues, one of her animals mistook her face for dinner and ripped out her tongue and part of her cheeks, leaving her seriously disfigured and partially blind. That description fits well with the growing myth that she jumped on cars that parked near her island.

The tragic story has no happy ending. It evolved to include Dog Lady's murder by the Iron Coffins motorcycle gang that took up residence on the island. The gang allegedly kept her body in a coffin as a souvenir, but they couldn't imprison her ghost. Her spirit continued to haunt the island.

A slight twist, but with some common threads, is a second story told about Dog Island. In 1943 a young woman was held prisoner in a shed on the island. She was abused and repeatedly assaulted by four men. Since this is a PG travel book, we'll skip the most disturbing details of this version. But it concludes with her giving birth to a baby that lived feral among the dogs on the island.

Paranormal groups who have visited the island claim to have witnessed glowing red eyes, captured voice recordings, and seen colorful orbs around different parts of the island as well as found scattered animal bones.

On a night of a full moon, you may want to get in your car and take a short drive up to Monroe, Michigan, and howl at the moon as you seek the legend of the Dog Lady Island . . . if you dare.

Spoiler: a local who lives nearby says, "I live in the closest residence to the island, I have never seen sh__."

[There are references that this legend had enough interest to become a book, and that a movie was set to be released in 2017, but research and Amazon.com books don't bear this out.]

<<>>

Ghosts of the River Raisin Battlefield. The site where hundreds of soldiers were killed has the dubious reputation of being one of the most haunted sites in Michigan. Several people have claimed to see apparitions of American soldiers dressed in 1813 military uniforms. Electronic voice phenomena have allegedly been recorded— some sounds are said to be cries of agony as soldiers lay dying. There are also fuzzy photographs claiming to be human figures in doorways, windows, and on the actual battlefield.

The Detroit River

The Detroit River flows 24 nautical (28 land) miles from its source on southwestern Lake St. Clair to its mouth on northwestern Lake Erie. The River is 574 feet above sea level and is an important cog in one of the busiest water transportation systems in the world, used by both huge freighters and small pleasure craft. It connects Michigan's Lakes to the St. Lawrence Seaway and the Erie Canal. The river is also part of the international border between the United States and Canada.

In its early days, the river carried birchbark canoes laden with furs. The Iroquois traded with Dutch settlers before the area was claimed by the French explorers as part of New France. The French named the river *Rivière du Détroit*, which meant *River of the Strait* since it connected two lakes (Lake Erie and Lake St. Clair).

Great Britain took possession of the Detroit River and surrounding land from the French at the conclusion of the French and Indian War. The waterway next passed to the newly formed United States during the American Revolution, but it was not turned over by the British until 1796.

During the War of 1812, the river was a barrier between the Michigan Territory and Upper Canada which was still ruled by the British. The Civil War brought Union fears that the Confederate States would cross the Detroit River from Canada to launch an attack.

By 1907 the Detroit River carried 67,292,504 tons of shipping commerce through Detroit to locations all over the world, causing *The Detroit News* to run a headline calling it "the Greatest Commercial Artery on Earth." With all that activity came a price. The wetlands that the Detroit River shoreline boasted a century earlier were lost to industrial pollution, contamination, and deep shipping channel excavation.

During Prohibition, the river was the pipeline from Canada, where alcohol was legal, to the United States, encouraging the new business of rum-running. The Detroit River, Lake St. Clair, and the St. Clair River were estimated to have transported 75% of the smuggled liquor that found its way to thirsty Americans. It was an era that gave rise to the violent and ambitious Purple Gang whose bootleggers and hijackers rose to prominence in the early 1920s. A decade later, the hoodlums self-destructed due to their own brutality and avarice. In the short span of five years during its heyday, the gang was estimated to have killed five hundred, a record topping fellow-bootlegger Al Capone. The Purple Gang was suspected of participation in everything from the St. Valentine's Day Massacre to the Lindberg kidnapping.

Today, the Detroit River serves a wide array of economic and recreational purposes. Habitat restoration projects are underway by the Environmental Protection Agency, aided by Friends of the Detroit River.

Belle Isle Park sits in the middle of the Detroit River. Its 987 acres offer a conservatory, aquarium, museum, giant water slide, swimming beach, and golf course.

Much of the lower portion of the river is an International Wildlife Refuge. In the heart of Detroit, the river has been developed as an International Riverfront, the focal point of which is the Renaissance Center, a group of seven interconnected skyscrapers.

Along the river's banks perch the cities of Detroit, Grosse Pointe Park, River Rouge, Ecorse, Wyandotte, Trenton, and Grosse Isle. The river divides Windsor, Ontario, and Detroit, Michigan. The Ambassador Bridge, the Detroit-Windsor Tunnel, and the Michigan Central Railway Tunnel connect the two cities.

The **M.V. Montrose** was a 444-foot British freighter on her fifth trip into the lakes. On July 30, 1962, the one-year-old vessel from London, England, docked at the Detroit Harbor Terminal near the Ambassador Bridge. She had just added a 200-ton load of aluminum to her prior cargo of fine wines from France.

The shipmaster, Captain Ralph Eyre-Walker, and George Beatty, a Canadian Great Lakes pilot, were on the bridge communicating with the upbound *T.J. McCarthy*, whose captain was waiting for the *Montrose* to depart. The *McCarthy*, an automobile carrier, intended to stay tight to the western side of the river, make a wide turn toward the east, and dock. The *Montrose* captain felt his ship was not clearing the dock fast enough for the incoming *T.J. McCarthy* and called for full speed as they headed across the river.

At the same time, making one of its five weekly trips from Port Huron to River Rouge, the tugboat *B.H. Becker* prepared to dock near the Ambassador Bridge. The *Becker* pushed a 200-foot barge, the *ABL202*, loaded with 1,600 tons of cement by-products. The tug's Captain Fuller looked skyward on that pleasant summer night. As his eyes drifted back to river level, he saw something on his starboard bow that no captain wants to see. A ship he could not avoid. The *Montrose* had pulled away from the dock and begun its rapid cross of the downbound shipping lane. Captain Fuller sounded several warning blasts and radioed the larger ship crossing his bow to warn the *Montrose* of the *Becker's* presence. Fuller threw his engines into reverse to slow the tug's forward movement while his wheelsman shone a bright spotlight on the barge it pushed.

By the time the crew of the *Montrose* saw the tug and barge, it was too late to avoid a collision. The barge's reinforced square bow struck the *Montrose,* tearing a hole

48-feet long and 24-feet wide in the *Montrose*'s hull. Captain Fuller's crew donned life jackets and raced to the bow of the barge. If the barge sank, they feared her heavy cargo might pull the tug down with her. The barge's port bow sustained significant damage, but she wasn't taking on water. The *Montrose*, on the other hand, began to tilt to port with water gushing through her exposed rib cage. The ship's propellers were lifted above the water, and she rolled over on her side beneath the Ambassador Bridge where she settled in 35 feet of water.

The Wreck of the Montrose. Courtesy of Pixabay Free Images.

The captain of the *McCarthy* was close to the injured ship. He saw and heard what happened, and would later testify that he observed the lights of the barge and noted no warning from the *Montrose*.

The hapless *Montrose* was the largest foreign ship to go down in the river since it had opened to foreign trade. It was also Detroit's biggest tourist attraction that summer. Gawkers stood on the banks or boarded smaller boats to get a closer view.

The ray of sunshine from the disaster was that no one was injured or killed. One of the sad misfortunes of the calamity was the loss of the fine French wines to the fishes.

4. Dearborn

Dearborn is part of the greater metropolitan Detroit area. Whether it technically sits on the coastal waterways might be questionable since it lies on the Rouge River, a tributary, three miles from the Detroit River. The Rouge River has been dredged and widened to allow large freighters access to Ford Motor Company. Dearborn's proximity to the major waterways, its history, and its museums make it a worthy inclusion to your travels.

Before the influx of European and Middle-Eastern immigrants, the area around Dearborn was home for thousands of years to indigenous peoples, primarily Algonquin speaking Potawatomie, Odawa, and Ojibwe. In the late eighteenth century, French farmers settled ribbon farms—long, narrow strip farms that fronted the Rouge River and the Sauk Trail.

At the end of the Seven Year's War in 1763, France ceded all of its territory east of the Mississippi River to Great Britain. With American independence, more European-Americans settled in the Dearborn area. Dearborn Township was formed in 1833 and the village of Dearbornville was established in 1836, each named for Henry Dearborn, a general in the American Revolution. Henry Dearborn later served as Secretary of War under Thomas Jefferson. In 1893 the area of Dearborn was incorporated but remained mostly rural and agricultural.

In the twentieth century, Detroit underwent significant industrial growth that spread to Dearborn, which had established itself as a city in 1927 to avoid being devoured by the expanding Detroit.

Over the years, Dearborn has held an unsavory reputation for racial segregation, so much so that it is said that Orville Hubbard, Dearborn Mayor from 1942-1978, considered it unlawful for African Americans to live in his suburb.

The land between Dearborn and Fordson, which later became part of Dearborn, was bought by Henry Ford for his Fair Lane estate and for the Ford Motor Company Headquarters. Henry Ford, born on a farm in Dearborn in 1863, remains, even after death, one of his hometown's favored sons. The open land of Ford's holdings is planted with sunflowers and his favorite crop, soybeans. Neither are harvested.

Ford may have been an economic success and industrial role model, but his reputation is tarnished by his anti-Semitism. Numerous books about the iconic tycoon include compelling discussions of his bigotry. Many of those books are available in Dearborn's Henry Ford Centennial Library. Writing about Ford and the Holocaust Memorial Center in Farmington Hills, Brian Dickerson, a *Detroit Free Press* reporter says, "Henry Ford's anti-Semitism is about as well-kept a secret as Donald Trump's contempt for Rosie O'Donnell." (Dickerson also calls the Holocaust Memorial Center "a deceptively modest venue that may be, pound-for-pound, the most thoughtfully curated museum in America.")

Today the city of Dearborn has the largest proportion of Arab Americans of any city in the United States.

Henry Ford's Fair Lane Estate in Dearborn and River Rouge.
Courtesy of Pixabay Free Images.

Henry Ford Museum and Greenfield Village, 20900 Oakwood Boulevard, Dearborn. Opened to the public in 1933 as the Edison Institute the museum is dedicated to the innovation of American Genius. The complex is the largest indoor and outdoor history museum compound in the United States and is visited annually by nearly two million people. An educational treasure, it possesses one of the largest collections of Americana in the country.

Greenfield Village led the way in preserving historic buildings, relocating them to its grounds, and sharing their significance.

In 1962 the museum earned a Michigan Historical Marker. In 1963 it was added to the State Register of Historic Sites. In 1969 it was added to the National Register of Historic Places, and in 1981 it was designated a National Historic Landmark.

Among its vast historical collections are the presidential limousine of John F. Kennedy, Abraham Lincoln's chair from the Ford Theatre, the Wright Brothers' bicycle shop, the bus on which Rosa Parks refused to relinquish a seat, and Thomas Edison's laboratory.

<<>>

Arab American National Museum, 13624 Michigan Avenue, Dearborn. The Arab American National Museum opened in 2005 and is the first museum in the world devoted to Arab American history and culture. The museum attempts to show visitors the Arab American story through a timeline of exhibits. It also seeks to replace misconceptions with truth about Arab Americans. The museum offers three permanent exhibits showing contributions of the Arab civilization to science, mathematics, architecture, medicine, and the arts. Construction of the museum cost fifteen million dollars. Donors included Chrysler, General Motors, the Rockefeller

Foundation, Saudi Arabia, and Qatar. The museum is a part of the Smithsonian Affiliations.

The Arab American National Museum.
Courtesy of Wikipedia.

<<>>

Automotive Hall of Fame, 21400 Oakwood Boulevard. This museum is a tribute to those honored as innovators, inventors, and pioneers of the industry. Founded in 1939 in New York by a group called The Automotive Old-Timers, it has over 800 worldwide honorees. The organization moved to Washington, D.C. in 1960, sharing space in the National Automobile Dealers Association building. In 1971 it moved to Midland, Michigan, and then in 1998, it relocated to its present location of 25,000 square feet in a building adjacent to the Henry Ford Museum.

● THE FAMOUS OR INFAMOUS WITH TIES TO DEARBORN

Henry Ford, the man synonymous with the auto industry, was born on July 30, 1863, in Wayne County. His father had immigrated from Cork County, Ireland. Henry was the founder of Ford Motor Company. He died on April 7, 1947, in Dearborn. He was 83. (See preceding sections for additional discussion.)

<<>>

Edsel Ford was the only child of auto tycoon Henry Ford. As such he was groomed to run the company on his father's retirement. He served as the second president of Ford

The Edsel.
Courtesy of Pixabay Free Images.

Motor Company from 1919 until his death in 1943. His death, at the young age of 49, caused his father to step back into control Ford Motor Company until it passed to Edsel's son Henry Ford II. Edsel was a patron of the arts and also underwrote the polar expeditions of Admiral Richard Byrd. Edsel had the dubious posthumous honor of having the Edsel automobile named for him. The car was aggressively advertised. When it reached showrooms, the buying public considered it overpriced and ugly. It never made the auto company any profit. By the time Ford Motor Company gave up the venture, it had lost $350 million, or the equivalent of nearly two and a half billion in today's dollars. Instead of the honor it was intended to bestow on its namesake, the word Edsel became synonymous with commercial failure.

<<>>

Nancy Milford is an author and biographer best known for her book *Zelda* about the wife of F. Scott Fitzgerald. Milford chose the topic of Zelda Fitzgerald for her master's thesis, but interest in the subject matter, as well as Milford's writing style, turned it into an acclaimed biography that spent 29 weeks on *The New York Times* best-seller list.

<<>>

Chad Everett's name at birth was Raymon Lee Cramton, but he changed the moniker to Chad Everett before becoming a TV star. He is best remembered for his seven-year stint as Dr. Joe Gannon on the medical series, *Medical Center.*

<<>>

George Peppard had the kind of good looks that preordained a career in Tinseltown. He played Hannibal on the A-Team but was also a film actor with roles in *Breakfast at Tiffany's, The Carpetbaggers,* and *How the West Was Won.* After the highs and lows of his acting career, George wanted to go home. He is buried in an unpretentious grave next to his parents in Dearborn's Northview Cemetery.

<<>>

Congressman John David Dingell Jr. was the longest-serving member of Congress in history. He represented Michigan's 12th District for 59 years. Dying of metastatic prostate cancer, he faced his last day of life on February 7, 2019, writing a final column that was published in the *Washington Post.* He referenced the great stain on our country's moral fabric as its legacy of racial discrimination. He also said, "In democratic government, elected officials do not *have* power. They *hold* power in trust for the people who elected them. If they misuse or abuse that public trust, it is quite properly revoked (the quicker the better)."

5. DETROIT

Detroit is the largest city in Michigan. The greater Detroit metropolitan area is home to more than four million people. It ranks, after Chicago, as the second-largest city in the Midwest. It is a city that brings to mind Motown, Jimmy Hoffa, the Lions, and the auto industry. To do this city justice, it can't be covered in a travel guide of wide scope. Its history, its culture, its attractions deserve their own book. Fortunately, there are several good guides out there including, *Wildsam Field Guides: Detroit* from the American City Guide Series and *Lonely Planet* that in 1918 named Detroit the second-best city in the U.S. to visit. If you plan to make it your destination and spend time in the city, you will want to pick up a comprehensive guide. For the traveler just passing through, here are ten spots worth a stop.

Detroit Institute of Art, with over 100 galleries and 65,000 works, is one of the most significant art collections in the United States.

<<>>

Detroit Riverfront includes the RenCen and the People Mover. The RenCen is the General Motors world headquarters. The seven skyscrapers that make up the RenCen include the Marriot at the RenCen, the third tallest hotel-only skyscraper in the Western Hemisphere. The Detroit People Mover is a light rail system that operates on an elevated single track that loops through the city's business district. It services 13 stations and connects offices, sports arenas, courts, exhibition centers, hotels, and shopping.

<<>>

Eastern Market. A huge open-air marketplace, opened in 1841, the Eastern Market still draws crowds every Saturday. With over 150 vendors, you can find almost any specialty food and a beautiful selection of flowers.

<<>>

Motown Museum. As its name suggests, this museum is a tribute to the Motown Sound that produced so many talented singers and groups.

<<>>

Charles H. Wright Museum of African American History opened in 1997. This 125,000-square-foot museum is dedicated to portraying the African American experience.

<<>>

Detroit Historical Museum chronicles Detroit's history from the fur trade era to today.

<<>>

Greek Town was originally settled by Germans, but as they moved out, it became home to Greek immigrants, who established businesses in this culturally important neighborhood.

<<>>

Henry Ford Museum and Greenfield Village (See Dearborn listing in this guide.)

<<>>

Walking Tours include the Civic Center, Broadway, People Mover, Greek Town and a look at the well-preserved architecture of some of Detroit's most famous buildings.

<<>>

DNR Outdoor Adventure Center is a museum that brings the outdoors inside and showcases Michigan's natural resources.

● A FEW OF THE FAMOUS OR INFAMOUS WITH TIES TO DETROIT

Sherilyn Fenn appeared in TV series *Twin Peaks*.

<<>>

Piper Laurie was born Rosetta Jacobs on January 22, 1932, in Detroit. She won the Best Supporting Actress award in 1976 for her role in *Carrie*.

<<>>

Carl Levin was born in Detroit on June 28, 1934. A member of the Democratic Party, he served as a United States senator from Michigan from 1979 to 2015 and was the longest-serving U.S. Senator in Michigan history. He died at age 87 on July 29, 2021.

<<>>

Harry Morgan, born Harry Bratsberg in Detroit on April 10, 1915, played Sherman Potter on the TV series *M*A*S*H*. His career spanned six decades.

<<>>

Bob Seger, singer and songwriter, was born on May 6, 1945, at Henry Ford Hospital.

<<>>

Tom Skerritt was born in Detroit and starred in the movie *Fighting Back*.

<<>>

Edward Donald Slovik was born in Detroit in 1920. He was a troubled youth, imprisoned for various charges, deemed unfit for military service, married, was reclassified as fit for military service, and drafted by the army to fight in WWII.

More than 21,000 soldiers have been court-martialed for desertion since the American Civil War, and 29 have been given death sentences, but Slovik was the only one executed. His sentence was carried out by a firing squad on January 31, 1945.

<<>>

Lily Tomlin played a wealthy spinster in the 1984 movie *All of Me*. Her co-star was Steve Martin. She was born in Detroit on March 3, 1913.

<<>>

Robert *Wagner* was a Detroit native and starred as the suave crook Alexander Mundy in *It Takes a Thief*.

● MOVIES AND BOOKS WITH TIES TO DETROIT

Movies

8 Mile. The 2002 movie about a white rapper trying to make it in music dominated by African Americans. The movie starred Eminem, who was from Detroit, and Kim Basinger. The movie made it to #1 at the Box Office.

<<>>

The Execution of Private Slovik. The 1974 movie starring Martin Sheen about the desertion and subsequent firing-squad death of Edward Slovik. (See The Famous or Infamous with Ties to Detroit.)

<<>>

The Irishman revives the public's curiosity about the disappearance and assumed murder of Jimmy Hoffa. With an all-star cast including Robert De Niro, Al Pacino, and Joe Pesci, and directed by Martin Scorsese, the movie met expectations and was nominated for several academy awards. Have a huge bowl of popcorn beside you if you watch this Netflix winner because the film runs three hours and 29 minutes.

<<>>

Other movies set in or with ties to Detroit: *The Betsy, Beverly Hills Cop* (Eddie Murphy played a streetwise Detroit cop), *Bird on a Wire, Dream Girls, Evil Dead, Garfield the Movie, Out of Sight, Presumed Innocent, Red Dawn, Renaissance Man, Robocop, The Rosary Murders, Scarecrow,* and *The Virgin Suicides* are among the many movies you might consider if you plan to spend time in Motown and want to absorb some of the vibes.

Books
Harriette Arnow published ***The Dollmaker*** in 1954. The novel told the saga of a family transplanted from Kentucky to Detroit.

<<>>

Elmore Leonard, novelist famous for his crime fiction and suspense novels, was raised in Detroit and lived in Bloomfield Hills. Several of his books, including ***52 Pickup***, are set in the Detroit area. Leonard was also a screenwriter.

<<>>

Joyce Carol Oates moved to Detroit in 1962 and taught at the University of Detroit before moving to Ontario. Oates' first novel, **With Shuddering Fall**, was published while living in Detroit. She was 26 years old at the time of its publication. She has since earned honors and awards too numerous to mention including the U.S. National Book Award.

• GHOST STORY

The Ghost of Benny Evangelist

Evangelist Family and Benny Evangelist.
Courtesy of Pixabay Free Images.

Late at night the moon peeks from behind clouds and shimmers off the Detroit River. If you look deep into the shadows of the Motor City, you may glimpse Benny Evangelist's headless ghost trudging along the streets near St. Aubin and Mack at the edge of the Eastern Market. His disembodied screams are garbled. Unlike ghost stories sewn from whole cloth or those born solely of vivid imagination, this tale originates in a true crime.

In the late morning hours of July 3, 1929, realtor Vincent Elias walked up the steps to the Evangelist front door. Inside the home at 1587 St. Aubin Street, lived Benjamino Evangilisto, who had by that time anglicized his name to Benny Evangelist, his wife Santina, and their four children, Angeline, 8; Mathew, 5; Jean, 4; and Mario, 18 months. Their green house with its wide front porch greeted the unsuspecting realtor with no harbinger of evil.

Elias had sold the Evangelists a farm near Marine City and was calling to collect his money. He knocked repeatedly, then twisted the doorknob, and pushed the door open. He shouted his neighbor's name. There was no answer. He stepped farther inside.

We know from newspaper accounts what awaited Elias, but the descriptions vary slightly. In one, Benny Evangelist sat ramrod straight at his desk, hands folded across his chest. His severed head lay on the floor inches from his feet. In another account, his body was hacked to pieces, and the head placed on a living room chair where it stared vacantly at the realtor when he entered. Both versions continued with Elias hightailing down the front steps, putting distance between him and the butchery, before he called the police.

After entering the house, responding officers followed the bloody footprints to the second floor where they found Santina Evangelist tangled in the bedsheets, her head smashed and nearly severed. Lying in her arms was 18-month-old Mario, the youngest of the Evangelist children. The toddler was also dead, his head crushed.

The police continued their gruesome inspection. The corpses of the three remaining Evangelist children waited down the hall. Two were dead in their beds, the third slumped on the floor where she dropped in a failed escape attempt.

In the following days, detectives speculated that the occult, mystical healing, insanity, greed, vampires, blood, black magic, and heresy flourished inside the dwelling, and each played a role in the depravity. The July 4th weekend drew every law enforcement officer in the city to join the manhunt for the family's killer or killers.

The coroner placed the time of the massacre at midnight or the early hours of July 3, 1929. The witching hour or the devil's hour is the time from 3:00 a.m. to 4:00 a.m. It is associated with supernatural forces and black magic. Benny Evangelist was no stranger to those forces. He did his best work between the hours of midnight and 3:00 a.m. The authorities took a close look at the self-described mystic's background as they pieced together the case.

They learned that Benny had arrived in the United States with his older brother Antonio when Benny was fifteen. The boys came from Naples in 1902, part of the largest Italian emigration in history. Between 1880 and 1915, four million Italians fled poverty, poor wages, and high taxes. Often, they came from rural areas, were uneducated, and hoped to carve out their piece of the American dream. Many expected to return to their homeland with pockets full of gold. Benny and Antonio, like most of the emigrants, settled along the Eastern seaboard. The siblings prospered in Philadelphia. Benny sharpened his carpentry skills at the same time he developed an interest in the occult. He described visions from a god that had little resemblance to the Catholic god of his family's faith. He started peddling potions and hexes and established a cult based upon his own teachings. Antonio couldn't tolerate his brother's new tastes and cut all ties.

Benny, needing a friend, or perhaps looking for a father figure after his brother kicked him out, began a relationship with another Neapolitan, Aurelius Angelino. What impact this relationship had on twenty-year-old Benny two decades Angelino's junior, no one knows. The police speculated that the two men fed on each other's psychopathy. In 1919 Antonio was institutionalized in the county mental asylum. His wife secured his release. The same day he returned home, Angelino expressed his gratitude to his spouse by picking up a club and trying to kill her. She ran outside. Her deranged husband locked the door and then murdered their twin four-year-old sons in a scene too macabre for description. This horrific incident involving his friend sent Benny fleeing the area.

He moved to Detroit where his actions showed definite signs of mental imbalance. He wrote the Evangelist bible and inscribed it, "My story is from my own views and signs that I see from 12 to 3 AM. I began on February 2, 1906, in Philadelphia, PA, and it was completed on February 2, 1926, in the city of Detroit, County of Wayne, State of Michigan." The result was a four-volume set of books, titled *The Oldest History of the World: Discovered by Occult Science.* These books captured the essence of Benny's faith and became the center of his cellar sanctuary adorned with paper-mâché gods, three pictures of a child laying in a coffin (later identified as Benny's child), and an altar. A wig, and beard that police believed Benny wore when giving his readings, along with symbols of devil worship, voodoo, and several Catholic icons including a Christian cross were also found. The police collected women's undergarments neatly tagged with the owner's name. These may have been part of the voodoo. From his dungeon-like edifice, Benny ministered to his cult members, practiced faith healings for which he charged $10, and preached sermons. Benny's physician described him as insane.

The funeral for the Evangelist family was a spectacle. Three-thousand people showed up, more from curiosity and to hear grisly details than from sympathy.

To this day, the matter remains an open cold—very cold—case.

The Evangelist home was demolished in the 1940s. In the weed-ridden lot that is its legacy, roams the ghost of Benny Evangelist, one Italian immigrant who would never return to his homeland. He would remain in Detroit where his headless ghost wanders the area of his former home.

6. Belle Isle Park

Steeped in history, this 987-acre park, the largest city-owned island park in the United States, sits in the middle of the Detroit River. It became Michigan's 102nd State Park on February 10, 2014 when the City of Detroit entered an agreement giving the city ownership and the Michigan Department of Natural Resources management responsibility.

The park is accessed by the McArthur Bridge and provides spectacular views of both the Detroit and Windsor skylines.

The island offers visitors the Anna Scripps Whitcomb Conservatory, an aquarium, the Dossin Great Lakes Museum, a nature zoo, tennis courts, giant slide, 15 acres of wooded area, botanical gardens, watercraft rentals, three lakes, swimming beach, athletic fields, and picnic areas. A Michigan Recreation Passport is required for entry.

Rich with history, Belle Isle was settled by French colonists in the eighteenth century. They named their beautiful island the less than flattering *Ile aux Cochons* or Hog Island because livestock were allowed to roam free. The name was changed during a July 4, 1845, party at Belle Isle to honor the daughter of Governor Lewis Cass.

The conservatory and the aquarium were designed by Detroit architect Albert Kahn, who also designed Cadillac Place and the Ford Rouge Factory.

During World War II, the island was used as a staging ground for a re-enactment of the Pacific Island invasion by the Navy and Marine Corps. The local citizenry watched an island invasion, minus the death and bloodshed.

In the late 1800s, the island became home to a large herd of Eurasian fallow deer, but the herd was decimated by disease and inbreeding. In 2004 the last of the herd was captured and moved to the Detroit Zoo and nature center on the island.

LAKE ST. CLAIR

Lake St. Clair is a small lake in the company of giants, Huron to the north and Erie to the South. With 160 miles of shoreline, it averages 22.5 nautical miles from north to south and about 21 nautical miles from east to west.

Its 430 square miles of water offer plenty of recreational opportunities. The lake empties into the Detroit River and is part of the navigable waterway from the Atlantic Ocean through the St. Lawrence Seaway and Great Lakes that provides a critical water highway into the country's heartland. Native Americans called the lake *Waawiyaataan* meaning whirlpool. The Mississaugas had a village near the lake in the seventeenth century.

Early French mapmakers called it *Mer Douce* or Sweet Sea as a reference to its freshwater compared to saltwater oceans. On August 12, 1679, French-Catholic explorer René Robert Cavelier, Sieur de La Salle, first navigated the lake. It was the feast day of Saint Clare of Assisi, and the lake was named in Saint Clare's honor.

The lake is six miles northeast of Detroit bordered by Michigan and Ontario, Canada. The governments of the U.S. and Canada work together to maintain a 27-foot-deep shipping channel through the otherwise shallow lake. The lake is fed by the St. Clair River, which connects to Lake Huron. The mouth of Lake St. Clair empties into the Detroit River.

7. GROSSE POINTE AND GROSSE POINTE SHORES

Grosse Pointe, a waterfront city located eight miles north of Detroit, became heavily populated in the early 1900s as one of Detroit's first commuter suburbs. Grosse Pointe Shores is the smallest of the five Grosse Pointe communities adjacent to one another and referenced simply as The Pointes. The Pointes occupy just over 10.4 miles of land mostly within Wayne County with a small portion in Macomb County. Grosse Pointe Shores has a beautiful shoreline on Lake St. Clair. Grosse Pointe (the city), along with Grosse Pointe Park and Grosse Pointe Farms, are referred to as the southern points. They are older and more densely populated than the northern points of Grosse Pointe Woods and Grosse Pointe Shores.

The City of Grosse Pointe has several blocks of mansions and architecturally important homes, including the Ralph Harmon Booth House (315 Washington Road), the John M. Dwyer House (372 Lakeland), the Waterman House (330 Lincoln), and the Murray Sales House (251 Lincoln). The homes are not open to the public, but make an interesting drive.

Grosse Pointe Shores, along Lake St. Clair, has no retail and is strictly residential. Its best-known house, and one that is open to the public, is the Edsel and Eleanor Ford House (1100 Lake Shore Road).

The Edsel and Eleanor Ford House situated on 87 acres of lakeshore property became the residence of Edsel and Eleanor in 1928. It sits on a plot of land known as Gaukler Point. For the wealthy son of Henry Ford, who was the second president of Ford Motor Company, money was no object and the house reflects the Fords' opulent taste. Although

The Edsel Ford Home at Christmas.
Courtesy of Bob Royce.

undeniably extravagant, the lavish estate manages to feel homey. The kind of place where you imagine grandchildren frolicking without being too harshly restrained.

The buildings were designed by architect Albert Kahn with whom the Fords traveled to England for ideas. They became enchanted with the architecture of the Cotswolds. Edsel and Eleanor wanted Kahn to design a house that would resemble the closely assembled village cottages typical of that rural region.

The gardens were laid out by renowned landscape designer Jens Jensen who favored a long view giving visitors a beautiful garden as an entrance to the house.

In 1979 the property was listed on the National Register of Historic Places. In 2016 it became a National Historic Landmark. Construction was a two-year process with meticulous attention to detail responsible for the lengthy building period. The kitchen counters, for example, are sterling silver.

The Edsel and Eleanor Ford Home.
Courtesy of Pixabay Free Images.

The house features an extensive art collection including original Paul Cezanne and Diego Rivera paintings as well as Renoir, Degas, and van Gogh reproductions.

The grounds had several outbuildings, including a gatehouse along the beautiful lakeshore that provided apartments for many of the staff. It also featured an eight-car garage with a device to rotate cars so they didn't need to back out. This gatehouse was often mistaken for the main house.

Edsel died in the house in 1943. Eleanor remained there until her death in 1976 at which time it was her wish that the estate be used for the benefit of the public. Today about 20 of the 60 or more rooms are open for viewing.

• The Famous or Infamous with Ties to the Pointes

Anita Denise Baker, the famous songstress, was born on January 26, 1958, in Toledo, Ohio. She lived a hardscrabble life, abandoned by her mother when she was two, moved to Detroit by her foster parents who died when she was twelve. After that, she was raised by a sister. From difficult beginnings, she rose to be the popular singer of soulful romantic ballads. She received eight Grammy Awards out of 18 nominations. She currently lives in Grosse Pointe Park.

<<>>

The Ford Family. Numerous members of the Ford family including Edsel Ford II, Elena Ford, Henry Ford II, Martha Firestone Ford, and William Clay Ford have lived or currently live in Grosse Pointe.

<<>>

Kirk Harold "Gibby" Gibson attended Michigan State University where he was an All-American wide receiver in football. At the suggestion of Spartan football coach Darryl Rogers, Gibson also played baseball in his last year at M.S.U. He was a first-round draft pick of the Detroit Tigers baseball team and the seventh-round draft pick of the St. Louis Cardinals football team. He chose a baseball career.

Grosse Pointe Blank. John Cusack plays a depressed assassin who returns to his high school reunion. The movie was a box office hit.

8. ST. CLAIR SHORES

St. Clair Shores, 2020 population 59,195 is located 13 miles northeast of downtown Detroit. On the shores of Lake St. Clair, it is part of the Metro Detroit area. Fourteen miles of canals set St. Clair Shores apart from other Michigan cities. Originally a farming area settled by French and German immigrants, the village transitioned into a resort and entertainment area that took full advantage of water-related recreation.

St. Clair Shores became a city in 1951, giving up its claim as the largest village in the U.S. It was a popular local playground for gamblers, bootleggers, and tourists. Jefferson Beach Amusement Park was the place to go for a good time. The Amusement Park opened in 1927 with the longest roller-coaster in the United States. A fire destroyed much of the park in 1959, and coupled with changing taste in recreation, the park's decline was inevitable.

The city is home to the longest-running preliminary pageant of the Miss America organization in Michigan. Beginning with its early lakeshore entertainment, the city retains strong ties to Detroit's music industry. St. Clair Shores is also known for its hockey program and called itself Hockey Town before the Red Wings got their start.

•MUSEUM

The Selinsky-Green Farmhouse Museum, located behind the St. Clair Shores Public Library, shows how a typical late nineteenth century farm settler lived. The Selinskys, Polish immigrants, came to Erin township (now St. Clair

Shores) in 1868. They purchased land and built a saltbox house which they sold to their daughter when she married German immigrant John Green.

Green's descendants lived in the house until 1974 when the State Highway Commission bought the house and the land on which it sat to make way for the 1-696/I-94 interchange.

The house was moved to its present location and is owned by the City of St. Clair Shores under the direction of the Historical Commission. Volunteers have restored the farmhouse, and it is now operated as a museum. It is listed on the Michigan State Register of Historic Sites.

• A PARK

Veteran's Memorial Park, 32400 Jefferson Avenue. This lovely park is only mentioned here to warn you not to go! Visitors have driven considerable distances to take their children to the Splash Pad only to find this is a residents-only park. It is open to the public for Wednesday concerts.

• OTHER STOPS TO CONSIDER

The Nautical Mile is located between Nine Mile and Ten Mile Roads on a mile-long lakefront strip of Jefferson Avenue. The mile's most prominent building is the 28-story residential Shore Club Sky Tower with a rooftop beacon that can be seen for many miles. The Mile displays a nautical-themed street-scape with marinas, antique dealers, restaurants, and retail establishments.

The Nautical Mile.
Courtesy of
Pixabay Free Images.

<<>>

Annual Memorial Day Parade. If you are in the area over the Memorial Day weekend, you may find it difficult to maneuver around St. Clair Shores as it hosts its annual Memorial Day Parade with musical acts, dancing, floats, and bands. One of the largest parades in the Midwest, it draws upwards to 100,000 people.

● THE FAMOUS OR INFAMOUS WITH TIES TO ST. CLAIR SHORES

George Allen. An NFL football coach and a member of the Pro Football Hall of Fame, Allen was born in Virginia, but the Allen family moved to St. Clair Shores when George was a child. At Lake Shore High School, he earned varsity letters in football, track, and basketball.

<<>>

Patti Smith, singer, songwriter, poet, musician, and author was an essential part of the New York City punk rock movement. She lived in St. Clair Shores during most of the 1980s. She earned the unofficial title of punk poet laureate and is most remembered for her song "Because the Night," which was co-written with Bruce Springsteen. Smith won the National Book Award for her memoir, *Just Kids*. In December 2010, Smith was honored by inclusion on the *Rolling Stone Magazine*'s list of 100 Greatest Artists.

<<>>

John Augustus Ziegler Jr. was president of the National Hockey League and a member of the Hockey Hall of Fame. Ziegler was born in Grosse Pointe in 1934. His family moved to St. Clair Shores, and John graduated from Lake Shore High School in 1951. He attended the University of Michigan where he earned both an undergraduate degree and a law degree. He practiced law, initially joining the firm of Dickson-Wright and then opened his own practice before becoming President of the NHL.

- ● GHOST STORY

A Travel Channel episode of the *Dead Files* featured a house in St. Clair Shores. The owners of the house called the producers of the show claiming they were terrorized by ghosts of the most frightening ilk. A team of investigators, consisting of a medium and a retired New York City detective, traveled to the home.

The wife who lived in the haunted dwelling described having her hair pulled several times while showering, and also while she was in the basement—not endearing little tugs, but violent yanks.

She alleged she had been scratched and burned and suffered constant headaches and nausea. The family had two sets of twins. One pair that looked about eight years of age described seeing ghosts and hearing voices. The children suffered nausea. The family attributed their problems to evil within the house. The medium perceived a graveyard with several dead children of the home's former owners. These deceased children could be the unsettled dead who are menacing the current occupants.

9. NEW BALTIMORE
INCLUDES LISTINGS FOR ANCHOR BAY
AND FAIR HAVEN

Located on the north coastline of Lake St. Clair, New Baltimore boasted a population of 12,913 in the 2020 census. It was originally called Ashleyville, got its first post office on September 20, 1851, was incorporated as a village in 1867, and as a city in 1931. As early as 1796, French settlers chose the waterfront for their farms and homes.

The city's water accessibility connected residents to the region's navigable transportation system and allowed them to operate port facilities with piers extending a hundred feet or more into Lake St. Clair. The area's economic base included lumber and building materials, creamery products, barrels, brooms, bricks, and coffins.

When the automobile changed the state's transportation patterns, the city began catering to resorters by offering hotels, salt baths, taverns, and even an opera house.

•MUSEUM

Grand Pacific House Museum, 51065 Washington Street. Frederick Losh used locally made bricks to construct this building in 1881, and it was first operated as an Italianate Hotel. Losh prospered by catering to the tourists drawn to his small city. The hotel was later converted to a boarding house that remained open until 1986, when it was sold to the New Baltimore Historical Society and became a museum. It is furnished with antiques and period pieces. Located on the main street that runs through New Baltimore, it makes a nice stop to stretch and take a short break.

• A PARK

Walter and Mary Burke Park, 36300 Front Street, located at the end of Washington Street, offers a swimming beach, fishing, changing area, restrooms, boat launch, picnic area, grills, indoor and outdoor pavilions, swings, and a universally accessible playscape to delight the little ones. The park claims it has the tallest flag in Michigan.

THE ST. CLAIR RIVER

The St. Clair River is the part of the St. Lawrence Seaway that joins Lake St. Clair to Lake Huron. Both Lake St. Clair and the St. Clair River are sprinkled with many islands including Harsens Island, Russell Island, Squirrel Island, Dickenson Island, Bassett Island, Seaway Island, and Walpole Island. There is also Gull Island, site of the Jobbie Nooners (See description under Algonac). The River has three channels, the North, South, and Middle Channel, each winding its way into some of the loveliest lakeshore in the United States.

The South Channel is about ten miles long and empties into Lake St. Clair. The North Channel, which flows past Algonac, is about six miles long and ends at Anchor Bay. The Middle Channel, approximately three miles from Algonac, runs a distance of seven miles to Muscamoot Bay.

The St. Clair River is 39 miles long and has depths ranging from 40 to 50 feet and in certain areas even 90 feet deep. It also has shallow spots that could prove dangerous to an inexperienced freighter captain. Watching freighters along the St. Clair River is addictive because they get up-close-and-personal. The River is narrow and at times it seems you can reach out and touch a passing ship. Nowhere else will you get such a spectacular view of these huge vessels. They come from all over the world and make their way from Lake Huron to her sister lakes, transporting their cargo. Benches dot the shoreline allowing locals and tourists to fritter away their time watching the action and listening to the freighters' horns.

In local marshes, you will sight swans, herons, and ducks. The area is home to 150 species of birds. The wildlife, as well as the opportunities for fishing, and recreational boating, make this a natural choice for summer activity. Fishing is an angler's dream come true. Walleye is arguably the best game fish in Michigan, although many local restaurants insist Lake Perch is their house specialty. Both are easily caught, even by an amateur. The lake and river are filled with salmon, bass, and trout. The spring smelt run is always popular.

Experienced divers enjoy the challenge of the St. Clair River near Port Huron. It is an exciting dive spot where the speed of the swift waters can exceed four knots. The river can be seductive with its lure of shipwrecks and other artifacts, but at times, it can also be treacherous. Divers should not tackle these waters without appropriate training, as both their diving expertise and physical stamina will be tested. Because this narrow channel is one of the busiest waterways in the world, divers must be savvy and skilled at diving in an area of extremely heavy boat traffic. The river has special rules: It is one of the only spots in Michigan where a diver is not required to tow a dive flag: Boats have the right of way. Divers must put out two flags, one at the point of entry and one at the exit point of their dive. Because of the often-congested boat traffic, divers treat this area as an overhead environment dive, surfacing near their point of entry.

On good days, the underwater visibility can be up to 80 feet and the ecosystem is one of the most diverse found in the Great Lakes. Although winter diving would seem to be out of the question, there are always a few courageous souls who brave the frigid waters—for the thrill and bragging rights that go with diving into the St. Clair River during the bitter Michigan winter.

10. ALGONAC

Algonac, population 4,023 according to the 2020 census, refers to itself as the Venice of Michigan because of its vast waterway system of rivers and channels. As early as the mid-1600s, the French Sulpician priests, Dollier de Casson and Gallinee, explored this area around Lake St. Clair and the St. Clair River. Adrien Joliet paddled along the St. Clair River's shores about 1669. Joliet's trip met with disaster when his canoe overturned, and he lost all the maps and information he had collected. In 1697 another French Priest, Father Hennepin, traveled to this area and named the river St. Clair because he landed on the feast day celebrating Santa Clara.

After these early explorers paved the way, fur traders began making repeated voyages in search of pelts. Beaver furs were especially popular with affluent French society. Michigan became a territory in 1805, but the earliest permanent residents in Algonac settled there around 1815. In 1821 there were only four taxpayers in the area that later became Algonac. These solitary taxpayers lived in log cabins, and it is unlikely they generated a great deal of revenue for the young state government. By 1836 there were many more farmers in the Algonac area, which was then known as Manchester or *Pointe Du Chene*, the latter meaning Point of the Oaks. In the spring of 1836, the settlers organized the Algonac and Pointe Du Chene Company and plotted the village of Algonac. Their plotting became official in 1843. Henry Rowe Schoolcraft, an agent in charge of Native American affairs, named the city in honor of the Algonquin tribe living in the area. Translated from French, the word Algonac means place of the Algonquin.

For over half a century, Algonac was home to a world-wide boating empire built by Christopher Columbus Smith and his four sons. It was appropriately, if not imaginatively, named the Chris Smith and Sons Boat Company. The Chris-Craft plant employed many residents and became a leader in building powerboats. Algonac remains famous for its numerous speed-boating events and fishing contests. Its location on the St. Clair River has helped define the city.

●Museum

Algonac/Clay Township Historical Society Community Museum, 1240 St. Clair River Drive. The museum is housed in the Bostwick Building, which was built in 1849 in the Greek Revival style. It houses exhibits about local history, local schools, boat building (including Chris-Craft), boat racing, hunting, fishing, and military artifacts.

● Lighthouses

Old South Channel Range Lights. Located off the southeastern tip of Harsens Island, these two lights were built before Abraham Lincoln became president. They are unique because it takes both to guide the great freighters into the South Channel. The front light is 30 feet tall, the rear light 40 feet tall. A ship's captain lines up the two lights and enters the channel to the south of them. The lights opened the channel to 24-hour shipping.

South Channel Front Lighthouse. Courtesy of Pixabay Free Images.

A second unique feature of the Old South Channel Range Lights is the man-made, mini-islands on which they stand. Construction on the lights began in 1855 and was completed in 1859. The front light began to lean in 1875 and was repaired using the stone and timber crib from the original construction. In 1990 the light was again leaning, and a steel cell filled with limestone was placed around its base to offer additional temporary support. In 1996 a permanent seawall was constructed around the front light.

Once described as "The Toughest Little Lights on the Lakes," the lights are on the National Register of Historic Places. Restoration efforts are being undertaken by a hard-working, non-profit staff to save these marvelous pieces of history. The rear light, even though constructed in the same manner and from the same materials, managed to withstand the elements better than the front light, although it, too, eventually needed major foundation work. The rear light had a keeper's house standing next to it until 1930 when it succumbed to vandalism, age, elements, and general deterioration.

● OTHER STOPS OR EVENTS TO CONSIDER

Jobbie Nooner. No discussion of Algonac is complete without mention of the *Jobbie Nooner*. Sue Kulman, an Algonac librarian, describes it as a huge bi-annual bash currently held on Gull Island. It creates monstrous problems for local law enforcement officials as well as for the United States Army Corps of Engineers responsible for Gull Island. But, if you plan to be in Algonac the Friday before the 4th of July or the first Saturday in September, you can guarantee your vacation photos will be interesting.

The annual celebration began in 1975 when Lee O'Dell, a jobber in the auto industry, decided he wanted to take his co-worker and friend, Lee Wagner, out for a birthday blowout. They decided to ditch work for the afternoon or pull a *nooner*. They, and some of their friends, got together on their boats and started to party. That was many decades ago, but the craziness continues. It has grown from seventeen men to nearly five thousand attendees with more than one thousand boats headed to Gull Island's *Mardi Gras of the Midwest*. The event comes with all the revelry, music, and insanity synonymous with the New Orleans version.

The original *Jobbie Nooner* was in Anchor Bay. Only later was Gull Island, an uninhabited island at the entrance to the South Channel, determined to be a better site for this popular celebration. If you are going, you might want to arrive early, although by definition, the party starts at noon. Take lots of sunscreen, no glass bottles, and pick up after yourself. Leave the children home; this rowdy diversion is not suitable for them.

Jobbie Nooner. Courtesy of Pixabay Free Images.

<<>>

Colony Tower, M-29 (Pointe Tremble). This steel-framed water tower is a local landmark, built in 1925 by the Chicago Bridge and Iron Works. It held the main water supply for the Colony on the St. Clair, a secluded residential community established outside Algonac during the early 1920s. The tower, which resembles a lighthouse, is 136 feet tall, and once held a 60,000-gallon water tank. A light on top helped guide aircraft and boat navigation in the area from 1925 through 1937 at which time lighting the tower became cost-prohibitive.

<<>>

St. John's Wet Prairie, Clay Township, (just outside Algonac). Six-tenths of a mile east of the Colony Tower on the north side of the road with a gravel parking lot, you will find 87 peaceful acres of lakeplain prairie. This globally imperiled ecosystem is perfect for canoeing, fishing (no motors), nature study, photography, hunting, and bird watching. Lakeplain prairies are relatively flat, occurring on sand ridges overlying clay. High water tables fluctuate seasonally and over the years with the rise and fall of the Great Lakes. Fires were also important for maintaining lakeplain prairies. It is estimated there are as many as 160 different plants, including blazing star and tall sunflower. Grasses such as big bluestem and Indian grass are found in this marshy area. You can watch great blue herons glide to the ground or search for rarer species of birds.

<<>>

Harsens Island. The Champion Ferry takes you for the short ride to Harsens Island located at the top of Lake St. Clair at the mouth of the St. Clair River. Perhaps the greatest attractions of the Island, which is rather secluded and isolated, are its freshwater deltas, wildlife, and the opportunity for freighter watching. Sportsmen are attracted to the hunting and fishing offered on the Island. Until 1960 Harsens Island was called *Sans Souci*, a name given to it by its first postmaster. The loose translation from French is "carefree" or "serenity with your surroundings."

<<>>

Walpole Island. You can take the Walpole-Algonac Ferry for an eight-minute ride to this First Nation Village called Bkejwanong, meaning "where the waters divide." (Passport required.) The Village is located between the United States and the Canadian mainland on the North Shore of Lake St. Clair. It has been occupied by the original people for over 6,000 years and continues to be home to Ojibwe, Potawatomie, and Odawa. With a common heritage, these three tribes formed the Council of Three Fires, which survives to the current time as a political and cultural council.

Walpole Island possesses one of the richest and most diverse wetland areas remaining in the Great Lakes Basin. There are oak savannas, tallgrass prairies, and Carolinian forests. The wildlife is plentiful and guides are available for a waterfowl hunt. You can enjoy bird-watching (on your own or with a guide), or take guided nature tours. Walpole Island attracts hunters and fishers from many parts of North America. Check the web for a listing of places where you can get hunting and fishing licenses.

The Walpole Island Heritage Center or *Nin da waab jib*, meaning "those who seek to find," was founded in July 1989 as the research arm of the Walpole Island First Nation. The Bkejwanong Territory was not included in any of the eighteenth or nineteenth century land surrenders or treaties, and Walpole Island First Nation continues to assert and exercise Aboriginal title to its territory, unceded lands, and waters.

• GHOST STORIES

The Ghost of the Morrow Street Bridge. A stranger and more contrary tale you will not read in these pages. This is the tale of Annie Smith, although her true name has never passed a storyteller's lips.

Annie was a mere sixteen years old, but her soul was much older. She remembered her mother; the smell of her lilac soap, the sparkle of her eyes when she laughed. Annie was nine years old when that laugh was extinguished. Her mother's life came to a devastating end. Annie became surrogate mother to Emma, her youngest sister, born the same day their mother died. The mother's death left Annie responsible for two brothers and a second sister, all born in the years between Annie and Emma.

Without his wife, Annie's father became distant and unapproachable to his young children. Annie did what she could to keep the family together and provide the love her younger siblings needed.

When she turned fifteen, Annie thought life would get easier. Her sisters were old enough to help her with household chores, and her brothers could take care of themselves. Annie dreamed that she might soon have a life of her own. She smiled thinking of the red-headed, freckle-faced farm boy who lived a mile down the road.

It was late March, and the mean Michigan winter dumped one final snowstorm on the little Algonac community where Annie and her family lived. Two soldiers, heading south from Port Austin to join up with Grant at Appomattox, were forced to seek shelter for the night. They knocked on the family's door. Annie's father invited them in, treated the military men like visiting royalty, and brought out his best moonshine. The men talked about Mr. Lincoln, the country, and farming. Annie smiled, watching her father become more animated than she had seen him since her mother's death. He ordered her to bring out extra blankets and make a pallet in front of the fireplace for their guests. She was pleased to do as she was bid.

It took only a few hours for Annie's happiness to turn sour. She was awakened in the middle of the night to the smell of nasty, liquored breath on her face. A rough, calloused hand covered her mouth and whispered that if she was quiet no one would get hurt. Annie barely had time to think of her sisters sleeping soundly in a single bed only a few feet from her own.

It was over in an hour-long minute. Annie lay in silence until dawn. The soldiers were gone. She boiled a pan of water and tried to wash away the filthy feeling that clung to her body like the ripped and sweat-soaked nightgown.

In 1865 hers was a story best borne in silence—a memory best suppressed. Annie's life might have returned to a semblance of normal had her belly not begun to grow. It wasn't a situation she could share with her father. She corseted her waist and wore looser clothes. No one paid much attention.

It was late November, and the weather was warmer than normal. The full moon intermittently peeked out from dark clouds that threatened a menacing squall. Her first pain came at 9:30 p.m. Everyone in the house was asleep. The farm family's day was charted by the rising and setting of the sun.

Snoring loudly from the soothing effects of alcohol, Annie's father could sleep through a storm, or the agonizing screams of childbirth. But, unlike their father, Annie knew that her brothers and sisters would awaken to any sound she made. She silently put on her high-top shoes without lacing them completely, grabbed her raggedy coat, and tied it about her with a length of rope. She picked up a small knife and a tiny embroidered blanket and made her way into the woods. For the next five hours, she suffered the pain alone—unless you counted the random owls and hawks that occasionally checked her progress. When the final push brought her new daughter into the world, Annie used the small knife to cut the cord.

She whispered the name Annabelle and wrapped the child in the tiny blanket she had lovingly and furtively stitched over the past year. She held the baby close for a few moments, listened to its soft breathing, then laid the precious bundle under a tree and headed toward home.

The infant's cries weakened as Annie put distance between her and her child. When the whimpering was almost inaudible, she could stand it no longer and retraced her steps to reclaim her baby. Before she reached Annabelle, the crying stopped. The clouds covered any illumination from the sky, and the young mother searched in vain.

Annie's physical pain was masked by anguish of the incomprehensible act she had committed. Annie took the rope she used to tie her coat about her and hung herself at the foot of Morrow Bridge. The next morning, Native Americans hunting in the area were the first to see her corpse swaying in the wind. They cut her down and took her body into the village to return to her family.

When settlers, including Annie's father, arrived at the village, they presumed the Native Americans had murdered the young girl. Her blood-soaked dress was the evidence they needed to conclude this was not a natural death. The settlers began firing on the band of Native Americans, killing many.

Over the years there have been reports of glowing green orbs in the area of the bridge and sightings of a bloody woman, beseeching anyone coming near, to help her find the abandoned infant. There are stories that if you go on the bridge and honk your horn three times, you will hear a baby cry. There have been reports of a woman's ghost seen through flames of fire on the road nearby.

One version of the tale sets forth most of the details recounted above, but it does not include the physical assault. Perhaps it was just the boy down the road who fathered the child? Many variations are told, mixing and matching details.

The most interesting attempt to get at the truth was offered by Francis Sampier, who made the ghost the subject of a film about the Morrow Street Bridge Ghost. He said, "The legend started around the 1950s, when a donkey was seen running through the woods. People rumored it was a monster, so the old folks called it the Morrow Road Monster. Then it was rumored to eat babies. Somehow over decades the mother was added to the story, and it became her baby that was eaten. Next, it morphed into a ghost on the road looking for her child."

All because a donkey ran loose!

<<>>

The Harsens Island Ghost. What's a man to do when ghosts inhabit his house? Call Ghost Busters, of course. Or in this case invite them to bid on the chance to spend a night and investigate.

That is what Bob K. did. Bob owned a house on Williams Street on serene and peaceful little Harsens Island. He had owned the residence for thirty years and lived in it for twenty. He had several sons, a daughter, and a wife, all of whom experienced the ghost's presence in the home. After Bob and his wife moved out, one of his sons lived there for a few years. This son reported seeing shadowy people folding clothes and described sleep paralysis and night terrors. He felt that one upstairs bedroom increased his "desires," including that for alcohol.

After the son and subsequent tenants moved out, the house remained unoccupied for several years. The last renters before its abandonment could not contend with the unexplained lights, burning smells, mysterious electrical malfunctions, and loud echoes that defiled the place.

Bob K, not knowing what to do with a haunted house that he couldn't rent, brought in professionals. He ran an ad on eBay that brought several responses from psychics or mediums willing to pay for the opportunity to investigate the paranormal activity in the dwelling.

The Michigan Ghost Society submitted the winning bid. As for what made the house so angry, these ghostbusters claim to have contacted three spirits that may shed light on the situation.

Isabella is the spirit of a woman who worked for a family that owned the house before Bob. Since Isabella did not actually live or die in the house, it is unclear why her spirit remains there.

Timmy is the ghost of a four-year-old boy who was killed by an automobile in front of the house. He was innocently riding his trike when the tragedy befell him. It is relatively easy to see why he might be unhappy.

The third ghost has no name, but is believed to be Timmy's uncle who accidentally ran his car over poor little Timmy. The uncle could be contending with a lot of guilty feelings and anger. Maybe he is shunned in the afterworld.

There may be additional ghosts residing at the Williams Street address, but those are the ones identified by the ghost hunters of the Michigan Ghost Society. During their investigation they described sensations of being choked in the upstairs bedroom. One member of the society contends she was scratched by one of the ghosts. She was wearing a T-shirt and a jacket, and yet claims she sustained a mark that went from the base of her neck down her spine. She suffered several smaller scratches as well.

The Ghost Society used everything from high-tech photography equipment, which was said to have revealed interesting white spots, to spirit sticks to figure out what was happening inside the house.

One thing appears clear: these ghosts are not the mild-mannered Casper types. They want no one in the house and have been heard whispering that visitors should get out.

11. MARINE CITY

Marine City, 2020 population 4,124, occupies a central location along the St. Clair River District. It is one of three international crossings to Canada on the St. Clair River. A quick ferry trip allows a visitor to step off in Sombra, Ontario.

Marine City is a former lumbering town with lovely Victorian homes along Main Street. You will also see registered historical sites like Holy Cross Church and the Nautical Mile. The latter is one of the premier places on the St. Clair River to watch freighters and other marine traffic.

Freighter passing Nautical Mile.
Courtesy of Judy White, Marine City Chamber of Commerce.

In the 1800s, Marine City was a prominent shipbuilding community. In1818 Sam Ward traveled from the East Coast, teamed up with Reverend Gabriel Richard of Detroit, and bought land north of Bridge Street. They established a shipyard at the foot of what is now Broadway Street, and together built some of the finest ships to sail the Great Lakes. For half a century, Marine City's primary industry was shipbuilding. At one time there were five shipyards along the Belle River, which winds through Marine City and provides the perfect opportunity for canoeing before it flows into the St. Clair River.

Parks dot Marine City's shoreline. Their numerous benches invite you to choose a book and idle away the afternoon.

This area of Michigan's Thumb was first home to Native Americans, and then settled by the French, followed by German farmers. Today more than 30 percent of the population can trace its heritage to the hardworking German immigrants.

Marine City celebrates the end of its cold winter with the annual Spring Salmon Festival. Summer brings more celebration and beckons antique enthusiasts from far distances. If you travel this route in the fall, you will have the opportunity to enjoy the magnificent change of colors.

Marine City describes itself as a quaint town in a bustling world. Its downtown boasts turn-of-the-century street lamps, fine and casual dining with great river views, and shops to explore.

Main Street Victorian.
Courtesy of Bob Royce.

● Museum

Pride and Heritage Museum, 405 South Main Street. Exhibits include artifacts from Marine City's nautical history and a fully-equipped blacksmith shop. The museum attempts to bring Marine City to life with three distinct displays: the Maritime, the Lifestyle and Business, and the Commercial Gallery. The highlight of the exhibits is a 4½ by 36-foot diorama showing life on the Belle River in 1885 when five shipyards engaged in producing the finest ships on the Great Lakes. The museum has designed complete furnished rooms dating back 150 years.

● BEACHES, PARKS, AND TRAILS

Algonac State Park, 8732 River Road. A place to indulge in long walks and enjoy the globally significant lakepin prairies and oak savannas. These special habitats include 19 species on the state endangered, threatened, and special concern lists. Prairies and oak savannas require periodic burning to remain healthy.

The park is home to some of the rarest natural communities in Michigan. The Blazing Star Prairie across from the archery range is the best place to view prairie plants, birds, and butterflies. The park contains approximately 1,500 acres with a half-mile of St. Clair River frontage. It is open all year, offering a variety of activities including hiking, trap shooting, small and big game hunting during the fall and winter seasons, and cross-country skiing. From the park you can also spend an enjoyable day watching the freighters move along the St. Clair River.

The park has modern campsites located in two campgrounds. It has three modern toilet/shower buildings, electric service, and a sanitation station. The day-use area has a picnic facility with shelter and restroom facilities. The Algonac State Park provides access to the Bay to Bridge Trail.

<<>>

Marine City Beach, at the end of South Water Street, is the place where crowds gather on a hot day.

Enjoying the sunshine and water at Marine City Beach.
Courtesy of Judy White, Marine City Chamber of Commerce.

• LIGHTHOUSE

Peche Island Rear Range Lighthouse. Now located on the coastline in Marine City, this lighthouse was originally built in 1908, off Peche Island, Ontario, at the head of the Detroit River. It marked the narrow passage from Lake St. Clair into the river. It served from that location for three-quarters of a century.

In 1983 the lighthouse was scheduled for decommission and demolition. That same year, a group of historic-minded citizens of Marine City stepped in to halt the destruction and move the lighthouse to the waterfront in Marine City. The move required a healthy dose of imagination and an even greater degree of tenacity. The job was completed successfully in spite of the fact that the lighthouse weighed 35 tons, stood 66 feet tall, and was 14 feet in diameter.

The lighthouse has no current utilitarian function but adds charm and interest to the waterfront. It is a piece of preserved maritime history.

Marine City Lighthouse.
Courtesy of Judy White,
Marine City Chamber of Commerce.

• OTHER STOPS TO CONSIDER

The **Nautical Mile Walkway** on Huron Street is the place for a summer stroll. You can gain access at the Ferry Landing.

<<>>

Holy Cross Catholic Church.
Courtesy of Bob Royce.

Holy Cross Church, 610 Water Street. This grand old church has a historic-site designation. It is located on a piece of land long known as Catholic Point, given to the church by President John Quincy Adams. The current structure was built in 1903.

<<>>

73

Canadian Stops to Consider

Take a 10-minute ferry ride to Sombra, a quaint little town in Ontario, Canada. (Passport required.) The Spanish word for shade or shady place, *sombre*, was the inspiration for naming this tiny hamlet. Early surveyors found themselves in such a dense forest that the sun could not penetrate. The original people in the area were Shawnee. Sombra was first recognized as a municipal entity in 1826, and for many years, due to a lack of adequate drainage, was called Mudtown. Don't let that prior dismal appellation dissuade you from visiting this charming village with its bird's-eye view of the St. Clair River. You will likely consider it one of the gems of your trip.

<<>>

The Sombra Museum. Housed in a turn-of-the-century Victorian in the heart of Sombra, Ontario, this museum built in 1881 was originally the Bury home. It is presented today with eight rooms furnished as they would have been in the late 1800s. You can experience the hominess and warmth of the kitchen, and the elegance of the dining room which displays silver, crystal, and china from the period. The parlour and music room offer a peek at the entertainment of the time. Even the children's bedroom is filled with toys and clothing of the era. The home provides an excellent example of Victorian architecture, and the furnishings make it feel authentic.

The museum also features a maritime heritage exhibit, which illustrates the importance of the St. Clair River and the Great Lakes to the history of the area. There is an Agricultural and Technology Room which highlights tools used in farming, smithing, logging, cooperage, photography, and butter making. A reference room has archives, cemetery records, and photos of businesses, ships, schools, and churches in the area. The 1930 log cabin characterizes the lifestyle of early Sombra pioneers.

Moore Museum, 94 Moore Line Road, Mooretown, Ontario, Canada. Mooretown is fewer than ten miles north of Sombra and easily accessible by the Marine City Blue Water Ferry followed by a short drive north on St. Clair Parkway. The ferry transports autos as well as passengers. The museum grounds contain a historic riverside village. Among other buildings, it includes a one-room schoolhouse reminiscent of Michigan's early country schools.

The village's historic Trinity St. Clair Chapel, built in 1919, was formerly the Trinity Anglican Church. The church highlights the importance of religion in the community and appears fully equipped to serve with its wooden pews and stained-glass windows. The village has a functional blacksmith shop demonstrating the essential need for a smithy's skills in the early communities.

The Moore Museum 150 Year Celebration. Courtesy of Pixabay Free Images.

A Rear Range Light (lighthouse) from 1890 is preserved on the grounds—retired after guiding ships up the St. Clair River for 92 years. You can visit the original Mooretown Railroad Station. The Reilly Victorian Cottage introduces you to the home life of a bygone day. It features a sitting porch for enjoying the river breezes. The village's more modest Log Cabin shows the home of a settler living in the 1800s and displays handmade quilts and a kettle for dipping candles. The Exhibit buildings house a wide variety of artifacts ranging from a ten-thousand-year-old Mastodon bone to a storefront and miscellaneous marine equipment.

12. ST. CLAIR

Historical accounts are inconsistent regarding the origin of the city's name. According to one source, the name St. Clair pays tribute to General Arthur St. Clare, governor of the Northwest Territory, which included Michigan before it gained statehood. Another account attributes the name to Father Hennepin who traveled through the area on the feast day of Santa Clara.

In 2020 the city's population was 5,485. Settlement of the area began under the British flag in the 1700s. Development was aided by the area's location on the St. Clair River, and St. Clair became the site of a local fort. There are historical landmarks and many of the homes of the early seafaring families remain today. The marina has one hundred slips if you plan to arrive by boat. The visitor to St. Clair has a choice of competing activities including Alice Moore Woods, Imagination Station playground for children, and a spectacular walkway for a stroll along the river on the longest freshwater boardwalk in the United States. All combine to make your visit memorable.

Salt may be Michigan's least publicized natural resource. St. Clair County lies on a sheet of salt. About six hundred million years ago, during the Paleozoic Era and up through about two hundred thirty million years ago, seawater flooded the Michigan basin many times. This seawater receded or simply evaporated, leaving behind mineral deposits known as rocksalt (halite), liquid brines, lime, and sandstone. Early settlers used salt to preserve game. It was critical to survival on the Michigan frontier. Mastodon and musk oxen remains are often found where there are salt seeps. Native Americans used salt as a form of money to barter between tribes.

As Michigan entered the twentieth century, it led the country in the production of salt and many natural salines.

In 1887 the Diamond Crystal Salt Company began tapping the area's vast underground deposits. Cargill Salt (formerly Diamond Crystal) operates a large solution salt mine and evaporation facility in St. Clair. This is the only plant in the United States that produces Alberger salt, which is prized in the fast-food industry.

At Port Huron, St. Clair, and Detroit hot water is pumped into the salt to form artificial brines, which are then pumped and used in the manufacture of salt and in the chemical industries. There are no longer any active salt mines in Michigan. All salt is obtained by the hot water pumping method. In 1886 Diamond Crystal Salt opened a factory in St. Clair. Akzo Salt Company bought Diamond around 1990, and the current owners, Cargill Salt, bought the business from Akzo.

Next winter if you pull out the bucket of salt to de-ice your driveway, or anytime you reach for the salt shaker to flavor your popcorn, remember you owe a debt of gratitude to St. Clair.

• BEACHES, PARKS, AND TRAILS

Avoca Rail Trail. The St. Clair County Parks and Recreation Commission purchased the trail from the CSX Railroad in 1999. It offers 9.82 miles of paths for walkers, hikers, bicyclists, and horseback riders with both paved and unpaved sections. The Mill Creek Railway Bridge, once used for trains, is now a pedestrian walkway, and the highlight of the Avoca Rail Trail.

<<>>

Bridge-to-Bay Trail, 547 North Carney, runs along the shoreline of St. Clair County and is diverse in style and landscape. The 37½-mile trail takes you past state and municipal parks, museums, gazebos, and lighthouses. It starts in Algonac State Park and ends with continuous travel to Greig Park in St. Clair. Other sections north include Marysville, Port Huron (with a section under the Blue Water Bridge), and Fort Gratiot Township. It connects community to community for walkers, joggers, strollers, inline skaters, and bicyclists of all ages. Various sections include boardwalks, river walks, rail trails, safety paths, and bike paths. The trail is a cooperative effort involving the Parks and Recreation Commission and cities and townships located along the St. Clair County Shoreline. To access the trail in St. Clair, turn from Riverview onto Brown Street. The trail starts at Brown and Carney, or you can enter at Greig Park.

<<>>

Greig Park, 547 North Carney. This is a city park with a play area called Imagination Station and a pleasant 1½-mile nature and interpretative trail through the woods that features planked walkways over marshy areas. There are restrooms and a picnic area.

<<>>

St. Clair River Walk. If you have traveled to St. Clair, it would be a shame to leave without walking the longest freshwater boardwalk in the United States.

13. MARYSVILLE

Marysville was incorporated as a city on October 28, 1919. Its 2020 population was 9,639. The city's original name was Vicksburg after E. P. Vickery who built a sawmill in Marysville in the 1840s. Mr. Vickery sold his mill in the 1860s, and the town was renamed for the new owner's wife, Mary. In this lumbering era, the mill was an important part of existence and naming the town or village after the mill owner (or his wife) was a significant honor.

Marysville, like St. Clair, is situated on a salt flat. Visitors can enjoy Marysville's 58-acre city park on the beautiful St. Clair River.

78

• MUSEUM

Marysville Historical Museum, 887 East Huron Street, displays several rooms, each with a single theme, such as Pioneer's Parlor, Marine Room, Native American History, and Fashion Display.

• A PARK

Marysville City Park, Huron Boulevard and Riverview. This is a lovely, treed park with a playground, zero-depth splash pad for tots, picnic tables, restrooms, grills, two boat launches, beach with changing rooms, and terrific views from the 1.2-mile boardwalk along the river.

Marysville City Park. Courtesy of Pixabay Free Images.

LAKE HURON

Lake Huron reaches depths of 995 feet and has a water surface of 23,000 square miles. Her shoreline stretches more than 3,800 miles if you include her 30,000 islands. She has a length of 206 miles and a breadth of 183 miles. She is either the fourth or fifth largest lake in the world, depending upon whether you include the Caspian Sea, which is saltwater, on your list. She has the second largest surface area of the Great Lakes. The Great Lakes are estimated to hold six quadrillion gallons of fresh water. If that is anywhere near true, then Huron must hold well over a quadrillion all by herself. That number boggles the human mind.

Unfortunately, other than what the geologist tells us about her creation, the lake has no recorded history until humans came in contact with her and then, mostly only when they began keeping records. The history we have of her earliest people comes less from them than from the explorers and settlers and traders who arrived later on the lake's shores and offered their European view of the area and its people. That perspective must be considered incomplete, clouded by the customs and beliefs of the newcomers, and somewhat suspect in its description of the indigenous communities living there.

The early French explorers of the sixteenth century came to the New World with a three-fold policy: find better trade routes to the East, exploit the natural resources of the new land including its fur-bearing animals, and missionize the native people. The newcomers were not terribly successful, however well-intentioned, in either the first or last of these goals, although they did manage to exploit the fur trade for many years.

So intense was the desire to reach China that Jean Nicolet met the Winnebago Indians, in what is now Wisconsin, dressed in Oriental silks with patterns of flowers and birds. The Native Americans may have dismissed his costume as no stranger than those of the Jesuits, who came to Christianize them wearing long black robes unsuited to the densely forested and primitive land.

It is a curious fact that Huron was the first Great Lake discovered. Of the chain of five, she sits smack in the middle. It seems logical that early explorers would first have stumbled upon Ontario. A direct path from the Atlantic Ocean would have led to Lake Ontario. However, fear of the Iroquois inhabiting the region of Lakes Erie and Ontario kept European explorers away from those lakes, despite their closer geographic proximity to the American east coast.

Jacques Cartier began exploring Canada in 1535 and gave the French their first claim in New France. He entered through the St. Lawrence Gulf and traveled a short distance inland on the St. Lawrence River, oblivious to the lakes behind and ahead of him.

Champlain reached the tip of Lake Huron at the Georgian Bay during his explorations from 1609 to 1615. Like Cartier, he was unaware of Huron's sister lakes or the great waterway passage from the Atlantic to Lake Superior and Michigan via the St. Lawrence River. He named Huron *La Mer Douce* or the great freshwater sea.

In 1669 Louis Joliet was sent by Champlain on a journey to take supplies to Father Jacques Marquette, a Jesuit priest, who had established a mission at Sault Ste. Marie. Joliet was unable to carry out his assignment because of threatened tribal wars on Lake Superior. While at the Sault, he rescued an Iroquois prisoner who was about to be killed at the stake. Joliet took his new charge back to Quebec, and the prisoner suggested they follow a route directly south from the St. Mary's River.

That was the first time Europeans had descended Lake Huron to the St. Clair River. Joliet continued through Lake St. Clair and the Detroit River eventually coming upon Lake Erie. With continued good luck, Joliet might have discovered the whole water system from the Sault to the Niagara River. However, growing fearful of a band of Andaste Native Americans, he landed about halfway through the length of Lake Erie, hid his canoe, and proceeded eastward by an overland route.

Rene-Robert Cavelier, Sieur de La Salle began a journey in 1679 that took him through the entire Great Lakes Waterway system. Eventually La Salle traveled down the Mississippi and arrived at the Gulf of Mexico in 1682. He had constructed his vessel, *Le Griffon*, just above the Niagara Falls, and sailed through the lakes to Green Bay, Wisconsin. On the return trip, *Le Griffon* became the first major vessel to vanish in Lake Huron. There is more than one story about where her bones rest.

French cartographer, Nicholas Sanson, on his misshapen, but somewhat accurate, 1696 map of the Great Lakes called Lake Huron, *Karegondi*, which simply meant Lake in the language of the local Native Americans. Sanson labeled Lake Michigan *Lac De Puans* or Lake of the Stinking Things.

The above chronology gives credit where recorded history has decided it is due. There is, however, every likelihood that Étienne Brûlé was the first European to travel extensively in the Great Lakes region, and it is he, perhaps, who first saw much of the lake now known as Huron. Unfortunately for Brûlé he could neither read nor write, so he kept no journals of his travels. As is almost always the case, the glory for discovery went to the explorer or explorers who kept a recorded version of their exploits.

Champlain had sent Brûlé, then a very young man, on a mission that undoubtedly took him into the far reaches of the Great Lakes. Brûlé adopted the dress of the Native Americans and learned the Algonquin language. He would have been a great asset to the French in these regions, except for his disloyalty. He sold his services to the English in their ongoing warfare with the French over control of the area. Brûlé was considered a traitor by Champlain. Brûlé was eventually killed in a drunken brawl, and some historians say his body was cannibalized by one of the local tribes.

The name for the lake that has endured, Lake Huron, comes from *Lac De Hurons* which was another name often designated on early maps. The Hurons were the Native Americans living in the area during the time of the French exploration.

By whatever name, she remains majestic and mysterious, and as alluring as awesome. Human words mean nothing to her. Man's love affair with this Great Lake doubtless began when the first human walked through a dense forest that opened to reveal her immense and dazzling splendor. She has afforded a watery highway for travel. She has provided sustenance in the form of her whitefish and salmon, her walleye and perch. She has offered recreation and a means to cool off on those hot, muggy, 90-degree, Michigan summer days. These gifts she gave to the first people reaching her shores, and she continues to graciously extend them to everyone visiting her today.

But Lake Huron demands respect. The fury of storm-driven, 30-foot waves has terrorized many a hapless sailor. Thousands of sunken ships pay a silent, ghostly testament to her raging power. We recognize her unpredictability and watch safely from a distance when her mercurial temper flares, her white caps warning of her anger; even then, we are transfixed by her dark mood.

We always forgive her, unable to hate something so noble and glorious. When she turns a cold shoulder, and a gloomy sky melts into her murky gray waters, we stay inside and watch her sullen movements. In her more melancholy moods, the rhythmic pounding of her waters lulls us to sleep.

She makes us laugh: watching children belly-flop against her surface, watching water skiers take ungainly tumbles, or on occasion, watching wet-suited body surfing in a winter blizzard. She helps us keep things in perspective. She existed many millions of years before us and will likely go on many millions of years after. She makes any minor crisis seem irrelevant, for it too shall pass, and she will go on.

We are awed by her almost unfathomable size. She may not be an ocean, but standing on her banks, unable to see land on the other side, we must concede she is a mighty big body of water.

Walking Lake Huron's Shores

If you walk Lake Huron's shores, you'll find beach glass, driftwood, Petoskey Stones, and plenty of skipping stones. (Your right to walk the shoreline of the Great Lakes is discussed on page 2 of this guide.) Along Huron beaches, you will also find **Pudding Stones.** These are conglomerate rock. That description helps you identify them. You are looking for a rock that appears to have smaller rocks (usually black or red, although sometimes brown or pink or even purple) embedded in it.

These sedimentary and metamorphic stones were formed a billion years ago. Sedimentary rock is made from layers of sediment. Little bits of earth, broken down and worn away by wind and water, are washed downstream where they settle to the bottom of lakes, rivers, and oceans in layers. One layer of earth is piled atop the next and pressed down until the bottom layers slowly turn into rock.

The metamorphic aspect of the rock references the fact that it was changed, or metamorphosed, by great heat or pressure. When the sedimentary rocks were buried deep beneath the earth's surface, the millions of years of heat and pressure changed them into a different form. Both igneous and sedimentary rocks are subject to the metamorphic process. Limestone turns into marble, sandstone becomes quartzite, and shale turns into slate.

The white or gray in the Pudding Stone is quartz sand which has cemented itself together over millions of years. Mixed with it is a combination of other pebbles and stones of various sizes, shapes, and colors. Some of these rocks may even contain fossils. Pudding Stones are also referred to as quartz conglomerates, meaning they are composed of quartz and various other minerals. If you have a keen eye, you will find these unusual stones along the shores.

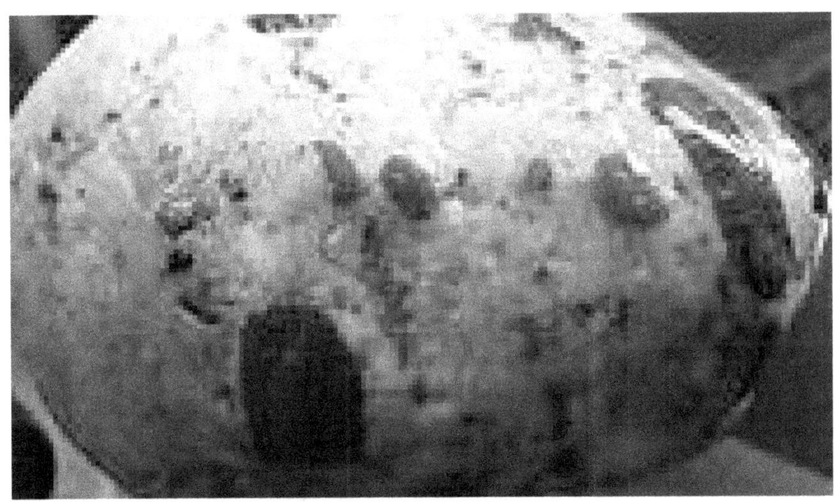

Pudding Stone.
Courtesy of Pixabay Free Images.

Le Griffon may be the first ship on Lake Huron to be designated a ghost ship. Some argue she is the first ship to go down in the Great Lakes, but others claim that dubious honor goes to the *Frontenac*, lost in Lake Ontario in early 1669. If the *Frontenac* went down earlier, *Le Griffon* may be the first big ship to vanish in Lake Huron. *Le Griffon* was built by René-Robert Cavelier Sieur de La Salle, weighed forty-five tons, and had five guns. She was on her maiden voyage in 1679 and had sailed across Lake Erie, Lake Huron, and Lake Michigan. She picked up a load of furs and was headed back through Lake Huron on her return trip when she went down with all six of her crewmembers. She has been followed to the depths of Huron by more than a thousand ships, but perhaps because *Le Griffon* was first recorded large vessel, her crew is the angriest. Or, perhaps it is the persistent rumors of a mutiny that make her rest uneasy.

Look into the mist some foggy morning, and you may see her sail by.

Le Griffon Woodcut by Father Hennepin. Public Domain.

<<>>

The Storm of 1913.

The **Charles Price,** the **Isaac Scott,** the **James Carruthers,** the **Wexford,** the **Regina,** the **John McGean,** the **Hydrus,** and the **Argus.** Eight huge freighters sank in Lake Huron during The Big Blow. It was a killer-storm, the likes of which had never been seen before, and the fury of which would never be seen again. While the remains of the ships that went down that night may belong to a specific beach or city, the magnitude of the disaster is best understood by the story that uniquely belongs to Lake Huron.

The Ojibwe have a legend that explains November's fury. They attribute the whims of the winds to two spirits: Gitche Manitou and Matchie Manitou. Gitche Manitou is a good wind spirit that favors Ningabianinodin, the pleasant and steady West Wind. Gitche Manitou also loves the gentle South Wind, Jawaninodin, that brings the pleasant summer breezes.

Matchie Manitou, on the other hand, is an evil wind spirit that favors Kiwedininodin, the terrible North Wind, or Wabaninodin, the evil East Wind that breeds many of the Lake's tempests.

When the winds become schizophrenic and seem unable to find their direction, the Ojibwe believe it is the two spirits competing to test their wind-summoning strengths. The maelstrom of 1913 made Lake Huron the playing field of the competing winds. At some point, as in many sporting events, the game got out of hand. During that November weather aberration, a dozen or so longships became Gitche Manitou and Matchie Manitou's playing pieces.

Settlers in the Thumb area, oblivious to the legends of Gitche Manitou and Matchie Manitou, spent November 9 in their own houses of worship. When they entered their

87

churches, the weather was an unseasonably warm 80 degrees. Mother Nature could not decide if she was headed to December or retreating to August. The heat, so uncharacteristic of November, begged a last day at the beach.

As a Lexington congregation sat in their pews singing *Shall We Gather At the River*, the music was drowned by sounds like that of ricocheting buckshot. Pellets of ice, snow, and sleet peppered the handsome stained-glass windows and the temperature dropped at least 50 degrees by the time the pastor sent ushers to take up the collection.

On the lake two days earlier, one seasoned captain had predicted the white hurricane, but crews of other ships were ignorant of his warning. Captain George Holdridge captained the steamer, *Robert W. Bunsen.* On November 7, he was downbound on Lake Huron. His crewmen believed the unseasonably hot weather and placid lake were cooperating with their efforts to get their last haul of the season behind them.

Captain Holdridge saw it differently. He had been a sailor all of his life. He had sailed the salt waters of the China Sea, where he developed an internal barometer that told him with no uncertainty what was coming. On this November morning, as his ship briskly traversed the glassy Huron surface, Holdridge grew concerned about what his internal weather equipment predicted. The sky was copper-colored and although the sun was out, he could not distinguish it. The world was cloaked in surrealistic garb. When the *Bunsen* was off Harbor Beach, Holdridge announced to a crewmate, "Boy, you're going to see a storm such as you never saw before!" The Captain then called down to the engine room and ordered his chief to give it all he could; they needed to make time. He knew the storm was coming; he just was not sure when the monster would strike.

About the same time church let out, the *James Carruthers*, the *Wexford,* and the *Hydrus* entered Lake Huron headed downlake. They ignored the warning flags and lights hoisted in accord with maritime procedure. These ships had endured rough seas on Superior and hoped Huron would afford them better conditions.

At the far end of the lake where the St. Clair River gives way to the big lake's open water, the *Charles Price*, the *John A. McGean,* and the *Isaac Scott* charted a northern course at daybreak. Warnings in both Sarnia and Port Huron signaled the folly of their actions. With heavy gale warning flags flying in a hundred ports as early as the preceding Friday morning, it seems foolhardy that ship captains blithely ignored the threat. But November storms didn't frighten them, and they needed to make every minute count before the close of navigation for the season. Chances were taken. For many it was the last run of the year, and they were eager to get home. They didn't know it would be the last run of their lives.

The storm started no more threatening than many wild November squalls originating on Lake Superior. By the time it reached Huron two days later, it had mutated into a witch's brew beyond anything seen before or since. It was birthed by an unusual and horrific confluence of factors. A massive low-pressure system had spawned in the Aleutians and moved steadily over the Canadian provinces on a course headed for Superior. A second low-pressure system, born in the Rocky Mountains, beat a northeasterly path from lower Minnesota to join the first. The marriage of these two colossal fronts brought savage and sustained winds and rough seas. The fickle gusts started from the east, turned in minutes to the south, or north, or even west, as though they could not make up their minds from which direction they wanted to pummel the sea.

This was bad, yet predictable. What came next was unprecedented. A third low-pressure system originating in the Gulf of Mexico swept northward from Georgia in an abnormal route. This diabolical third front covered the east coast with record-breaking snowfalls and hurricane-strength winds.

Straight from the docks of lower Lake Huron, the three fronts converged, creating a cataclysm like no other. The lake convulsed and churned under the assault of hurricane-strength winds. The snow raged down and sideways in 80- and 90-mile-per-hour gusts in a gale that lasted for at least twenty-four hours.

Lake Huron lies in a geographic area where cyclonic storms can and do come up quickly—often without warning. The lake also has its own peculiar and distinctive danger spots. One of the foremost is the Six Fathom Bank that lies almost due east of the Black River and Port Huron. It is in the center of the lake and not too far from what would normally be considered by ship captains to be a fair uplake or downlake course. The earliest explorers like Father Louis Hennepin received warnings from local Native American tribes to avoid that area and stay close to the coast because the sands made navigation dangerous when they were disturbed by high wind.

During the storm of 1913, ship captains operated blind. The storm reduced visibility in most parts of the lake to mere feet. Captains gave up trying to stay on course and fought to stay afloat and avoid collisions. In one instance, their efforts may have been sabotaged by a lightship keeper's unwillingness to authorize a payment of $25. The operator of the light had been offered the services of a Canadian tug to tow her back to her assigned station. He balked because he was not authorized to make the expenditure. It is one of the unnecessary horrors of such natural disasters. During foul weather, ship captains depended on the lightship stationed offshore at the mouth of the St. Clair River to guide them safely from Lake Huron into that narrow river channel. By midday on Sunday, November 9, 75-mile-per-hour winds drug the lightship and her anchors two miles east and two miles southeast, leaving her up against the Canadian shore. By a cruel quirk of fate, her light and fog signal continued to operate, guiding unsuspecting ships into the waiting trap of the Corsica Shoal. This tragic circumstance claimed the *Northern Queen* and the *Matthew Andrews.*

Captain Joseph Lampoh had successfully brought the *Andrews*, loaded with iron ore, down the length of Lake Huron through the early hours of the vicious storm. Relying on the signals from the lightship, he then steered her aground at Kettle Pointe, Ontario.

In fairness, although both the *Northern Queen* and the *Matthew Andrews* were forced ashore by misdirection and these vessels sustained heavy damage, the crews lived to tell the tale of the Storm of 1913. The crews of ten others (two in Lake Michigan) did not. What we know of their ordeal is speculation supplanted by the accounts of vessels, like the *Hanna*, that passed them as she headed to shore and relative safety.

We love tales of adventure, and there will always be a romanticism connected with sailing the seas and braving its dangers. But on Sunday, November 9, and Monday, November 10, 1913, it can be said with absolute certainty that no captain or crewman considered himself (or herself, because a couple of women went down too) caught in a web of romantic circumstances. Theirs was a raw and ugly struggle for survival and, unlike sentimental formulaic plots, there would be no triumphant happy ending.

Romance was starkly absent as these terrorized men and women clutched slippery railings with numbed fingers and fought desperately to keep from going over. Giant sheets of ice, intent upon capsizing their colossal freighters, repeatedly swamped them. Romance must have been miles from their minds as they sought last-minute reprieves from a god who seemed to have momentarily lost track of them, but with whom they were intent on making final peace. Every gesture, every act was a meaningless effort in futility. They were going down.

Some of their distress calls were heard on shore, but there was no possibility of sending assistance. Aboard, they got out the life rafts and vests, both useless and trivial protection against a sea that sent waves 35 feet high exploding over them—waves capable of taking a flat-bottomed ship, over 500 feet in length or nearly twice the distance of a football field and weighing several hundred tons, and flipping her turtle-style to the bottom.

The best they could hope for was an easy death. Perhaps for a few lucky victims, death was instantaneous, a blow to the head by flying debris. For others it may have been blessedly brief as they gasped for two or three minutes to suck in fresh air, but were doused by angry water that filled their straining lungs. For the remainder of the crew, it meant freezing to death. Floating around them, the last earthly sights they would witness were carnage from their ships and the bodies of their mates.

The morning it all ended, a farmer saw what appeared to be several men covered with ice walking out of the water. Upon closer inspection, he discovered frozen corpses bobbling upright in the waves, held in that position by their worthless lifejackets.

Altogether, eight long-ships vanished in Lake Huron that wretched night. So spiteful was the storm that the final resting place of the *James C Carruthers* remains a mystery.

The *Wexford* moldered in an unknown grave until 2000. The *Hydrus* was not found until November 2015, more than a century after she sank. The 416-foot long, 4,700-ton vessel was discovered sitting upright on the bottom of Huron and was identified by a sign bearing her name found inside the engine room.

When the White Hurricane ended, it fell to the living to pick up the pieces. The final death count from the Big Blow is estimated at 248. Of those, 178 perished in the original Sweet Water Sea, Lake Huron. These numbers are considered fairly accurate, but back then ship rosters were not kept in a precise manner. Many crewmen were not listed by their full or legal name. Local cemeteries where they are buried honor them only as Skip or Red. Some may never be acknowledged.

The number of victims would have been greater if the ships had carried passengers. These were cargo ships, and the crew of the largest numbered 28. Two sets of twin ships perished: the *Charles S. Price* and her sister ship the *Isaac M. Scott*, and the *Argus* and her sister ship the *Hydrus*.

The eight ships that perished in Lake Huron during the storm of 1913:

Vessel	Lives Lost	Length in Feet	Capacity in tons	Value in 1913
Charles S. Price	28	524	9,000	$340,000
Isaac M. Scott	28	524	9,000	$340,000
James Carruthers	`19	550	9,500	$410,000
Wexford	17	270	2,800	$125,000
Regina	15	269	3,000	$125,000
John A. McGean	23	452	7,500	$240,000
Argus	24	436	7,000	$130,000
Hydrus	24	436	7,000	$130,000

The *H. M. Hanna Jr.* and the *Matoa* were also deemed total constructive losses, but because they made it to shore, there was no loss of life.

The following is the best account available of what happened to each of the great ships that perished.

The **Charles S. Price** was seen by Captain A.C. May of the *H.B. Hawgood* on Sunday afternoon, November 9. Captain May had steered his ship some distance up Lake Huron before he realized the enormity of the weather conditions. He hauled around and started back for the relative safety of the St. Clair River. Near Harbor Beach, he saw the *Price.* She was moving north toward the worst of the storm.

It is clear that at some point the *Price,* too, turned around, because her remains were found close to the entry to the St. Clair River at Port Huron. Observers believe if she had managed to get an additional fifteen miles behind her, she might have survived. Instead, she was one of the great ships to "turn-turtle."

On Monday morning, November 10, Captain Plough of the Lakeview Lifesaving Station above Port Huron searched the tossing water with his telescope and spied what appeared to be the hull of a vessel. There were no masts or smokestack. Plough called Captain Tom Reid of the Reid Wrecking Company in Sarnia, who in turn, sent a big tug to investigate. Reid confirmed that a huge, flat bottomed freighter was flipped upside-down. The bow was about thirty feet out of the water, but the stern was submerged. It was not possible to tell the length of the ship nor could its identity be established, as the hull looked exactly like the hull of many other ships.

For six days, she remained a mystery ship amid speculation that it was the *Regina,* the *James C. Carruthers,* or the *Wexford.* Finally, William Baker, a diver from Detroit, plunged into the icy waters, worked his way around the hull, clutching the railings above him, and found the nameplate. He checked it twice to be sure. There was no indication of a collision, and there was no other vessel trapped under its bow. The wrecked boat's peculiar position was caused by trapped air that was escaping in a tiny, slow stream of bubbles. All doubt was gone. It was the *Charles S. Price*. The *Price* sank from sight on November 17, eight days after she had been tossed upside down by the monstrous sea.

For one woman, awaiting the news identifying the mystery ship, it was the end of uncertainty, but also the end of hope. She was the wife of second mate, Howard Mackley, and she finally knew her husband's fate. When the ship had passed Detroit early on Sunday morning, her husband had posted a letter to her. When the *Price* was abreast their home in St. Clair, he pulled the whistle in customary salute. Mrs. Mackley was there waiting to wave a response greeting. She watched his ship travel upriver until it was out of sight, unaware it was the last time they would perform their loving ritual.

For assistant engineer Milton Smith, who had looked at the weather forecast in Cleveland and decided to sit this one out, there was the relief of simply being alive. He had felt uneasy about the trip for days and tried to talk his friend and neighbor, wheelsman Arz McIntosh, into leaving with him, but McIntosh insisted he needed the money.

Of all of the ships that went down that terrible night, it was the *Price* that caused the most concern. No one believed a bulk freighter with its wide flat-bottom could possibly be flipped over and sunk like a toy boat in a bathtub.

<<>>

The **Isaac Scott** was also spotted by Captain A.C. May, as he headed for safety at the foot of the lake. Captain May encountered the *Scott* about five or six miles north of the Port Huron Lighthouse at approximately 3:30 p.m. on Sunday. May later described his feeling that the *Scott's* captain had been a fool to leave the St. Clair River, the very destination for which May was headed. It seemed inconceivable that the *Scott's* captain would make for the open waters of the storm-churned lake.

The *Scott* foundered farther up Lake Huron, near Pointe aux Barques. Relatively little sign of her was immediately found, other than one empty lifeboat with its canvas covering still intact. The lack of drifting bodies and artifacts suggested she capsized quickly without providing the crew enough warning to make even vain attempts to avoid certain death.

<<>>

The **James C. Carruthers** was a Canadian ship making her third voyage. Because the captain's name was William H. Wright, and the manager of Marine Affairs for the company owning her was also named Wright, the boat was nicknamed the "All-Wright boat." For three days after the storm, panicked family members and the ship's owner waited for the final word of whether the *Carruthers* was lost. Evidence began drifting in—a lifejacket, an oar, a piece of debris believed to have been part of her cabin. Bodies began appearing and quashed lingering hopes. The ship's owner predicted they would never find Captain Wright, who under all circumstances would go down with his ship. Perhaps more astonishing is that the *Carruthers* has never been found.

One amazing story of survival came out of the sinking of the *Carruthers*. Days after the storm, Thomas Thompson was summoned to Goderich by his daughter, Mrs. Edward Ward of Sarnia. She told her father that she had just identified the body of her brother, John Thompson. The elder Mr. Thompson arrived, and like his daughter, identified his son's body. The waters may have been unkind, but there was no mistaking the J.T. tattoo, the scars on his nose and leg, and the two deformed toes. Father and daughter set about making funeral arrangements.

96

Meanwhile, in Toronto, John Thompson was surprised to read about his death in the newspaper. Without calling, he hopped a train for Sarnia and arrived in time to crash his own funeral! He had not been aboard the ill-fated Carruthers.

<<>>

The **Wexford** spewed its bodies and cargo on the Canadian shores. Even after the snows melted, the beaches were white with her 96,000 bushels of spilled grain. The *Wexford* remained invisible for eighty-seven years until she was finally discovered in 2000 near Grand Bend, Ontario.

Out of every natural disaster, there is always one story of someone lucky enough to have missed a train, a plane, or in this case, the ship that meets tragedy. During this storm, it was James McCutcheon, a sailor on the *Wexford*. After the storm, he was among the small army of people who rushed to the lakeshore to identify bodies. He had missed the train to Sarnia where he planned to board the *Wexford*. McCutcheon had been late and missed his ship on only three occasions in his life. The first time the ship caught fire and sustained heavy casualties. The second time the ship was wrecked and suffered a heavy loss of lives. As he stood surveying the bodies of his dead shipmates, he uttered the understatement of the disaster, "I'm the luckiest guy alive."

<<>>

The **Regina** went down in mystery and speculation. The bodies of crewmen from the *Price* and the *Regina* floated to shore together. Sometimes the waves threw them into each other's arms. Twelve men, later identified as being from the crew of the *Price*, were found wearing the life jackets of the *Regina*. The explanation that makes the most sense is that the two ships collided before sinking and in those moments before they went under, men slipped and slid from the deck of one doomed ship to the other. Perhaps believing one ship might survive, some crewmen may have jumped to the more stable of the two. During the pandemonium that must have broken out, men likely grabbed whatever life preservers were available with no consideration for which ship it came from.

If a collision did take place, one of the ships had to limp for many miles before going under, since the *Price* was found in Port Huron, and the *Regina* was found thirty miles farther up lake between Lexington and Port Sanilac.

The *Regina* may have been the most ill-equipped vessel to venture forth and vanish in the Great Storm. When it was all over, it would not have made a difference. She was making her last trip for the season and Captain McConkey was eager to get home to his wife and two daughters. At Sarnia he picked up a heavy load of iron pipe that was lashed to his deck before he headed into Lake Huron. His ship's broken communication equipment prevented him from knowing how severe the storm warnings were. It is believed that the ship made it as far as Saginaw Bay when the brutal winds forced her to turn back.

Water began to freeze everywhere on the ship. The crew put on life preservers and readied the lifeboats. By 11:00 p.m., the captain was the only man left on the ship. People on shore heard his mayday pleas, but in the face of 90-mile-an-hour winds and 35-foot waves, they were helpless to offer any assistance. The captain was a frightened 34-year-old husband and father who only wanted to see his family again. His body was found nine months later, along with his watch and his diary. He was the last of the crew to be found. His ship was not found for 73 years.

Missing from the *Regina* when she sank was George Gosby. Three weeks earlier, Gosby stumbled over a hatch cover and fell into the hold as the *Regina* was loaded. Initially feeling sorry for himself for having to sit out the remainder of the season, he had reason to consider it his lucky break.

The **John A. McGean** floundered and sank about 75 miles north of Port Huron and slightly north of Harbor Beach. The *McGean* was captained by the colorful Dancing Chauncey Ney, who as his nickname suggests, loved to dance. He liked to be in port on Friday and Saturday nights so he could catch the local dances. He never left the dance floor until the band played its last tune.

One of the *McGean's* life rafts drifted onto the beach with its gruesome crew of three dead men lashed to it. A second *McGean* raft carried a single body. The frozen bodies of most of the remaining crew were found washed ashore and scattered randomly along the sand and rocks. A few remained, bobbing in the water. All were accounted for except Chauncey Ney whose last dance partner was an angry Lake Huron.

The **Argus** was the only ship to sink that day before the eyes of horrified witnesses. Captain Walter C. Iler of the steamer *George C. Crawford* was fighting his own battle on the rogue and rampaging sea when he witnessed a scene he would remember forever. Captain Iler was attempting to turn his huge vessel around but meeting with little success when a temporary lull in the wind helped him right his ship and escape the raging waters. Sometime late Sunday afternoon, between snowy whiteouts, he caught sight of the *Argus* laboring strenuously beneath her heavy load of coal. Her bow and her stern appeared suspended by huge waves going in different directions, leaving the cargo-heavy midsection unsupported in the gap between the waves. Iler watched her crumble like an eggshell and disappear.

Captain Paul Gutch of the *Argus* washed ashore with no lifejacket. Mrs. William Walker was a second cook on the

Argus. When her body floated out of the water, she wore the lifejacket marked Captain—likely an unselfish act of heroism, but for naught. No life jacket protected against the whirling white waters made foamy by ice and snow.

<<>>

The **Hydrus**, twin sister ship to the *Argus*, was the ship with the worst recovery rate for bodies. Several are believed to have washed onto the rocky shores of the Saugeen Native American Reservation. Speculation suggested that the Native Americans, because of cultural beliefs, were hesitant to touch the bodies. Shifting winds and currents may have carried some of the dead to places where no one would find them. Two lifeboats with bodies of seamen from the *Hydrus* were recovered, but it was 102 years before the wreckage of the *Hydrus* revealed itself.

In the storm's aftermath, several bodies washed ashore with watches still on the victims' wrists. Many of the watches stopped between 8:00 p.m. and 11:00 p.m. on Sunday, November 9. The weather bureau reported that the highest winds on Lake Huron came between six and eight o'clock that evening.

While Lake Huron buried many secrets beneath her turbulent waves that awful night, she did give up another. Near Harbor Beach, fishermen found a body and wreckage from a tug, the *Searchlight,* which had vanished with all hands aboard in 1908. The violent storm had unearthed her watery grave.

<<>>

Less than a year after the big storm, the Great Lakes offered a possible demonstration of how those freighters capsized in November 1913. On May 8, 1914, the *Kirby* sank in a relatively modest storm. The *Kirby* was regarded as seaworthy, but she sank almost without warning. The investigation revealed that a great wave crashed over the port bow, submerging the deck. The weight of the water pushed the bow downward and tipped the stern high in the air. Before the *Kirby* righted herself, a second wave came at her and stood the boat in a position with her hull poised out of the water. A third deadly wave then caught her from beneath. She heaved upward, stood motionless for thirty seconds, and then plunged to the bottom.

Captains of the ships that managed to get ashore during the Storm of 1913 reported their vessels being struck by waves coming from all directions.

Immediately after the Storm of 1913, the death count and human suffering were foremost on everyone's mind. Later, it became apparent that the White Hurricane had also destroyed one of the Thumb's major industries. Docks crumbled at Harbor Beach, Lexington, Forester, and Port Sanilac. They were never rebuilt. The great cargo freighters no longer stopped at these small towns. The transportation of goods moved inland to the railroad. Shipping and transportation in the Thumb had changed forever.

Today, meteorologists would call the Storm of 1913 a weather bomb. To many of the Thumb's people it was the end of the world as they had known it.

The Days Michigan Burned.

The Horrific Fires of 1871 and 1881. In the late 1800s, two tragic fires, a decade apart, had a profound impact on the citizens who lived along Lake Huron. From Port Huron to Mackinac City, fields roll gently to Huron's shores, and these cataclysmic infernos changed forever Michigan's Sunrise Coast.

You don't have to put out the fire
when all is burned out. Unknown.

Everything in the path of the two massive fires lay in ruins. Counting the dead and calculating the loss was left to the survivors. The rich lumber industry had turned to ash.

In the early days of its recorded history, Michigan was one giant forest. Timber was a valuable resource. The area seduced lumber barons intent on making their fortunes. Many who fell under the spell were not disappointed. Their success rates were better than those of gold prospectors who stampeded San Francisco about the same time. More money was made from the sale of Michigan timber than from all of the gold mined in Alaska during the Yukon Gold Rush.

Dozens of sawmills marked the landscape along the rivers and tributaries of Sanilac, Huron, and Tuscola counties. Small towns devoted to lumbering sprouted on the shores of the Great Lakes. Lumbering was the lifeblood of their early economies, and the mill was the heart pumping that blood.

Although it was a time when the white pine was king, numerous farms had been cleared and cultivated. When the final flames of the two great fires were extinguished, most of the farms had been razed.

The Fire of 1871
It would be difficult to find anyone who has not read a historical account of the Chicago Fire of 1871, but many are unaware of the tragedy that befell Michigan that same day. Both fires started on October 8. That day and the next will always be known as the Days Michigan Burned.

August and September that year had been unseasonably dry. Not a drop of rain had fallen in two months. The severe drought was superimposed on Michigan's irresponsible and greed-inspired lumbering practices. The conflagration that roared into the Thumb demanded payback for human imprudence. The fire began on the west side of the state on October 8, and by October 9, the Thumb was in full-reddened fury.

Before it became the enormous wall of fire that rolled across the entire width of Michigan, the fire had modest beginnings. Many small brush fires burned, started by farmers clearing their land. They multiplied and ran together, their proliferation fed by the dry air over the land rather than the moist air from Lake Huron. The wind changed direction often, and carried chips of burning wood and sparks from these smaller fires to ignite new blazes. Eventually it became one huge sheet of flames.

It was called a "Tree Top" fire because it was fueled by gigantic piles of treetops left behind as lumbering operations took the valuable trunks and littered the forest floors with useless tops. The limbs and pine slash became tinder to fuel the relentless flames. The accumulated needles and twigs held heavy amounts of resin, and when combined with the leaves, treetops, and other dried organic matter, this mixture burned with intense heat. These fires roared hottest at ground level and destroyed everything in their paths. At some spots, the direction seemed arbitrary, as the flames jumped a house here or a barn there and picked up again on the other side. Just as often as not, when the wind changed, the fire returned, and consumed what it missed the first time.

Farmers, who awakened to screams of "fire," struggled to hold back the onslaught. Some gave up and scrambled out of harm's way, looking back to see their homes, livestock, and meager possessions destroyed. Others, who stayed, succumbed to the smoke and flames and left only their charred remains to document their deaths.

The relentless, racing devastation sent people from Forester and other lakeside villages into the water. Those fortunate enough to salvage a boat embarked on the lake and covered themselves with wet clothing and quilts. Their only hope, their only prayer, their only salvation, was that their Lake would stop the devil-driven hell.

Some desperate farmers tried to outrun the firestorm. One family climbed into their wagon, covered themselves with wet blankets, and headed for a stream a half-mile away. They arrived seconds before the wagon began to burn. They dove into the shallow water, again covering themselves with wet blankets to squelch the embers that rained down on them. There was nothing more to do but wait for the inferno to recede and pray they would be alive when it did.

It took Forester a mere half hour to burn to the ground. Some people stood at the lake's edge contemplating their choice of death—drowning or burning.

At Sand Beach, currently the city of Harbor Beach, William Mann was awakened by a neighbor with news that fire was coming. Mann and his wife made desperate attempts to bury some of their most critical tools, hoping to save them for the daunting task of rebuilding that they knew would face them if they escaped alive from this furnace.

The Mann farm stretched to Lake Huron. When it became clear their lives were in danger, Mr. Mann sent his children to the shore, instructing them to wade in the water and remain there until it was safe to come out. Mrs. Mann remained to help her husband battle the blaze. The oldest child, Rachel, age seven, carried the baby on one hip, and the others tagged along as their father had ordered.

The children were not the first to arrive at the lakeshore. Several other neighbors were already standing in the waves, soaking their clothes, and hoping to escape death since the flames could not follow them into the water. But the waves were ferocious that night, riled by the same gale force winds that spread the fire. Some women and children were unable to stand in the onslaught of the water's rush and were thrown repeatedly back against the beach.

Jim Huxtable arrived at the shore dragging a large open boat. With his family safely aboard, he prepared to shove off and head for open water where they might all breathe a little easier. The smoke was becoming as dangerous as the fire. Seeing the terror in the eyes of the young Mann children, he took pity on them and loaded them aboard.

The little group rowed out only a short distance before everything on land disappeared behind the dense smokescreen. During the night, the wind picked up and Mr. Huxtable tried to row closer to shore so the waves would not capsize his crowded vessel, but the shore was not where it was supposed to be. Huxtable shouted out to anyone who might be on the beach. He received no reply.

When the sun finally rose on a new day, Huxtable found himself far out into the lake and could not see land in any direction. One child had died during the night. The ship and its twelve survivors carried no food, and everyone was drenched and cold and hungry. For three days, they continued to drift.

On the morning of October 12, Mr. Huxtable saw land in the distance. He rowed to the Canadian shore, and there, in the town of Goderich, they buried the dead child.

It was feared that Mr. and Mrs. Mann were dead. But a local newspaper carrying the pathetic story reached the parents, who it turned out, had miraculously survived. The family was reunited in Port Huron in one of the few happy endings during the tragedy.

Thousands of acres of valuable lumber were gone by the time the fire burned out. It is estimated that the dwellings, barns, household goods, winter provisions, grain, and livestock of between 4,000 and 5,000 people were destroyed.

<<>>

The Fire of 1881

The horror Michigan residents believed was behind them returned a decade later with even greater enormity and intensity. The conditions were similar. There had been no measurable rainfall in two months. The area was parched.

And this time Michigan's Thumb was more densely populated. In retrospect it seems as though the first hideous fire was a mere prelude. The aftermath of the earlier blaze turned the attention of farmers to the land being sold cheap by struggling lumber companies. In spite of the drought conditions, many of those farmers spent time clearing their land of trees and stumps and the new growth that had sprouted after the previous fire. They were aided in their task by shovels, picks, handsaws, and matches. Of those tools, matches were the most effective. Brush fires were built to clear the timber, and in a situation reminiscent of the 1871 fire, dry kindling and gale winds again created a lethal combination.

In many places, the fire of 1871 had deadened the green timber and allowed it to dry out and become tinder for this second, more hellish fire. There is an old proverb that says wood already touched by fire is not hard to set alight. Nowhere did that have a more literal meaning than in Michigan's Thumb in 1881.

On September 5, a month and four days short of the tenth anniversary of the 1871 fire, this second conflagration took only four hours to travel across the entire width of the Thumb, leaving 150 people dead in Sanilac County alone.

More than 14,000 people living in the Thumb were left destitute; 1,521 homes were destroyed, 1,480 barns were reduced to rubble, 51 schools were nothing more than ashes. When the remaining county death tallies were added to Sanilac's, the final figure rose to over 300. Scores more died later of smoke inhalation or complications from their burns. The number of seriously injured or blinded was staggering.

The flames of the inferno advanced with such speed that they overtook galloping horses. The fire was so scorching hot that it burned buildings and trees to the ground with the only trace they ever existed a powdery ash residue covering the scarred earth. Horrified onlookers described the blaze as soaring a hundred feet high.

Some hapless victims in the Thumb had warning before the flames showered down on them; blinding smoke filled the air long before the flames were visible. Lamps were lit mid-day due to the sooty darkness.

Stories abound of the victims' desperate survival measures. Families crowded into wells and remained huddled there for several hours before summoning the courage to crawl out; some didn't survive long enough to crawl out.

One such tragedy befell the Freiburger family living in Austin Township. Frantic to escape the raging fire, they jumped into their shallow well, where searchers later found their suffocated bodies. A local cemetery marks their deaths with eight headstones. In Wheatland Township, six bodies were found on a burned-out farm. Neil and Mary Erhart and their newborn baby daughter were among them; the infant's future extinguished before the flames were put out.

Parisville, barely a dot on the map, contributed 28 victims to the final death toll. Yet just east of this small village, the Lemanski family surprised the blaze by doing the only thing that seemed to make sense in such a catastrophe. They dropped to their knees and asked God to spare them. They later described a miracle; the flames parted and went around them. Out of gratitude, the family erected a cross at the site.

In Bad Axe, the winds began at noon. By 1:00 p.m., the city was enveloped in darkness. Residents heard a strange roar. It was the sound of the approaching flames that would soon storm down from heaven. As the fire swept into town, people were lifted into the air and set down again by winds generated from the intense heat. Four-hundred people huddled in the new brick courthouse and watched as the buildings around them turned to rubble. A group of about thirty men inside the courthouse sanctuary made frantic trips to the pump for water to keep the walls and floors of the building wet. When the first group was overcome by smoke and exhaustion, a second shift of men took over. They watched in horror when the darkened hardware store across the street burst into a bright red glare as kerosene and gunpowder ignited. The fire moved so quickly that it traveled from Bad Axe to the lakeshore in less than two hours.

Amidst dire warnings, postman Ira Humphrey took the words "the mail must go through" to a new and fatal level. Despite the inferno blazing in the Thumb, he continued to make his daily rounds—even after warnings from several people that the area was too dangerous. He replied that he was delivering the mail, and he had to go on. He finally came to a clearing where the onlookers were adamant that he stop. He unharnessed his horse and proceeded a short way to get a better look. He reported to the group that he thought he could make it, and with that, he began walking in the direction of danger. His clothes caught fire. He removed his vest and jacket and rolled in a field trying to extinguish the flames. Another wave of fire surged toward him.

When rescuers recovered his body, the crystal of his watch was melted. His horse found its way to a local farm where the owner was fighting his own heroic battle against the blaze. The neighbor could not personally deliver the sad information about Mr. Humphrey's demise to the waiting Humphrey family. He wrote a note, attached it to the horse's neck, gave the horse a swat on the rump, and sent it home carrying the grave news.

One local farmer recalled that a neighbor's team of oxen came through the fire alive but lost their hooves. Another neighbor turned six hogs loose, and the only trace he later found of them was six large grease spots several yards from where he had set them free.

Perhaps the most ill-advised actions of the disaster were those of a man, who believed his death was imminent and slit the throats of his livestock to spare them suffering. He then took his shotgun and placed the barrel in his mouth ending his own life. The fire passed all around his place and left his buildings untouched.

Surely the most poignant image of the fire was that of a young mother, her charred remains found in a crouched position on the ground, with her five children kneeling and encircling her. One hand of each child rested in her lap.

After the fire subsided, William Bailey, a sergeant in the U.S. Army Signal Corps, was sent to the area to take an accounting of the situation. He talked to the survivors and shortly after the fire wrote his description.

> "The flames came rushing on, sometimes in huge, revolving columns, then in detached fragments that were torn by the winds from the mass, and sent flying over the tops of trees for a quarter of a mile to be pushed down to the earth again. Flames were seen to leap many feet higher than tall pines, and everywhere over the burning country sheets of flame were flying in every direction. The flying sand and smoke blinded people, who walked in the gathering darkness into fire-traps. Those who escaped were blind for weeks. Half-naked creatures made their way into village streets, often bearing the charred remains of the dead with them. Many found refuge from the fires in the lake, and even there they were suffocated by the smoke blown from the shores. The cinders, falling in the water, made

a lye, so that it was necessary to go down several feet under the surface for drinking water."

Bailey also noted that sailors felt the uncomfortable heat seven miles out on chilly Lake Huron. The heat withered leaves on trees two miles from its path and cooked vegetable patches of corn, potatoes, and onions turning them to stew in fields otherwise untouched.

Even for those fortunate enough to have walked, limped, or crawled out of the ravaged area, life was a shamble. They were homeless. The forests, which in the past had always offered lumber to build or rebuild their homes, were gone. The crops which they had recently harvested were destroyed. The water was unsafe to drink. They had no source of food, and winter was approaching. Many needed medical help which was not available. The air was polluted with the stench of dead animals rotting and awaiting disposal.

It took weeks, if not months, for the enormity of the disaster to reach the outside world. All telegraph lines were down and the railroad tracks so littered with debris that no trains could pass. When the staggering circumstances became known, headlines across the country told story after horrible story:

"Tremendous fires in Sanilac and Huron Counties," "Richmondville Destroyed," "Deckerville Reported Burned," "Many People Horribly Burned," "Wholesale Devastation," "Entire Townships Become Roaring Furnaces," "Counties Left in Ashes," and "Survivors Fled to the Lake to Escape Inferno."

There was no other news worth telling during the next few weeks. The damage estimates rose above two million at the value of the 1881 dollar. Two-thousand square miles, more than a million acres of forest, were reduced to cinders in an afternoon. Entire villages had vanished. The hours of

11:00 a.m. to 4:00 p.m. on Monday, September 5, saw the brunt of the damage, but the fires refused to die until rain came on September 7. Those rains helped save the village of Lexington which had been fighting vigorously to hold back the blaze.

Relief committees were set up to deal with the devastation. The American Red Cross was just getting organized in New York. Clara Barton sent her agent, Julian Hubbell, to Port Huron to investigate what could be done. In response to his report, Ms. Barton coordinated aid efforts by the fledgling organization. She raised money and sent food, bedding, medical aid, lumber, farm equipment, and other supplies to the victims. Her effort was small in comparison to that of local agencies, but the long-term importance to Barton's organization was great. The need for an organization ready to step in and be available to raise money and supplies in time of disaster was apparent. The American Red Cross, now respected and relied upon worldwide, first offered its assistance to the victims of the Thumb Fire of 1881.

<<>>

Thumb lumbering had barely survived the fire of 1871. In many areas that earlier fire had burned only the treetops, killing the underlying trees, without reducing them to ashes and soot. Lumber mills managed to stay in business by harvesting the trees that had survived, and by cutting up those that died but had not yet rotted. The second, more deadly fire of 1881 sealed the fate of mills and lumbering in the Thumb. The King was dead.

14. PORT HURON/FORT GRATIOT

As the St. Clair River meets Lake Huron, you find yourself in Port Huron. Locals lump the areas of Port Huron and Fort Gratiot together and will insist they are going from a neighboring farm community to Port Huron to shop at

Meijer's or Walmart, both of which are in Fort Gratiot, or technically Fort Gratiot Township.

Port Huron bills itself as the Maritime Capital of the Great Lakes, which gives insight into the city's self-image and its global role. The waterways, including the St. Clair River, Black River, and Lake Huron give the area a strategic role in shipping commerce. Port Huron has also been designated a Michigan All-American Cool City.

The area was originally inhabited by Native Americans who were joined in the early 1700s by a few French families who settled along the Black River. It's easy to imagine canoes gliding almost silently along riverbanks lined with tall pine forests. Tribes met in the area for various ceremonies and to settle disputes. Burial mounds have been uncovered near the river south of Water Street.

In 1686 a small fur trading fort was constructed in the vicinity now known as Port Huron and/or Fort Gratiot. Fort St. Joseph, a timbered blockhouse, was built by the French to protect against possible British interference with the French fur trade.

A year later, about two hundred French fur traders, thirty French soldiers, and five hundred Algonquin Native Americans, under orders from Marquis de Denonville prepared to attack the Six Nations Iroquois Confederacy during the Iroquois Wars.

With a lack of supplies and no orders from the governor, the fort's commander, Louis-Armand de Lom d'Arce de Lahontan, Baron de Lahontan, burned Fort St. Joseph on August 27, 1688, and moved to Michilimackinac.

In 1814 Charles Gratiot brought a group of men to the area and built a small military post that was named in his honor. Fort Gratiot occupied the land between Mansfield Street and Scott Avenue, from the St. Clair River to the Black River. It was established to protect the waters of Lake Huron against the British in the War of 1812. By 1822 the fort was abandoned, and by 1826 it lay in ruins, only to be rebuilt in 1829. The most lethal attack against the fort was not by man, but by disease. The fort occupants suffered an outbreak of cholera that resulted in many deaths. Soldiers fled in fear for their lives. Their bodies littered local roads where they dropped when the plague finished with them.

In 1866 a murder was committed at Fort Gratiot. Two men went fishing. Only one returned, and he told a story of how his companion fell overboard. When the body washed up on the shore the bullet hole told a different tale. This old-time CSI-type drama resulted in a charge of murder against the surviving fisherman who was hanged for his crime.

The fort was open for a period during the Civil War to enlist soldiers for the Union but was permanently closed in 1879. The land was split up and became many businesses. The city received 20 acres for Pine Grove Park. It is believed that the first street developed in Port Huron was Water Street. Some of the original buildings were constructed on Water and Military. The earliest residents of European descent came to the city of Port Huron in 1790.

Sawmills sprang up along the Black River in the early 1800s. They heralded the era of the lumber baron. The two fires in the Thumb, and the resultant elimination of much of the forest bounty, brought the end to the lumber mills. The last existing mill was the Howard and Son Mill, located east of the railroad bridge. It burned in 1903. The Black River became quieter without boats carrying lumber, but the Lake remained active with the great freighters carrying ore.

In 1886 initial plans began for the world's first international submarine railway tunnel. It connected the United States and Canada—Port Huron to Sarnia. It was August 30, 1926, before the tunnel under the St. Clair River was completed. Steam whistles and honking automobile horns signaled the news, and the city went crazy in celebration. The tunnel has been subject to two sabotage attempts, one that was foiled, and the other so ineffective that it did no damage.

Seven hundred men worked seven days a week in three eight-hour shifts to build the tunnel. The tunnel caused several deaths, as men were overcome by fumes when they attempted to reconnect railroad cars that had become uncoupled. One child was born in the tunnel.
Passenger trains no longer run through the tunnel, and it is only used for freight trains. If you stand aboard the *Bramble* in Seaway Terminal when a train goes underneath, you will hear and feel it.

The Blue Water Bridge also connects the United States

The Blue Water Bridge. Courtesy of Bob Royce.

with Canada, from Port Huron to Sarnia. The initial bridge was built in 1938. When the second span was added in *1997*, extensive renovation took place on the original span as well. The Blue Water Bridge is the only bridge owned jointly by Michigan and Canada. The second span opened to traffic on the morning of July 22, 1997—a time and date that had been kept secret to avoid glory-seekers lining up to be the first to cross. The bridge is an architecturally magnificent backdrop to the waters of the St. Clair River and Lake Huron. International Flag Plaza offers a place to relax and admire the bridge's structural beauty.

Today the Black River and Lake Huron are fishing and recreational bodies of water. They enrich the lives of those who live in Port Huron and those who visit.

As you drive into Port Huron from the south, note the beautiful Victorian homes that remain along the waterway between the Seaway Terminal and the drawbridge. If traffic is moving too fast for you to appreciate the old architecture, consider parking your car and walking along these few blocks.

Port Huron offers something to suit everyone's taste, from shopping to dining, from fishing charters to sightseeing, from theatre to museums. And a lot in between.

• MUSEUMS AND GALLERIES

Carnegie Center/Port Huron Museum, 1115 Sixth Street at Wall Street. The Museum was built in 1904 and originally served as the city library. Andrew Carnegie, the famous philanthropist, provided the money for this beautiful classical building. It became a museum in 1968. Inside are permanent and traveling displays.

The museum is home to over 15,000 objects and archival items related to the pre-history, history, and culture of the Blue Water Area. There is also genealogical information, and you can tour a pilothouse. The second floor contains marine artifacts of the Great Lakes.

Port Huron Museum. Courtesy of Bob Royce.

Anchors and a log house built in the late 1850s by Conrad Kammer are on the museum grounds. The cabin was originally constructed in Casco Township southwest of Port Huron. Several generations of the Kammer family lived in it. In 1981 new owners were intent on tearing down the structure and rebuilding. By that time, the exterior had been covered with layers of siding. When the treasure beneath was discovered, the owner donated it to the museum, and it was moved to the current location.

Kammer Log Cabin. Courtesy of Bob Royce.

Huron Lightship Museum, 800 Prospect Place, docked in Pine Grove Park. When retired from active service in 1970, the Huron was the last lightship (a floating lighthouse) on the Great Lakes. She was the third lightship placed at the Corsica Shoals where it replaced an ineffective gas buoy.

The Huron Lightship.
Courtesy of Bob Royce.

Commissioned in 1921 as *Lightship Number 103*, she operated in southern Lake Huron at the mouth of the St. Clair River. The *Huron* was equipped with one acetylene lens lantern, a steam whistle fog horn, and a hand-operated bell. In 1970 she was decommissioned and replaced by an unmanned warning buoy light. The ownership of the *Huron* was transferred to the city of Port Huron.

The ship is on the National Register of Historic Places, is designated a National Historic Landmark, and has a State Historical Marker. The ship is well-preserved, with her operable light and fog horn still on board. She packs fascinating history on a short tour.

<<>>

The Knowlton Ice Museum, 317 Grand River Avenue. The ice museum is an unexpected little treasure. You may be wondering how interesting an ice museum can be. Prepare to be favorably surprised. This museum chronicles earlier times when families had no refrigerators, only iceboxes.

The museum contains a large collection of ice-industry artifacts, including a century-old ice delivery wagon. It also houses a large collection of classic photos documenting ice harvesting in the late 1800s on the Black River. You can watch a rare film of the ice business in the early 1920s showing an ice harvest in Wisconsin. If that was the extent of its exhibits, it would still be a worthwhile place to spend an hour. But the Knowlton Ice Museum has a large license plate collection, antique vehicles, and surprisingly, a doll and baby buggy room—a little something for everyone.

<<>>

Thomas Edison Depot Museum, 510 Edison Parkway, directly below the Blue Water Bridge. The museum chronicles the life and history of Port Huron's most notable, and perhaps favorite, son. Thomas Edison spent his childhood years in Port Huron. The museum is housed in the Grand Trunk Western Railroad Fort Gratiot Depot, a building included on the National Register of Historic Places. Trains connecting at this depot carried people and freight between Port Huron and Detroit, Port Huron and Sarnia, and Port Huron and other destinations. In its time, it was Port Huron's link to the greater world. Twelve-year-old Thomas departed the depot daily on the Port Huron to Detroit run and sold newspapers and snacks to finance his burgeoning quest for knowledge. Edison, who loved experimenting, marked all of the vials in his lab POISON, so no one would disturb them. The depot building was constructed in 1858 and became a major stop for immigrants. In 1881 more than 77,000 arrivals from other countries took their first steps into the United States here. The museum's exhibits demonstrate Edison's history of invention, family ties, the obstacles he overcame, and his ultimate triumph as one of the greatest—if not the greatest—inventors of his time. The museum has several hands-on, interactive displays and its own small theater.

The Thomas Edison Depot Museum. Courtesy of Bob Royce.

● BEACHES, PARKS, AND TRAILS

International Flag Plaza, located under the Blue Water Bridge, begins a river walkway that provides great views of the water traffic. The park honors those who respond to 911 calls in the U.S. and Canada.

<<>>

Lighthouse Park, 3002 Conger at Gratiot, provides a playground, swings, picnic area, sandy swimming beach, grills, and restrooms. This is an interesting park because the Fort Gratiot Lighthouse is next door, and the Blue Water Bridge is in view. Like most parks in Port Huron/Fort Gratiot, it also has scenic views of the river's marine activity.

<<>>

Pine Grove Park, 1204 Pine Grove, is described as one of the jewels of the Port Huron area, with its sweeping 1,500 feet of river view. It offers picnic areas, playground equipment, and shuffleboard courts. It is across the street from the Huron Lightship Museum.

<<>>

Fort Gratiot Bicycle Path and Nature Trail. Access at Keewahdin Road Beach (Turn toward the lake from M-25

119

at Keewahdin Road). Miles of paved pathways perfect for walking, biking, and rollerblading. There are several unpaved hiking trails throughout the marshland and a 40 acre preserve where you can watch swans, marsh hawks, geese, mallard ducks, and other birds and animals. A floating observation deck located on the east side of the pond is a wonderful place to watch wildlife.

<<>>

Wadhams to Avoca Trail. Access the trail from I-69 Wadhams Road Exit, (Wadhams to Lapeer to left on Barlett). The trail is open year-round. The Mill Creek Trestle is the showpiece of the Trail. Four overlooks provide breathtaking views and spots for picnicking. Take your cell, iPad, or camera. The trail is 10-feet wide and approximately 2.75 miles of the trail, starting at Barlett Road and ending at McLain Road, is paved. It is a place for running, cycling, and in-line skating. The remaining seven miles of the trail is unpaved and is surfaced with either limestone or gravel. Mileage markers are located every half-mile of the walkway.

• OTHER STOPS TO CONSIDER

Great Lakes Maritime Center at Vantage Point at the confluence of the Black and St. Clair Rivers. Acheson Ventures has revitalized and transformed a mile of waterfront property along the St. Clair River. Previously this stretch was industrial property that failed to capitalize on the fabulous views.

Dr. James Acheson, a local philanthropist, turned the area into a place for locals to enjoy and tourists to visit. At the south end of the property is the renovated Seaway Terminal, home of the tall ship *Highlander Sea*.

The Great Lakes Maritime Center, opened in 2006, has a long wall of windows offering a clear view of river traffic. Inside, at the Coffee Harbour, you will find a comfortable place to sit and enjoy a variety of coffees, soft drinks, deli sandwiches, and salads. Outside, along the waterfront, you can get fries at the French Fry Truck or a hand-dipped ice cream cone from the Ice Cream Trailer. There are a fishing pier and a promenade.

The Center offers a variety of activities and opportunities to learn about the maritime history of the Great Lakes. Information is provided as displays, speaker programs, and videos. A live underwater camera feed lets you view activity under the surface of the St. Clair River and follow ship movements. There is an outside observation deck for sunny summer days or an inside viewing room for days when the weather is less than optimal. You can bring your fishing gear and catch dinner from the pier. (Fishing license required.)

<<>>

McMorran Tower, 701 McMorran Boulevard. The tower was the last addition to the three-building complex that is

McMorran Tower. Courtesy of Bob Royce.

the site for many local entertainment events. It was completed in October 1965. A climb up the 188 stairs to the observation deck, 150 feet above the ground, allows you to survey the entire Port Huron vicinity. You can view the double spans of the Blue Water Bridge and the surrounding city and countryside. You can see the Black River, and if you give free rein to your imagination, you can almost picture canoes, and maybe even a Native American ceremonial meeting.

For those with less vivid imaginations, it is interesting to pick out local landmarks from this high perch. Wear shoes with a good grip because the stone steps get slippery.

The tower is only open in the summer because the moisture and snow of the winter make it too dangerous to climb. It is a worthwhile exercise in more ways than one.

<<>>

The Port Huron Trolley is also known as the Bluewater Trolley. You might not be able to get a cup of coffee for a thin dime, but ten pennies are all it will cost you to ride the unique Port Huron Trolley. The trolley tour recaptures the past of public transit and provides an overview of many Blue Water Area sights. The hour-long tour takes you past fifty points of interest including the Huron Lightship, Old Fort Gratiot Trading Post, Thomas Edison Depot, McMorran Arena and Tower, and the Museum of Arts and History. It's a bargain and a half.

<<>>

Sawmill City, 5055 Lapeer Road, (five miles from Port Huron, next to KOA camp). A fun-park with go-karts, adventure golf, batting cages, paintball, bank-shot basketball, hippo wet/dry slide, giant jumping pillow, and bumper-boats. Seasonal.

<<>>

Acheson Ventures *Highlander Sea*. Acheson Venture's tall-ship *Highlander Sea* is a 154-foot, gaff-rigged topsail schooner. When she is in port, you can view her from the deck of the Seaway Terminal. The vessel offers some day cruises. Acheson Ventures is dedicated to showcasing the marine history and lore of Port Huron and the Great Lakes.

<<>>

Huron Lady II. Just before the drawbridge in downtown Port Huron, driving south to north on M-25, you will see a sign for the Huron Lady. Daily, seasonal, narrated, three-hour sightseeing cruises, as well as romantic sunset and moonlight cruises are available. You can charter the *Huron Lady* for special events. It is wise to call for reservations.

<<>>

Victorian Homes on Military. San Francisco isn't the only city with statuesque Victorians. Driving north into Port Huron on M-25, you will pass many beautiful Victorian homes. Take time to enjoy them.

A few that are noteworthy

- 1501 and 1503 Military. This old house has been turned into rentals but retains much of its original charm.

- 1507 Military. The house was constructed in 1893. It has an interesting history; serving as home to a former Speaker of the House of Representatives and a speakeasy—not at the same time, of course.

1507 Military. Courtesy of Bob Royce.

- 1617 Military. The Lohrstorfer House. This is not a Victorian, but elegant nonetheless. It was built by Dr. Fred Lohrstorfer for his wife, Alice, who was described as spoiled, rich, and ungrateful. She thought the home was below the level of elegance she deserved. The marriage failed, and the Port Huron newspapers had ample fodder for many juicy stories from the messy public divorce.

The Lohrstorfer House. Courtesy of Bob Royce.

- 1623 Military. No history is available but worth a look.
- 1707 Military. The Davidson House B&B. An 1888 Queen Anne style home with seven fireplaces and jeweled and leaded glass windows. This elegant home is listed on the National Register of Historic Places and features loads of ornate woodwork.

The Davidson House.

The Thompson House/Castle.

Courtesy of Bob Royce.

• 1719 Military. The Castle, as it is called and bears a small placard to that effect, is a monster three-story, also known as the Thompson House. It was built by Mr. John Thompson who made his money in the coal business. Construction began after he returned from his honeymoon in France. He and his wife, Ida, lived in the castle with their only daughter Mary who enjoyed a very splashy, society wedding in the home.

• 1723 Military. Not an ornate Victorian but still an interesting old home.

• 1806 Military. This home features lots of bric-a-brac, a turret, leaded glass, and rounded-rooms common in Victorian architecture.

• 1905 Military. Lots of Gingerbread, 2003 Yard of the Year home, built in the Queen Anne style, and constructed in 1885 for a cost of $6,000. For several years, it was the Catholic League House and was then restored by new owners.

1905 Military. Courtesy of Bob Royce.

• 1906 Military. This home was built in the 1890s, and its earliest known resident was Charles Thompson, a furniture dealer. Like the other Victorians in this area, it is built in the Queen Anne style.

• 1909 Military. Leaded glass and a great front porch are noted characteristics of this lovely old home. It was awarded the 2005 Yard of the Year designation.

• 2015 Military. This house is called the Kathryn House, but additional details are unavailable.

• 2037 Military. Another lovely home worth a look but for which no historical information was found.

• The Harrington Hotel at 1026 Military (just beyond the ornate Victorians). This was once the grandest hotel in Sanilac County. It is currently an assisted-living community.

<<>>

Local Festivals. Port Huron offers many local festivals that you can check out online before visiting.

• Antique Yard Sale Trail, August. Trail from New Baltimore to Sebewaing. This is the big one if you like monster garage sales. M-25 will be crowded beyond capacity as cars pull off the highway and park in every haphazard fashion imaginable.

• Be a Tourist in Your Town, July. Offers a tour map and lots of free places to visit.

• Port Huron to Mackinac Sailboat Race, July. This is *the* big sailboat race of the season, drawing thousands of boaters and even more spectators.

• Studio Tour, Usually in October. This is a cooperative effort between Sarnia and Port Huron to open their art studios to visitors.

● LIGHTHOUSE

Fort Gratiot Lighthouse. Located at 2800 Omar Street in Port Huron, just north of the Blue Water Bridge, the Fort Gratiot Lighthouse is the oldest operating lighthouse on the Great Lakes. It was built in 1825 and named after the engineer in charge of the construction. The tower is 86 feet above the lake level.

Fort Gratiot Lighthouse.
Courtesy of Bob Royce.

The keeper's cottage and the fog whistle house are painted red. The lighthouse is red brick painted white. It is a classic example of an early nineteenth century style lighthouse. The tower collapsed in 1828 due to shoddy workmanship. It was rebuilt in 1829. Additional rebuilding was required in 1861. It is worth the climb to the top for the view.

● SHIPWRECK

The monument can be seen along the boardwalk near the foot of the Blue Water Bridge.

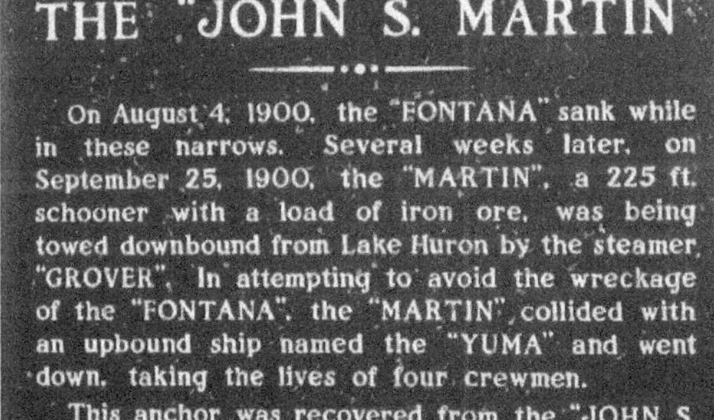

Courtesy of Bob Royce.

Also see The Big Blow, the Storm of 1913, for a history of other ships that went down near Port Huron.

● THE FAMOUS OR INFAMOUS WITH TIES TO PORT HURON

Thomas Edison, inventor and entrepreneur, moved to Port Huron in 1854. (See Museums in this section for more information about Edison's activities in Port Huron.)

<<>>

Herbert Warren Kalmbach was the personal attorney for Richard Nixon. It was a thankless job, and he was enmeshed in the scandal because of his fundraising activities. He served six months in jail and was disbarred.

<<>>

Terry McMillan, author, was born in Port Huron. Her novels and other works include *Mama, Disappearing Acts, Breaking Ice: An Anthology of Contemporary African-American Fiction, Waiting to Exhale,* and *How Stella Got Her Groove Back* (which was turned into a movie starring Angela Bassett), *It's OK if You're Clueless: and 23 More Tips for the College Bound, The Interruption of Everything, Getting to Happy, Who Asked You?* and *I Almost Forgot About You.* When McMillan was seventeen, she left Port Huron and moved to California. She attended the University of California at Berkeley. Her first novel recounted her childhood, and the setting, Point Haven, Michigan, is painted with her memories of Port Huron.

<<>>

Colleen Moore was born Kathleen Morrison on August 19,

Colleen Moore, age 21. Photo in the Public Domain.

1899, in Port Huron. She began her acting career during the silent-film era. After the advent of sound, she starred in the 1933 film *The Power and the Glory.* Her co-star in the well-received film was Spencer Tracy. Her list of film credits was long, and earned her notable wealth.

Moore's second love, after acting, was dollhouses. With the help of colleagues, she created the Colleen Moore Dollhouse and with it toured the country to raise funds for children's charities during the Great Depression. The dollhouse has been a featured exhibit at the Chicago Museum of Science and

Industry since the early 1950s. It is estimated that the nine-square foot dollhouse is worth close to ten million dollars. It enchants more than 1½ million people a year.

<<>>

John Burley Swainson was Canadian born but moved to Port Huron at the age of two. He served as a Michigan Supreme Court Justice and then as the 42nd Governor of Michigan.

<<>>

Harry Truman, the thirty-third president of the United States, spent a part of his honeymoon in Port Huron.

Courtesy of Bob Royce.

He returned from duty in World War I in May 1919. In June he married Beth (aka Bess) Wallace.

Truman's daughter Margaret wrote in her biography of Bess that "For the rest of his life, whenever Harry Truman wanted to regain the radiance of those first days with Bess, he simply wrote 'Port Huron.' For him it was a code word for happiness."

● BOOKS AND MOVIES WITH TIES TO PORT HURON

(See Terry McMillan under The Famous and Infamous with Ties to Port Huron.)

<<>>

Silent Star by Colleen Moore and ***Colleen Moore: A Biography of the Silent Film Star*** by Jeff Codori recount the film star's life. There are also several books about Moore's dollhouse. (See The Famous or the Infamous with Ties to Port Huron.)

The Ghosts of the Wind Wizards.[1] Michigan is a state surrounded by water so it makes sense that some of its most memorable ghosts sailed the seas. One particular bunch of sea captains was set apart from all others. Their numbers were small, but their powers colossal. No one knows for certain where they came from or how they became imbued with their unique skills. Oh, they could sail a ship straighter, faster, and more efficiently than a normal ship's captain, but those were the least of their talents. They carried with them, secreted away in a private alcove of their cabin, a thick, coarse, knotted rope. When the ship sat in the middle of Lake Huron, without a breath of wind to move it, a wind-wizard captain took out his rope, walked to the bow of his ship, and untied the first knot. The wind would pick up. If he wanted more breeze, he untied another, and another, until he was satisfied with the speed of his vessel.

As amazing as that feat may have seemed, the captain's true power—the one that saved many lives—came when the winds picked up. He retrieved his rope from its resting place and walked to the bow. There he tied a tight knot in the end of the rope. The winds died down. If the sea remained too choppy for the captain's taste, he tied another. When he felt the ship was no longer in danger, he returned to his cabin, stashed the rope, and poured himself a stiff drink.

When a wind wizard died, his ghost took residence in the ship of another wizard where he guided the younger man in the finer arts of their craft.

---

[1] This story first came to the author's attention when told to her by a Port Huron resident in response to a question about local ghosts. A similar version of the tale is included in *Spooky Michigan* written by S.E. Schlosser.

Perhaps it was a wind wizard with a grudge or a suicidal urge that summoned the winds of the Storm of 1913.

<<>>

The Spirits of the Sauk Warriors. The Sauk were a major tribe of Native Americans in the Thumb area of Michigan. Their name can be translated as People of the Yellow Earth. The word Saginaw means *Place of the Sauk,* and many roads, streets, and businesses in the Thumb, as well as one city, are named Saginaw.

The Sauk inhabited a large settlement on the banks of the Black River near what is now Port Huron. The Sauk were known for their fierce and warlike disposition toward other tribes of the area.

The Ojibwe, Potawatomie, Menominee, and Odawa banded together to battle their common enemy. They chose to attack at a time when they believed the Sauk men would be away hunting. They crept into the village and massacred the women and children. The Sauk warriors returned to a decimated settlement and were filled with inconsolable grief.

However, being outnumbered, the Sauk warriors could not engage in a head-on attack against the tribes that had wreaked havoc on their village. Instead, they made periodic forays into the villages of the tribes responsible for the attack.

They slipped in during the dark of night and burned a single hut, or killed a single enemy, and then slipped out under cover of blackness. The Ojibwe were convinced that the ghosts of the dead Sauk had returned to haunt them. Who can say that the anguished Sauk did not have assistance from the spirits of their deceased loved ones?

15. LAKEPORT

The village of Lakeport is located about 11 miles north of Port Huron and 68 miles north of Detroit along the lakeshore of Lake Huron. Lakeport was platted by Jonas Titus in 1837. He called the area's small stream Milwaukie Creek and the village Milwaukie City. The name came from the Potawatomie word *meno* or *mino* meaning good and *aki* meaning land. The name Milwaukie City was used until 1858. Titus never recorded his platting efforts, and when the village was replatted, it was also renamed. It became Lakeport because of its proximity to Lake Huron. For travelers, this isn't the place to discover fine restaurants (or even a McDonalds) or shopping. However, the Lakeport State Park may be worth your attention. If you are looking for isolation and a place to enjoy Lake Huron, usually in seclusion, Orchard Beach (See Beaches, Parks, and Trails.) may be worth trying to find.

● BEACHES, PARKS, AND TRAILS

Burtchville Township Park. Finding this 15-acre park can be tricky. At Burtchville (driving north), turn right from Lakeshore (M-25) onto Harris Road, and ahead of you, you'll spot this park. The park has tennis courts, a playground, pavilion, basketball nets, swimming beach on Lake Huron, rollerblade area, and lookout deck. The park area runs parallel to a street with cottages on the lake frontage. Most of the park is behind these cottages and without a view. At the north end of the park is a small, but pleasant, beach. The restrooms look ancient, and you better take your hand sanitizer. That said, it is a quaint little park.

<<>>

Lakeport State Park, 7605 Lakeshore Road, just north of Lakeport, consists of two units, one on each side of the community of Lakeport within Burtchville Township. Two campgrounds, a beachfront, and a camp store are on the north side, and a picnic area and beachfront are on the south side. The park is also divided east/west by M-25 with camping and picnicking on the lake side of M-25 and additional picnic facilities, parking, and restrooms on the west side (non-lake side). A footbridge over the highway connects the two areas. If you are picnicking on the lake side, you have to carry everything from a bit of a distance and cross the footbridge. The lake side has a playground, volleyball nets, and a swimming beach.

<<>>

Orchard Beach, on Beach Avenue, is about five miles north of Lakeport. This is a unique little beach. It is a couple of blocks off M-25, with only a small sign denoting its existence. It is about 150 feet by 200 feet of grassy, lakeside property that looks like a vacant lot missing only a "For Sale" sign. It has a tree or two but no services, no tables, and not even a port-a-potty. The grassy area slopes down to a small sandy beach with a seawall on each side of the property at beach level. The sign at the park entrance indicates that you can build a bonfire on the beach (make sure you extinguish it properly). This is not a family park (you would be running kids somewhere to find a bathroom every few minutes), but if you are coming on a weekend when you anticipate the parks of the area will be crowded to the max, you may find this tiny park less busy, and a nice place to spread a blanket under a tree, chill out, read a book, or just watch the water.

16. LEXINGTON

Lexington's population, over 2,000 at its peak, dwindled to 326 by 1940. The 2020 population was 1,172 thanks to its reincarnation as a resort village.

In 1830 Lexington became the first settlement north of Port Huron on the shores of Lake Huron. Today, signs at each end of the village announce its stature as The First Resort North. Lexington Township is the oldest township in Sanilac County. The county was mapped by Lewis Cass in

133

1822 when he was governor of the Michigan Territory. Sanilac County originally included all of Tuscola and Huron counties, except for a small area around Sebewaing. In those early days, there was nothing more than a trail through the dense pine forests connecting Lexington to Port Huron.

In 1837 John Smith brought his wife and twelve children to Lexington where he built a log house on the hill overlooking the lake on the south side of Huron Avenue. As beautiful as Lexington must have been in those days, with its huge pine and hardwood forests, Smith felt driven to leave after a few years because the place was simply becoming too crowded.

In 1840 Langdon Hubbard, age twenty-four, and his brother Watson and cousin R.B. came to Michigan from Connecticut to seek their fortunes as lumbermen and businessmen in the Thumb. The lumbering boom was well underway, and they obtained property and timberland in Lexington. Their company prospered, and later they moved north into Huron County. They built a dock in Lexington to facilitate the shipment of their lumber to market.

Lexington was known as Greenbush until 1846. Most of its original settlers came from Canada, and a few relocated from New England and the Middle Atlantic states. The Michigan Thumb was quite desirable with its rich forests, fertile soil, cheap land, and water access.

Three permanent boat docks were erected by 1870, initially for the shipment of lumber, and later for agricultural products. Fruit trees grew well in the sandy soil close to the lakeshore. Local orchards produced peaches, cherries, apples, pears, and plums. Berry patches provided raspberries, black raspberries, blackberries, gooseberries, and strawberries.

The first hotel was built of logs in 1840 at the site of the current Cadillac House. It was named the Mills Hotel after its owner Clark Mills. Mills owned the hotel for three years before trading it (some suggest as the result of a gambling debt) to his brother-in-law for a 40-acre farm near where the current Lakeview Hills Golf Resort is located. It is hard to say who got the better end of the deal. The Mills Hotel operated until 1859 when it was torn down and rebuilt as the Cadillac Hotel, which then opened on July 4, 1860. This second hotel was named for General DeLamotte Cadillac, who founded Fort Ponchartrain in Detroit. The Cadillac House has the local reputation of being haunted by a ghost named George. (See Ghost Stories in this section.)

The village was named Lexington in 1846 by Reuben Diamond, whose wife was a cousin of Ethan Allen who fought in the Battle of Lexington during the Revolutionary War. The village was incorporated in 1855.

The fire of 1871 spared Lexington because the townsfolk turned out to aggressively fight the flames. It helped that they had earlier carved clearings around the village. Equally important was the critical and much-welcomed rain that assisted their efforts. The local citizenry was instrumental in providing aid to those from farther north who had been left homeless by the ravages of that horrific inferno. (See detailed account of the Great Fires under Lake Huron in this guide.) Lexington is a charming village with an old-time feel. Its natural stone harbor is reminiscent of those along the Coast of Maine. The beautiful three-sided breakwater was built of huge boulders hauled from Rodgers City and was constructed by the United States Army Corps of Engineers. The walkway atop the breakwater is a striking place to take a cup of coffee and greet the new day on this sunrise coast of

Lexington Breakwater.
Courtesy of Bob Royce.

Lake Huron. Few experiences will leave you feeling more content and at peace with the world than watching the sleepy harbor awaken.

Many of Lexington's historic buildings have been preserved, including the 116-year-old General Store that still dispenses a variety of merchandise including nostalgic penny candy that no longer costs a penny. There's always a line of excited children picking out their favorites—piece by piece—to fill a bag.

Downtown Lexington. Courtesy of Bob Royce.

Lexington is at its best in the summer. There are free concerts in the park on Friday nights. It has a Fine Arts Fair that rivals Ann Arbor's in everything but size. Tierney Park, with its play area, beach, and picnicking, is a fine place to spend an afternoon with the family. In the second block of Huron (off Main toward the lake), you will come

Smackwater Development.
Courtesy of Bob Royce.

to the Smackwater Complex. In 1992 a local-boy-done-well, Adam Buschbacher, bought the property, and longing for the delightful old buildings that had been lost over the years, he built the current structure with its 32,000 square feet of space. The development complemented the existing turn-of-the-century architecture of the village, in part because Adam did not break ground until he had researched architectural styles and visited historic villages. He used only reclaimed bricks from demolished buildings in Detroit and Chicago. His attention to detail can be seen throughout in such touches as the oak floors and the cobblestone plaza in front. The development was subsequently sold to a buyer from Croswell, but the buildings still offer their special charm to today's visitors.

Whatever else you do in the Thumb, do not miss Lexington.

• BEACHES, PARKS, AND TRAILS
Lexington Park, M-25, three miles north of Lexington, has 42 grassy and shaded campsites, bathhouse, showers, pavilion, and day-use as well as beach, tennis courts, recreational field, and playground.

<<>>

Tierney Park, at the harbor in Lexington. The summer Concerts in the Park and other events are held here. You will find a nice beach, playground, picnic tables, barbeque grills, volleyball court, tennis courts, and a public bathhouse.

• OTHER STOPS TO CONSIDER
Lexington has a festival nearly every weekend in the summer including
Lakeside Spring Craft Show, June in Tierney Park
A&W Classic Car Show, June
Port Huron to Mackinac Sailboat Race, July

- *Music in the Park*, June to August
- *Port Huron/Lexington Sailboat Race*, August
- *Antique Yard Sale Trail*, August
- *Fine Arts Street Fair*, August
- *Thumbfest*, September
- *Bach Festival*, September

Check the village website for confirmation as times and events may change.

● SHIPWRECKS

The Thumb Underwater Preserve. Lake Huron is a glutinous lake with a voracious appetite. In the final accounting, she is believed to have devoured 40% of the Great Lake shipwrecks.

In 1980 the Michigan legislature enacted a law to preserve Michigan's endangered underwater resources. That law requires a special permit to remove any abandoned property from the Great Lakes bottomlands. From the Harbors of Lexington, Port Sanilac, Harbor Beach, Pointe aux Barques, Port Hope, Grindstone City, and the Saginaw Bay you can dive and explore shipwrecks claimed by the lake in her moments of fury. There are nearly four dozen ships in or near the waters of Huron's harbors. Those marked with * are popular dive sites.

- The ***City of Port Huron***, a steamer, foundered off Lexington's shores in 1876.
- The ***Eliza Strong**** burned and went down in 1904. She is located almost a mile from the Lexington Harbor (.9 miles) on a heading of 121 degrees in 28 feet of water. She rests upright on the bottom with her keel and some decking intact. She is a good dive for beginners.
- The ***Sport**.* a tug, lies three miles from Lexington Harbor on a heading of 98 degrees in 49 feet of water. She sank upright listing to her starboard side. Her cabin is missing. She was discovered by another tugboat and

became a popular dive site because she is the perfect depth for beginning divers. She went down in 1920.

▪ The **Regina*** was a victim of the storm of 1913. She lies 6.4 miles from Lexington Harbor on a heading of 45 degrees. She came to rest upside down with her bow facing north. She is considered a premier dive site in the Great Lakes. She was built in 1907. Her captain stayed with his ship. Nine months later his body washed ashore in Port Sanilac. The *Regina's* final resting place was not discovered until 1986. (See the Storm of 1913 under Lake Huron in this guide.)

▪ The **Mary Alice B*** is a new wreck found in the preserve and one of the more popular dive sites. She rests upright between Lexington and Port Sanilac. She is intact in about 54 feet of water.

● GHOST STORIES

The Cadillac House Ghost. George is the restless resident ghost of the Cadillac House. He tries to unnerve staff by rattling pizza pans, drinking beer, and otherwise being a nuisance. Still, you must feel sorry for George as he mourns his unrequited and cheating love.

Sitting with his sweetheart in the first booth from the door on a rainy April morning about a century ago, George had business to attend. Fearing that his lady-love was seeing his best friend, it was with a heavy heart that he departed Lexington to make the trip to Croswell.

George returned that evening earlier than expected. The innkeeper grinned and pointed up the stairs. George bounded up and opened the door to his love's room. As he had feared, she was not alone. Catching her in such a compromising position broke George's heart. His best friend broke George's neck by pushing him off the balcony.

George still wanders the Cadillac House hoping to convince his lover of the error of her ways.

Captain's Quarters. A seafaring captain is said to be drawn to the nautical motif and familiarity of this B&B. Perhaps it reminds him of his ship, or maybe it feels like home. There may also be a second ghost residing at Captain's Quarters. There are reports of a little girl staring from a front window. Some stories suggest she either lived there or stayed there for a night. No more details are known about either of these mysterious ghosts. Most guests enjoy the stories, and it seems these ghosts mean no harm.

<<>>

Ghosts of Lexington's Lost Sailors. If on a moonlight night you decide to walk the beach near Lexington Harbor, you may sense a disturbing presence. Try as you may, at first you will spot nothing but the million, shimmering diamond-like reflections of the moon on the black water. Look closer, and you may see wisps of white rising from the sea. Listen carefully, and you may hear the wailing of sailors whose ships went down in the tragic 1913 Storm. Several freighters sank that night, and pieces of their ships were scattered for miles along the Lexington beaches. Sailors lost in time are trying to make their way home to the loved ones who waited for them on shore that fateful evening.

17. Croswell

Note: This is a small detour from the shoreline route. You will have to decide if the following listings are worth your time.

Four miles west of the traffic signal in Lexington is another quaint Michigan village. Croswell's population is a skosh one way or the other of 2,447.

By 1899 the lumber industry was in full swing in Michigan's Thumb. Lexington had been growing for about a decade, its position on the lake making it a major trade center. Ephraim Pierce decided to seek an alternate source of lumber near Lexington. He wanted his new location to offer abundant timber and the means to transport it. He found his site, rich with forests, just five miles inland. It was a mile west of what is currently Croswell. Pierce recognized the value of the Black River for transporting lumber and generating power to the mill he set about constructing. His settlement was known simply as Black River until 1861 when it was renamed Davisville in honor of Randall Davis, who assisted Pierce in construction of the mill.

Two major players on the early Croswell scene were a land speculator named Truman Moss and his son-in-law Wildman Mills, the latter called Wild Man Mills because it was descriptive of his outrageous behavior. At his death, Moss owned 20,000 acres of land in Sanilac County. He was believed to be a millionaire back when being a millionaire meant something.

Mills, who like Pierce, understood the value of transportation, was instrumental in bringing the railroad to Croswell. It had been scheduled for construction in Lexington, but Lexington already had transportation thanks to the ships traveling the lake. Croswell residents were tired of having to haul their lumber and supplies over a plank road to Lexington. The objection to plank roads, although they offered a preferable alternative to rutted and muddy dirt roads, was the toll charge, often one or two cents per horse. The feud between the two cities vying for the railroad grew bitter.

An additional feud brewed in Croswell between the settlers on the west and east sides of the Black River regarding which side would get the locomotive. The west side had been renamed Falcon, the east side was called Croswell, and the two sides had separate post offices for many years. Somehow, although the manner is a mystery,

Croswell became one village. Falcon ceased to exist. The railroad was constructed on the east side of the river.

Croswell was incorporated as a village in 1881, and it became a city in 1905. Many of Croswell's buildings date back to pre-Civil War times.

There is a story about the stagnant waters in the area being such a fertile breeding place for mosquitoes that people were afflicted with a fever called the Seven Year Itch or the Michigan Itch. (And you probably believed the Seven Year itch was something that afflicted married people who were bored after that number of years of wedded bliss.)

After the railroad, the next major event in the Croswell history was the coming of Sanilac Sugar Refinery Company in 1901. The editor of the local paper announced, "Surely prosperity and plenty in large proportions is at hand . . ." At one time more than a thousand people were employed in harvesting sugar beets. The plant was designed to slice up to 600 tons of beets per day with plans to operate it 70 to 100 days a year. In 1945, two-hundred German prisoners of war were forced to help operate the factory. A sign in front of the factory today proclaims, ADDING A LITTLE LOCAL FLAVOR FOR OVER A CENTURY.

• OTHER STOPS TO CONSIDER

Croswell Swinging Bridge. The city is known for the MOTHER-IN-LAW BRIDGE, also called the CROSWELL SWINGING BRIDGE, which crosses the Black River at River Bend Park. This suspension footbridge was built in 1905 to provide greater access to the park and to assist workers in getting to their jobs on the east side of the river. Kids and grown-ups alike still enjoy running and shaking the bridge.

Bounce if you are brave enough, but hang onto the railings if you do not want to lose your balance and fall. Initially, the bridge consisted simply of two cables with boards attached. (There was likely very little jumping back then.) Eventually, two additional cables and fencing were added to provide handrails. Those additions helped stabilize the bridge. The improvements added to the safety of the bridge. You can only wonder how many people fell into the river trying to cross the river before the fencing.

At 139 feet, it is the longest suspension footbridge in Michigan. As you step onto the bridge you will see the sign, BE GOOD TO YOUR MOTHER-IN-LAW. The Swinging Bridge may make the short ride to Croswell worth the effort. River Bend Park also has a playground, pavilion, restrooms, and picnic tables.

Croswell Swinging Bridge. Courtesy of Bob Royce.

<<>>

Local Churches. If you've made your way to Croswell, check out the lovely architecture of two local churches, both located on Howard Street, the main street of town.

The Cobblestone Trinity Church. Courtesy of Bob Royce.

First Methodist Church. Courtesy of Bob Royce.

18. PORT SANILAC

Eleven miles north of Lexington sits the village of Port Sanilac with a population that hasn't yet reached a thousand (2020 population 673). An early landmark on the Thumb landscape, it was first known as Bark Shanty Point. Uri Raymond came to the area in 1848 and taught at the first school in Sanilac Township. He also built the first store, where he sold provisions to local settlers and provided a market for the shingles, tanbark, and cedar posts they produced. The Raymond Hardware has remained at the same location longer than any other hardware in Michigan, although it is now a True Value Hardware.

Raymond was interested in preserving the history of Port Sanilac, or Bark Shanty as he knew it. He wrote the following which gives us the origin of the name Bark Shanty.

"About the year 1830, a group of lumbermen came to peel the bark from the hemlock trees to be used for tanning leather. They built a shanty to live in and covered it with bark. When leaving in the fall, they left the shanty

144

standing, and it soon became a landmark to the sailors on Lake Huron, and they called the place Bark Shanty Point."

For a time, shingles were a form of currency in the area. Land was available to a homesteader for $1.25 per acre with a year to pay. Eighty-acres cost $100, and the sale of shingles brought $4 per thousand. A farmer could purchase an 80-acre piece of land for 25,000 shingles. A hardworking family could create a new life with nothing but strong backs and a goodly dose of sweat. If fortune smiled on them, they could even have it paid off in a year—no thirty-year mortgage hanging over their heads.

The settlement at Bark Shanty Point was organized by four lumber speculators: William Thomson, Anthony Oldfield, Quentin Thomson, and Joseph Moore. They traveled from England to Cincinnati in 1846 and formed the partnership of Oldfield and Company. They invested in pinelands in Michigan, built sawmills to turn the giant trees into lumber, and intended to get rich in the process. They chartered a schooner in Toledo and arrived at Bark Shanty Point on May 10, 1850. Between Port Austin and Lakeport, with Port Sanilac smack in the middle, more than 30,000,000 board feet of lumber was sawn in 1852.

Dr. Joseph Loop, who opened a practice in 1853, was another important Bark Shanty Point citizen. He remained in his practice until he died in 1904. He visited his patients by horse and buggy. The Loop House is now a quality museum in the village of Port Sanilac.

A post office was established at Bark Shanty Point in 1854, and the village name was shortened to Bark Shanty. In 1857 the village was renamed Port Sanilac, honoring Sanilac County and Sanilac Township, wherein it is located. One story of the derivation of the name is that it came from a Chief Sanilac, leader of a tribe of Wyandotte Native Americans. Others claim it came from the name of an Ojibwe chief. The third version claims it was named for a French fur trader, John Sanilac.

Port Sanilac Town Hall.
Courtesy of Bob Royce.

One of the early aids to navigation on Lake Huron was the Port Sanilac Lighthouse which was built in 1886. (See Lighthouse in this section.)

The first of the two catastrophic fires to hit the Thumb dealt a major blow to the small community. Hit again ten years later by a second roaring inferno, Bark Shanty witnessed the end of its lumbering days.

Development of the lakeshore got its start around 1915 when small summer cottages sprang up along the shoreline. Many current residents remain in Port Sanilac during fair weather and retreat to their main home in the Detroit area or, if retired, spend the cruel winter months in Florida.

Today, Port Sanilac is a charming village with a quiet way of life set against the magnificence of Lake Huron.

● MUSEUM

The Sanilac County Historical Society Museum and Village and Loop House, 228 South Ridge Street, Port Sanilac. This lovely old Victorian mansion is a worthwhile stop during your Thumb meanderings. Captain Stanley Harrison donated the Loop-Harrison Mansion to the

Historical Society in 1976, and it is one of the finest museums in the Thumb. As you walk through the house, imagine Ada Loop Harrison, the ghost from the story under Ghosts in this section, as she was when she lived there. The home was listed on the National Register of Historic Places in 1972.

The grounds of the Loop mansion showcase a historic village that includes a carriage barn, dairy museum, Platts General Store, Banner Log Cabin, Huckins Schoolhouse, and the Barn Theatre. The manicured lawns bustle with activity during the Annual Crafters Fair, the Log Cabin Heritage Days, and many other events.

The Loop-Harrison Mansion retains many of its original furnishings as well as some of Dr. Loop's medical equipment. It also displays artifacts of shipwrecks and the great fires. The home was built in 1872 and has twenty rooms. The carriage barn displays wagons and buggies, an old horse-drawn hearse, and farm machinery. The dairy museum contains vintage milking machines. Platts General Store allows you to browse a selection of gift items including local artwork, candy, and books on local history. The Banner Log Cabin is furnished with authentic pieces specific to the period. Huckin's Schoolhouse is a furnished, 1800s-era building typical of the early country schools in the area.

The Loop-Harrison Mansion.
Courtesy of Bob Royce.

The Barn Theatre, nearly 150 years old, is rustic theater at its best. The barn originally belonged to a local farmer who used it for storage in the winter. The barn had to be emptied every fall at the end of the theater season when all traces of the theater were replaced by farm equipment. After fifteen years of such starkly contrasting summers and winters, the Sanilac County Historical Society purchased the building, and now it is used exclusively for theater productions.

• BEACHES, PARKS, AND TRAILS

Horatio Earle MDOT Roadside Park, located on M-25 five miles south of Port Sanilac. This park has a historic plaque recounting the Storm of 1913. Although only a roadside park, it is a perfect place to pull off and enjoy a spectacular view of Lake Huron. Restrooms and picnic tables are available.

<<>>

Port Sanilac Municipal Harbor. Playground, public events (art shows, music in the park), restrooms, and fishing from the dock. (Fishing license required.)

• LIGHTHOUSE

The **Port Sanilac Lighthouse**. Two blocks east of the Municipal Harbor. This lighthouse is currently a private residence, but you can see it from the street or the parking lot that runs along its south side. The lighthouse was constructed in 1886 and sent out its first beams on the night of October

The Port Sanilac Lighthouse.
Courtesy of Bob Royce.

20, 1886. It originally burned kerosene but was electrified in 1929. The eight-sided tower continues to provide light to ships navigating the area. The house attached to the tower is red brick covered with ivy. It is worth a drive down Lake Street in Port Sanilac to glimpse this architecturally relevant lighthouse.

● SHIPWRECKS

Part of the Thumb Underwater Preserve. (See additional information under Shipwrecks and Underwater Preserves in Lexington listing.) Those marked with * are popular dive sites.

- The **Forester**, a schooner, was lost near Port Sanilac in 1898.
- The **North Star*** sank in a collision near Port Sanilac in 1908.
- The **F.B. Gardner*** sank on September 15, 1904, 6½ miles northeast of Port Sanilac. Equipment is scattered widely around the wreckage site.
- The **Charles A. Street**,* a 165-foot steamer, burned and went down in 1908. She lies 11½ miles north of Port Sanilac. It is a shallow dive, not more than 15 feet deep maximum.
- The **Checotah*** is a schooner that remains upright on the bottom, 12.2 miles from Port Sanilac Harbor. Her rear cabin, deck, and part of the starboard gunwale have pulled away from the ship. The winch, windlass, capstan port anchor, and steam boiler remain on the bow. This historic wreck is surrounded by several pulleys and other small artifacts. At the stern, are the ship's wheel, steering gear, and rudder. The *Checotah* went down on October 30, 1906. She rests in about 120 feet of water and is considered a site for more advanced divers.
- The **Col. A. B. Williams*** was lost in an 1864 storm. This 110-foot schooner is missing her masts and cabin but

otherwise is in fair shape. She lies 12½ miles northeast of Port Sanilac.

 ▪ The ***New York***** is a steamer that went down in 1876. She rests close to the *Checotah* in about 120 feet of water near Port Sanilac. She is recommended as a dive site for only more experienced divers.

● GHOST STORY

The Ghost of Ada Loop Harrison. Ada Loop lived a life of privilege by Port Sanilac standards. Her father, Dr. Joseph Loop, was the well-respected and beloved physician who ministered to the local population. He treated their ills, listened to their problems, delivered their babies, and in some cases tried futilely to stave off their deaths. Dr. Loop often took his medicine and advice to patients by horse-drawn buggy. The museum holds many of his physician's instruments and some early carriages.

Dr. Loop built his spectacular home in 1875, and it was magnificent by any standards, but compared to the log cabins and small homes of most of the populace, it qualified as a mansion. Ada lived her life surrounded by opulence.

After her marriage, Ada and her husband lived in the grand home. In the music room, she taught piano lessons to youngsters so thrilled to see the inside of the grandiose house that they accepted her stern demeanor and obediently practiced boring scales.

In 1925 the Model T Ford arrived in Port Sanilac. The contraption, called the Tin Lizzie, was produced from 1908 to 1927, and it was credited with putting America on wheels. It was also credited with putting Ada in her grave. There are several variations of the story. One describes Ada struck by the automobile as she crossed M-25 to collect rents from a tenant. Another says she was leaving a party, dressed in an exquisite, flowing, green gown when hit. A third version dismissed the Model-T altogether, and claimed Ada was killed by an out-of-control buggy. Each variation ends with her killed by a careless traveler riding along after dark without the benefit of lights. All agree the driver felt a sickening thump and got out to investigate. What he found was the dying Ada, her lifeblood seeping into the dirt. She was rushed inside the Loop home but nothing, including her father's medicine, could save her.

Today, behind the walls of the elegant Victorian, not all is as placid and serene as the exterior suggests. The tormented ghost of Ada Loop Harrison wanders the twenty antique-filled rooms but finds no peace.

Since becoming a museum, the Loop-Harrison house has seen its share of contractors doing repair work to the residence. These workers describe Ada Loop-Harrison pacing back and forth in the upstairs bedroom where she had slept as a child. She stops and stares out the window, contemplating the spot where she met her death. As she walks, her movements create a lingering chill in the air. It's enough to scare the kajeepers out of the bravest man on the crew.

Sometimes Ada haunts the grounds, and in recent years she has become fond of the Barn Theatre which stands next to the mansion. Theatergoers describe feeling her fingers touch them. They turn but see no one nearby. Theatre workers have experienced signs of her chicanery with a cup or a pen taken or moved. Ada enjoys the performances at the Barn, and only the most uncharitable would begrudge her a slight diversion from the drudgery of her otherwise unsettled life.

The most bizarre stories about Ada, however, are those involving current day motorists who report seeing a wisp of a woman ahead of them on Ridge Street at the exact spot where Ada was killed nearly a century ago. The drivers experience a thud and screech to a stop, certain they have killed someone. The poor motorists rush to local homes to report the accident and secure help, but when they arrive back at the scene, there is no body. Ada has returned home.

19. FORESTER AND FORESTVILLE

Forester's star came into existence in the mid-1800s shone brightly for a few decades, and then was nearly extinguished by circumstances beyond its control. In 2020 there were about 1,108 people in Forester Township. Like its sister cities of Port Sanilac and Lexington, Forester was heavily wooded when first settled, and the village was predicted to become a Thumb showplace. That expectation seemed to be fulfilling itself, as four hotels popped up in the thriving community.

Docks flourished along the lakefront to facilitate shipping. Then fate, and to a lesser extent man's carelessness, toyed with Forester's destiny. The fires of 1871 and 1881 destroyed the great forests for which it was named and ended the profitable lumber industry. The fires cleared the land, and the area residents turned to farming to sustain a way of life.

The storm of 1913 destroyed the Forester docks, and they were never rebuilt. The shipping industry was also lost to the small town. The railroad was built inland and became the source of transporting goods.

The fishing industry brought commerce to Forester but that, too, was dealt a death blow. The introduction of the lamprey eel to the lake decimated commercial fishing.

Today Forester is a mere specter of its former self. The tavern does a good business, and the churches manage to survive. The last hotel to remain standing is in ramshackle condition. For years it provided rooms to lumbermen passing through. In addition to a comfortable bed, it may have provided them with someone with whom to share it, as the persistent legend claims it was also a bordello. Now it stands empty; perhaps it is only nostalgia or lack of funding that prevents it from being torn down. The local cemetery holds the gravestone of Minnie Quay, one of the most frequently told ghost stories in Michigan.

Midway between Port Sanilac and Harbor Beach is Forestville, with a population of 128 as of the 2019 census. Like Forester, this is a one-blink town. Keep your eyes open wide, or you'll miss it. To say a place is small by Thumb standards means it is really, really, small. At the time it was first settled, Forestville was heavily timbered, and it was named for that natural bounty. Captain E. B. Ward built the first sawmill in the area in 1854. Forestville was incorporated as a village in 1895. It is a quiet place (consider that an understatement) with a small public beach.

• BEACHES, PARKS, AND TRAILS

Forestville Beach. Upon entering the tiny village of Forestville from the south, turn to your right at the first side street to find a park with a small, sandy beach and a boat ramp. The swimming area is rocky, and swimming won't be as much fun as it would be at the Forester County Park or Harbor Beach. On the other hand, you stand a greater chance of privacy and more tranquility at this beach. If you choose to stop here, you will find only an outhouse or port-a-potty, and you may prefer to use the bathrooms at the shops on M-25.

<<>>

Sanilac County Park, also called Forester Park, is located six miles north of Port Sanilac, 2820 North Lakeshore Road (M-25), along the scenic Lake Huron shoreline. This 68-acre park is one of the most handicap accessible campgrounds in the state. It offers a swimming beach, restrooms, showers, a park store, pavilion, nature trails, playground, recreation field, basketball court, horseshoes area, fishing, and 190 camping sites with 30-amp hookup and water.

● GHOST STORY

The Ghost of Minnie Quay. Mary Ann Quay listened to the argument between her husband James and their daughter Minnie. "Lucky that son-of-a—" Mary placed a hand on James' shoulder and shot him a stern frown. He bit his tongue in deference to his wife's sensibilities. After a few seconds, he continued his rant. "At least the ne'er-do-well knew enough to scram when I ordered him to git. Comes sniffin' around our back porch again, and my 12 gauge greets him." Unable to hold her peace, Mary blurted her opinion into the fray. "I'd rather my daughter was never born than married to a sailor."

Minnie lowered her head, shuffled her weight back and forth between her feet, and remained as silent as the gloom-laden air.

"And you, only fourteen-years-old." Mary glared daggers at the distraught girl. "What's a man near twice your age thinkin'?" The harsh words lengthened the chasm between parents and child. "I'd prefer a prayer over your still corpse, lying peaceful in its coffin. Such would inflict less cruelty than the pain we'd suffer if you were ruined by such a man." Strong, spiteful words filled with prophecy.

In 1876 farming and millwork were hardscrabble means of existence. Young Minnie Quay could hardly be blamed for seeking diversion from her dull, demanding life. Steeped in an aura of mystery, the sailors who docked at Forester offered the promise of dreams about to be fulfilled. They seemed worldly and wise and, in a few cases, distractingly handsome.

Like the heroine of a Greek tragedy, Minnie lost her heart. As her young seaman readied to depart her little hometown, he made a last visit to Minnie's house where he had slunk in the bushes and thrown a pebble against her bedroom window. Minnie rushed to his side, and he kissed away her tears with the promise he would return for her on his next trip through Forester.

Her frustrated father tried to reason with Minnie. "You are still a child," he said. "Give yourself time to grow up."

"What? End up like you, dirt poor, saddled with kids," Minnie asked. "Haven't you ever longed for more?"

"When you are older, you will find a suitable partner, a responsible, hard-working farm boy. He will not force you to forsake your family and move away. You seek to turn a fairy tale into reality. I promise you it won't work."

"Married to one of your industrious farm boys, the drudgery would kill me," Minnie said. "And if I refused that life, I'd die alone, a spinster, living with you and Mama, and never knowing love." Tears streamed down her petal-smooth cheeks.

Unable to convince his daughter that the affair was a mistake, and distrusting Minnie's obedience, James boarded off the second-floor hallway where it led to Minnie's room. He made an opening directly from his daughter's room into his and her mother's bedroom. Minnie came and went, first passing through her parents' sleeping chamber, subject to their scrutiny.

A month later, when her sailor's ship returned to port, the elder Quays locked their headstrong daughter in the house and took turns standing guard, convinced their efforts would deny her a way to yield to temptation.

Minnie considered ways to join her young man. But it was not meant to be. After her father had chased him off, she never saw her love again.

News reached Forester that several ships vanished in stormy Lake Huron waters that winter and spring. Minnie learned that aboard one of the ill-fated ships, her sailor plunged to his watery grave.

Minnie had been denied a proper goodbye. She had been denied a last time to gaze on his fair features and commit them forever to memory. She had been denied the chance to explain why she was not at the dock to greet him as she had promised.

She no longer spoke to her parents. She withdrew into her grief. On April 26, twenty-eight days short of her fifteenth birthday, Minnie's parents traveled to Port Sanilac. They left the inconsolable Minnie home with her youngest brother, Charles. The other Quay children went along on the trip.

Minnie estimated the time of her parents' return. When she figured they were less than an hour away from home, she tucked her little brother in for a nap. Then, with her pain unendurable, Minnie tied her long blond hair in red velvet ribbons, donned her gauzy, white, go-to-church-on-Sunday dress, and trudged toward the pier. She waved at a few neighbors sitting on the front porch of the hotel.

Minnie stood and contemplated the choppy waves. An onlooker heard her whisper, "Take me to him," before she stepped off the dock and slipped under the raw, numbing whitecaps that promised reunion with her sailor.

Several spectators rushed to Minnie's aid. Many hands grappled to reach her before she drowned. Her body eluded those hands for an hour. During the efforts, a bystander shook his head and muttered, "Early April is a cold time to test Lake Huron's waters."

Death provoked rumors. Gossip painted Minnie's sweetheart a married man who toyed with her naïve and youthful affections. A more romantic notion suggested he was sincere and never understood why his love was not at the pier when he arrived to see her.

Whatever the truth, if Minnie thought her spirit would be reunited with her sweetheart's in the icy waters of her Great Lake, she was as disappointed in death as she had been in life. Today a solitary and angry Minnie Quay haunts the beach near the ghost town of Forester, and as she shuffles along, she cries to young maidens she meets. "Forsake this world." Her beckoning, set against night winds, is eerie and persuasive. "Join me. Help me find my love."

But Minnie Quay is not at rest.
Or so the people say.
Her ghost still walks the lonely shore,
And you can see her to this day.
(Last verse of a local ballad.)

Minnie Quay's Grave in Forester Cemetery.
Courtesy of Bob Royce.

Author's Note: The dock from which Minnie Quay plunged to her death was destroyed in the Storm of 1913; any remaining wooden vestiges have long since rotted. A few of the rock piling supports can still be seen. At night, if you walk this stretch of beach, you may see Minnie's ghost bobbing back and forth between them.

20. HARBOR BEACH

The 2020 population of Harbor Beach was 1,574. The earliest settlers to this area arrived in 1836 and established a sawmill for processing lumber. The city was first known as Barnettsville. By 1855 the settlement had grown, and the town was renamed Sand Beach in recognition of its strip of sandy beaches that welcomed swimmers.

The local residents decided Sand Beach didn't quite fit either, so in 1899 they renamed their community Harbor Beach. In 1910 it was officially incorporated as a city.

Local stories suggest that in its early years, Harbor Beach was the location of a major counterfeit operation. Leonard "Pic" DeFrain recounts the tale in his book, *Thumb Memories.*

A Mr. Crane (maybe an alias he assumed while living south of Harbor Beach) was ostensibly a hunter and fisherman. Apparently, his real skill was coining counterfeit Mexican dollars and engraving bogus Canadian banknotes. Crane had previously lived in Philadelphia where he was employed by the United States Mint. He learned his counterfeiting skills as a minter. Crane did not try to pass the funny-money locally, so he was paid little attention by his neighbors. He had several shanties in the forests surrounding Harbor Beach for carrying out his illegal activity, but he sold his product in distant parts of the United States.

One of Mr. Crane's neighbors, Mr. Hiram Whitcomb, confronted Crane and told the counterfeiter that he (Whitcomb) was aware of Crane's real business. Further, he knew Crane was a fugitive from justice. After that Mr. Crane's activities became furtive, and he realized his neighbors had grown suspicious. He stayed in the area for another five years but acted more like a hunted animal than a friendly neighbor. Mr. Whitcomb saw Crane only once after their confrontation, and that was on an occasion when Crane returned to Harbor Beach to recover some ingot silver used for plating German silver dollars.

Mr. Crane was so skilled at his trade that even he sometimes became confused over what was real and what was counterfeit. On one distressing occasion, he mistook counterfeit money for genuine and put the real stuff into a melting pot and spoiled the whole batch.

While in Harbor Beach, you will want to see the Harbor Beach Breakwater Lighthouse which is best viewed from the Trescott Pier. (See Lighthouse in this section.) Plan to make stops at the Frank Murphy Museum, the Grice Museum, and the world's largest man-made harbor. (See Beaches, Parks, and Trails in this section.) You may want to spend a hot, summer afternoon on the beach or fish from the Trescott Pier. (Fishing License required.)

• MUSEUMS

Frank Murphy Memorial Museum, 142 South Huron Avenue, is dedicated to Harbor Beach's most famous native son. Frank was born in 1890 to John T. and Mary (Brennen) Murphy. He attended the University of Michigan Law School. After graduating, he returned home to practice law with his father and brother. On the museum lawn is a chronology of Frank's positions. It appears he averaged only a couple of years in each before he moved on.

Murphy was a politician who later served as an Associate Justice of the U.S. Supreme Court. Prior to that, he was the Mayor of Detroit, Governor General of the Philippines, Governor of Michigan, and a U.S. Attorney General. According to the Museum guide, Frank Murphy held as many offices as any politician in U.S. history, and what he accomplished in those offices was more important than the duration of each political stint. It is a good thing that was clarified, or we might wonder why he could not hold a job. Murphy wasn't a man who flip-flopped between jobs, but a man on his way to his calling, the Supreme Court of the United States. He remained there from 1940 until his career ended in 1949.

The Murphy Museum also serves as the city's Information Center. The family home next door contains part of the museum collection. The tour includes the Victorian home, early family living quarters, and the law offices of Frank Murphy. The tour gives you a respect for this humble man that you might not have if you simply looked at the dates on the plaque in front of the museum.

Murphy was an activist and fighter for civil rights. As he wrote in *Falbo v. United States* (1944), "The law knows no finer hour than when it cuts through formal concepts and transitory emotions to protect unpopular citizens against discrimination and persecution." There remains an argument that Murphy wasn't so much a legal scholar as a champion for the common man, and he sometimes allowed his decisions to be tempered by his feelings.

Murphy is best remembered for his vehement dissent from the court's ruling in *Korematsu v. United States* (1944), which

Murphy Museum.
Courtesy of Bob Royce.

160

upheld the constitutionality of the government's internment of Japanese-Americans during World War II. Murphy called the decision the legalization of racism and was one of the liberal justices to join the dissent. In the 1960s, along with William O. Douglas and Hugo L. Black, he opposed the conservative judicial restraint of Justice Felix Frankfurter.

Frank Murphy is buried in Our Lady of Lake Huron Catholic Cemetery in Sand Beach Township near Harbor Beach.

<<>>

The Grice Museum, M-25 north of Harbor Beach, 865 North Huron Avenue. Explore the late 1800s farmhouse with special exhibits, a barn, and a rural school. The farmhouse was built by James G. Grice who came to Harbor Beach in the 1860s. One hundred years later, the city of Harbor Beach purchased the property. Soon after, a group of local volunteers helped convert the house and surrounding area into a museum. There are over 2,000 artifacts in the complex which also exhibits agricultural machinery and farm implements.

● BEACHES, PARKS, AND TRAILS

Harbor Beach Bathing Beach Park and Trescott Street Pier, located in downtown Harbor Beach. This sandy swimming beach (or Harbor of Refuge as it is called) has a long pier that permits a view of the lighthouse as well as the opportunity to enjoy a leisurely day fishing. There is a playground area for children. The park has picnic tables, grills, restrooms, volleyball courts, and a lifeguard on duty during the summer swimming season.

A marker in the park describes the feat of Vicki Keith, who swam across Lake Huron from Harbor Beach to Goderich, Canada, where she arrived to a cheering throng of 400. She accomplished the swim between July 17 and

July 19, 1988. She swam 48 miles in 46 hours and 55 minutes.

<<>>

Wagener Park, 2671 South Lakeshore Road, (just south of Harbor Beach). This county park has 96 camping sites for RV and tent camping (some with views of the lake), hiking trails, a small secluded but rocky beach, fishing, picnic facilities, courtesy boat launch (maximum boat length of 14 feet), sanitation and bathhouse, running water, and electricity. Pets are allowed in the park.

● OTHER STOPS TO CONSIDER

Fishing. Harbor Beach has both a private launch and a large public marina. This port or harbor offers some of the best salmon fishing in Lake Huron. Besides salmon, you can try reeling in yellow perch, walleye, trout, and steelhead. (Fishing license required.)

<<>>

Sunken Ships/Diving. (See Shipwrecks in this section.)

● LIGHTHOUSE

Harbor Beach Breakwater Lighthouse. Constructed in 1885, this lighthouse is still active, although automated. It has a visibility of 21 miles. The best place to observe the lighthouse is from Trescott Pier. Upon entering Harbor Beach from the south on M-25, turn right on Trescott and drive to the end of the street. The lighthouse is beyond the fishing pier and sits on a freestanding crib off the long breakwater. It is not attached to land at either end so there is no way to walk or drive to it. Excellent tours are available.

The Harbor Beach Lighthouse was constructed to provide additional safety for ships traveling between the St. Clair River and the Saginaw Bay. The Fort Gratiot lighthouse sat at the south entrance to Lake Huron, and the Pointe aux Barques lighthouse sat at the bay. In

162

between was over 100 miles with no harbor of refuge. Big freighters, confounded by storms in this open area, were forced to tough it out. This situation resulted in many shipwrecks. The federal government acknowledged the danger and erected a lighthouse midway between the two existing lights.

The initial decision was whether to locate a lighthouse in Port Hope or Harbor Beach. It was estimated it would take 3,000 more feet of breakwater to construct it at Port Hope, so Harbor Beach won the lighthouse. The beacon first shone out in 1875 and could be seen from 13 miles. The Harbor Beach breakwater is 8,200 feet long. Construction consumed one million tons of iron, fifteen million board feet of lumber, and 48,000 cords of stone. The first year it was open, the harbor provided shelter to over 1,000 ships.

Harbor Beach Breakwater Lighthouse.
Courtesy of Bob Royce.

• SHIPWRECKS

The **Daniel Morrell** rests on the bottom of Lake Huron in the Thumb and is part of the Underwater Preserve.

The *Morrell* went down in 1966 near the shores of Harbor Beach where today each of her halves sits upright in about 200 feet of water. She stands as a testament that not all the ships that sank in Huron's November wraths did so in the late 1800s or the early 1900s before GPS and better weather-predicting tools. Even today, a great ship cannot always escape Lake Huron when she is riled.

On Monday, November 28, 1966, Harbor Beach was shrouded in snow from one of those blinding, wind-driven storms that warns Michiganders that winter is crushing down upon them.

The *Daniel Morrell,* a 356-foot iron ore carrier, was

The Daniel Morrell before she sank. Courtesy of Pixabay Free Images.

headed for her last run of the season when she began battling the blizzard. As midnight ushered out Monday, Tuesday arrived with the tempest growing angrier. Temperatures had dropped to 20 degrees. The morning hours terrified even the bravest of seamen.

At approximately 2:00 a.m., the ship was torn in two, and all aboard were tossed into the lake's frigid waters.

Deck watchman Dennis Hale made it to a lifeboat with three of his crewmen. Within six hours, two of the sailors lost their battle against the bitter elements. Several hours later the third of Hale's mates died. Hale, the lone survivor, wondered how long before he, too, would lose the struggle.

The storm continued spitting snow and ice with gale force as it tortured the near-dead sailor. On December 1, the body of a *Morrell* crewman was spotted by the vessel *G.G. Post.* Soon after, Hale was rescued by a Coast Guard helicopter. He was the only survivor of the wreck of the *Daniel Morrell.* Twenty-eight perished.

<<>>

Other ships of the Underwater Preserve. (For more information about the Underwater Preserve, see Shipwrecks under Lexington in this guide.) Listings marked * are popular dive sites.

▪ The **_Arctic_** was a propeller steamship that went down near Wagener Park/Harbor Beach in 1893.

- The ***Chickamauga***,* a double-deck schooner, foundered one mile north of Harbor Beach in 1919. She was removed to one mile outside of the harbor at a depth of 35 feet. It is accessible to novice divers.

- The ***Colonel Brackett***, a sail steamer, was stranded one mile northeast of Harbor Beach alongside the breakwater in 1890.

- The ***Dunderberg***,* a schooner, went down with her load of corn and passengers on August 13, 1968, when she collided with the *Empire State* six miles from Harbor Beach. It was a night collision, and it claimed the life of one of the six *Dunderberg* passengers. The ship remains in nearly perfect condition, resting at a depth of 155 feet.

- The ***George H. Wand*** was a sailing vessel stranded off Harbor Beach.

- The ***Glenorchy***,* a steamer, sank in a collision ten miles east-southeast of Harbor Beach in 1924. She carried a cargo of grain. She lies upside down at a depth of 356 feet.

- The ***H. A. Emery***, a sail vessel, was stranded in 1899, slightly more than one mile north-northeast of Harbor Beach while attempting to enter the harbor.

- The ***Marquis***,* a schooner carrying black stone, was lost north of Harbor Beach in 1892. She currently rests in shallows of ten feet.

- The ***Minnedosa***, a cannon four-masted sail vessel, foundered eight miles northeast of Harbor Beach while being towed by the steamer Westmount in 1905. All nine sailors aboard were lost.

- The ***Peshtigo*** is a wood steamer stranded 1,240 feet off the lighthouse at Harbor Beach.

- The ***R.G. Coburn***, a passenger and cargo propeller, foundered 6½ miles off Harbor Beach. In addition to passengers, she carried a cargo of wheat and flour. Thirty-two lives were lost when she went down about 8:00 a.m. on

October 15, 1871. Sixteen passengers, the captain, and fifteen of the crew, including every officer except the second mate, were plunged to a watery grave. Critics of the tragedy alleged that if the lifeboats had been properly handled, everyone aboard would have survived. Twelve crew and six passengers were rescued.

• The **St. Clair** is a barge that foundered 1 1/3 miles southeast off Harbor Beach in 1888. Five lives were lost.

• GHOST STORY

The Ghost of the Frank Murphy House. The Frank Murphy House is a local tourist attraction by day. By night something else may be occurring. The museum is operated by volunteers, and one of them believes that Murphy's younger sister haunts the family homestead. This volunteer has received phone calls from locals telling her that the lights are on in the house at night—long after the museum has closed.

These calls send the volunteer to the house to extinguish the source of such illumination. Yet upon arrival, the house is pitch-black dark. A quick check of the switches and lamps reveals nothing amiss. There are times in the winter when caretakers arrive and find the outside doors to the master bedroom suite open, although they had been tightly bolted. Snow covers the floor and the air seethes with unrest.

21. PORT HOPE

Known as the little town with the big welcome, Port Hope, 2019 population 250, was founded in 1855 and incorporated as a village in 1877. It was a busy logging, milling, and shipping port. Salt production was also an important industry. Early resident William Stafford, a lumberman in the area, built a boarding house to accommodate individuals working in or traveling to this growing community. In 1890 Richard Herman built the Herman Hotel, a stylish brick building that offered additional accommodations. Currently known as the Port Hope Hotel, it no longer rents rooms but remains in business as the local tavern, serving meals and spirits.

In earlier days, Port Hope had two long docks for deep-water sailing vessels and steamers. The schooner *St. Andrews* and the propeller-driven steamer, the *Swallow*, docked at Port Hope and serviced the Detroit area and the upper Great Lakes.

After the two great fires in Michigan, the community turned to farming as its major source of support.

● MUSEUM

Pointe aux Barques Lighthouse Museum, located in Lighthouse Park. (See Beaches, Parks, and Trails for additional information about Lighthouse Park.) President Polk ordered the lighthouse built in 1857 to guard ships from some of the most treacherous shoals in the lake. The lighthouse was automated in 1957 and is still in service, but the keeper's residence is now a museum, and the grounds are a lovely 120-acre park with modern camping. Parking is ample, and there is a gift shop inside the lighthouse. Relics from shipwrecks are located in some of the rooms. You can go through the lighthouse living quarters—both upstairs and down. You are allowed partway up the lighthouse tower.

● BEACHES, PARKS, AND TRAILS

Lighthouse Park, Lighthouse Road, ten miles north of Port Hope. This county park has 107 campsites and provides hiking trails, fishing, playground, picnic grounds, boat launch, park store, sanitation, shower, bathhouse, pit toilets, flush toilets, running water, electricity, group camping, tent camping, and RV spaces. There is no swimming beach.

<<>>

Stafford Park, North Street. A county park with 73 campsites. The park provides hiking trails, fishing, playground, picnic grounds, boat launch, sanitation, showers, flush toilets, running water, electricity, group camping, RV parking, and tent camping. There is a rocky, rugged, and reedy beach with pleasant views. (See also Port Hope Chimney under Other Things to See or Do.)

• OTHER STOPS TO CONSIDER

Michigan Nature Association's Whisky Harbor Nature Sanctuary, 2½ miles northwest of Port Hope, turn north from M-25 to Pochert Road, 1½ miles to the dead end. This nature sanctuary includes the Kernan Memorial Nature Sanctuary and the Thelma Sonnenberg Memorial Plant Preserve. You can enjoy unique rock formations, mudflats, native wildflowers, rare migratory birds, and artifacts washed up along the shore. The sanctuary is designed for hiking, birdwatching, and photography. MNA asks that you not use motorized equipment in the sanctuary and only take out what you bring in. This is not a park. It is a preserve area (natural state) with no restrooms, picnic tables, or other amenities. It is for those who can appreciate its ruggedness.

<<>>

Port Hope Chimney, located in Stafford Park. The chimney was built by William Stafford. It is all that remains of the lumber mill established in 1858 by John Geltz. The chimney is a remembrance of the pioneers, who by their courage,

Port Hope Chimney. Courtesy of Pixabay Free Images.

developed the area. It is Michigan's only chimney standing from the lumbering era.

<<>>

Port Hope Walking Tour. Pick up a Port Hope Village Walking Tour Map at any local business, and then stroll through town at your own pace. The points of interest include the Saw Mill Chimney, the Flour Mill, the Planing Mill, Port Hope Salt Company Site, Blue Town House, the Leuty-Peterson House (an excellent example of nineteenth century Carpenter Gothic architecture), Ogilvie Building (nineteenth century Victorian style), Stafford Home (currently a B&B), and Melligan's Store or Agricultural Hall (currently Main Street Antiques).

• SHIPWRECKS

The Thumb Underwater Preserve. See Shipwrecks under Lexington in this book.) The wrecks marked * are the most popular sites.

• The ***E. Cohen***, a schooner-barge, was stranded 8¼ miles, 158 degrees off Pointe aux Barques Lighthouse on Port Hope Reef. She went down in 1890 and was a total loss.

• The ***Frederick Lee***, a tug, foundered northeast of Pointe aux Barques in 1936 with five lives lost.

• The ***Hunter Savidge***, a sailing vessel, capsized near Pointe aux Barques Lighthouse ten miles and 45 degrees off Port Hope. She sank in 1899 with five lives lost. (See related Ghost Story.)

• The ***Iron Chief***,* a steamer, loaded with coal foundered off Pointe aux Barques in 1904. She rests at a depth of 135 feet.

• The ***John A. McGean*** was lost in the storm of 1913. Her entire crew of 28 perished. (See Lake Huron in this guide.)

169

▪ The **Keystone State**, a side-wheel passenger steamer, was bound for Milwaukee from Detroit in 1861. She was last seen three miles northeast of Port Austin. Wreckage foundered off Pointe aux Barques where the ship had sunk and carried 33 men to their watery grave.

▪ The **Philadelphia**,* a steel propeller, collided with the propeller *Albany* and took the *Albany* in tow. They both foundered trying to reach shore. The *Philadelphia* lies upright and intact in 124 feet of water, 5½ miles northeast of Pointe aux Barques Lighthouse. These ships went down in 1893 with the loss of 24 lives. The *Philadelphia* was loaded with iron stoves and packaged freight, and the *Albany* carried grain.

▪ The **Seaton**, a sailing vessel, went down in 1892, 1½ miles north-northwest of Pointe aux Barques Station.

▪ The **S. H. Kimball**, a sailing vessel, collided with the towing steamer *George Stone* and foundered 3.8 miles northwest of Pointe aux Barques. She went down in 1895, but the crew was saved.

● GHOST STORIES

The Ghost of the Hunter Savidge. The bones of the schooner *Hunter Savidge* lie in nearly 200 feet of water northeast of Pointe aux Barques, hurled there by convulsive winds that sprang from nowhere. It was late Sunday afternoon, August 20, 1899. It had been a sweltering, muggy day. Clothes stuck to bodies, and the smallest patch of shade was considered a blessing. The *Hunter Savidge* had waited for hours, every sail set and prepared. The crew hoped to catch the slightest puff of a breeze to ease them along their journey.

The two-masted schooner was built for the prosperous, lumbering Savidge family. 'Hunter' came from Mrs. Savidge's maiden name. Fred Sharptein captained the ship that day. He had brought along his wife Rosa whom he affectionately called Ma. One of their twin sixteen-year-old sons, John, had hired on for his first trip as part of the crew. Also aboard was Mary Muellerwies, wife of the ship's owner, and the couple's six-year-old daughter Etta. Mary and Rosa expected to enjoy a pleasant summer outing on the placid lake. The ship's first mate that day was Tom Duby.

The schooner had delivered a load of coal to a buyer in Sarnia, Ontario, and was sailing empty back to Alpena. Without warning, the air that had been stagnant and calm turned frenzied and caught the crew and passengers unprepared for the wind's punishing blows.

Fearing the worst as the storm bore down on them, Captain Sharpstein sent the women and young Etta below to the cabin where he hoped they would be safe. The maelstrom hit with such violence that it tipped the vessel vertical on the beam of its hull, trapping the women in the cabin. Visibility was limited in the roiling sea, thoughts were confused, and time was short—all factors that conspired against Rosa, Mary, and Etta who could not extricate themselves from their tomb.

As the ship capsized, the men on deck shot overboard into the frigid water where they had a fighting chance to survive. Most swam to the surface and grabbed the sides of the overturned wreck. Tom Duby drowned. John Sharpstein managed to break the surface and called to his father. Fred swam toward his panic-stricken, floundering son. John's heavy boots and clothing pulled him under. The frantic father watched from a few feet away as angry waves swallowed his child.

It was only minutes before the steamer *Alex McVittie* reached the site of the wreck and picked up survivors. Captain Sharpstein asked the captain of the *McVittie* to take the *Hunter Savidge* in tow, but the captain of the *McVittie* was hurrying north and denied the request. To avoid losing more time, he put the crew of the *Hunter Savidge* aboard the southbound *N. E. Runnels,* which took them to Sand Beach (now Harbor Beach). He was not inclined to squander precious time searching for people he believed were already dead.

Captain Sharpstein was horrified. He had seen the aft section of the boat still afloat just before rescue by the *McVittie,* and he believed that trapped air might afford the missing women and child a chance of survival for at least a short time after submersion.

Fred was convinced Ma was still alive. He had seen similar situations in his long career and knew of sailors who lived to tell him about them. At Sand Beach, Captain Sharpstein hired a tug, the *Frank W,* to take him back to the spot where the *Hunter Savidge* had gone under, but no trace of the wreckage or missing women could be found. A subsequent search by the lifesaving station crews failed to find any sign of the vessel, despite reports from other ships claiming to have seen the schooner floating up to four days later.

For months Captain Sharpstein walked the shoreline futilely searching for his wife and muttering, "Ma's out there somewhere," to anyone who would listen. Sigmund Freud published his famous landmark book *The Interpretation of Dreams* two months after the wreck of the *Hunter Savidge,* but it took no expert to figure out the cause of the nightmares the Captain endured each evening.

For years afterward, sailors insisted they saw the ghostly stern of the vessel suspended by the air trapped in the cabins and hull. Sometimes when the fog settled in, they saw the *Hunter Savidge* floating aimlessly with the winds. And they believe Ma Rosa Sharpstein is still out there waiting for rescue.

Postscript: Well-known Great Lakes diver and wreck finder David Trotter, began searching for the remains of the

Hunter Savidge in 1980 and finally found her in 1988, almost a century after she sank. Trotter dove the site for nearly a month before locating the nameplate that definitively identified the *Hunter Savidge.* Subsequent divers have tried to find the bones of the missing women and child, but with no success. One diver found a white porcelain cup buried in the sand of the wreck site, and when he gently picked it up, he noted the delicate handle had not been broken. A few feet away lay the matching porcelain teapot, civilized tokens of more genteel moments during the trip. A capricious storm killed innocent travelers but left bone china without a chip.

<<>>

The Ghost of the Pointe aux Barques Lighthouse. Built in 1857, this iconic lighthouse was named Pointe aux Barques, French for the Point of the Little Ships. The lighthouse sits at the extreme northern tip of Michigan's Thumb where the lake transitions into the Saginaw Bay. It is a rocky and dangerous stretch for ships. The light tower overlooks a 12-foot limestone bluff, while the light itself is 93 feet above lake level and visible for a distance of 16 miles. Mariners depended on the beacon to guide them away from the hazardous reef.

Peter Shook was appointed the first keeper of the Pointe aux Barques lighthouse on March 3, 1848. He placed the light in operation at the opening of navigation that year. On March 31, 1849, Keeper Shook was sailing to Port Huron, when his boat capsized. He and three others aboard drowned. Shook, forty years old at the time of the accident, left behind his wife Catherine and eight children.

After the news reached the Lighthouse Service, they appointed Catherine temporary keeper since she knew the job. She became the permanent lightkeeper of the Pointe aux Barques Lighthouse on May 15, 1849, making her Michigan's first female to occupy such a position.

Lighthouse keeper was the only non-clerical government job open to women in the late 1800s, and women were paid the same as their male counterparts. It was a physically demanding job with long hours and no vacations.

The widow Shook needed the job to support her family. She was, however, destined for more tragedy before another year passed. A fire broke out between the ceiling and the roof above the kitchen of the keeper's living quarters. Henry B. Miller, Superintendent and Inspector of Lights for the northwest lakes, blamed the fire on a faulty chimney. He sent a report to his superior outlining the gravity of the situation:

> "The circumstances of this fire is (sic) the more to be regrettable as the husband of the keeper but lately found a watery grave in Lake Huron, and this affliction on this account falls with a double severity upon the widow who was lately appointed in his place. By this catastrophe, the widow not only lost a considerable portion of her furniture, but was badly burned in her attempt to keep the fire from the main building. They have erected temporarily a small shanty, which is very uncomfortable and unhealthy. I therefore hope that no time will be lost in having the dwelling rebuilt."

By some miracle, Catherine and her eight children survived not only the fire but the subsequent harsh winter. The next summer, the house was rebuilt. Two years later, Catherine resigned her position. She passed away in 1860 and was buried next to her husband in the Oakwood Cemetery in New Baltimore, Michigan. Her spirit seemed troubled and unwilling to remain there.

Tourists report seeing a mysterious figure pulling back the curtains on the second floor of the empty lighthouse. Others have seen the grieving widow in mourning clothes walking the cliff searching for her drowned husband.

<<>>

Ghosts of the Pointe aux Barques Lifesaving Station.
Catherine Shook isn't the only ghost haunting the area
shoreline. Sailors moving into the mouth of Saginaw Bay
near the Pointe aux Barques Reef swear they have seen a
white lifeboat with seven men rowing out into the lake.

On April 23, 1880, the Pointe aux Barques Lifesaving
Station[2] crew honored their duty to assist a ship in
distress. The scow *J. H. Magruder* of Port Huron was bound
for Detroit with a cargo of lumber when she ran into
trouble.

The lifeboat plowed through Lake Huron without a hint
of a problem. The winds were from the east and mild before
they turned savage. But turn savage they did. Six men
drowned when their surfboat overturned in the raging
waters. One man lived to tell the tale. Captain Jerome Kiah
made it to the beach and lay there, barely alive. His agony
was fueled by both his physical condition and the
emotional trauma of losing "the poor, dead boys, who had
donned cork lifejackets and rammed their boat into the face
of death." The Michigan Lighthouse Conservancy kept the
following records and statements. Nothing could prove
more poignant than the words from those involved. A
statement was taken from Captain Conkey of the *Magruder*.
In part it read:

> "I left Alcona with a load of 187,000 feet of lumber for
> Detroit at noon the 22nd instant, wind north, fresh.
> Sighted Point aux Barques light at ten o'clock that night,
> wind east, light, but breezing up. Took gaff-topsails in at
> eleven o'clock. When abreast of light we commenced
> listing bad to starboard. Saw we were making great leeway
> and the lee rail under water. Discovered here, for the first
> time, that the vessel was leaking badly, with two feet of
> water in the hold. About midnight was laboring very
> heavy, with high wind and heavy sea. I feared we would
> roll over, and was satisfied we could not weather the reef.

---

[2] Lifesaving stations and crew were precursors to the Coast Guard.

Got both anchors ready and let go about 2 AM the 23rd, when she immediately righted. Had fourteen feet of water under the stern, and at every heavy surge on the chains she would drag anchor, the seas breaking over her bows. Hung a red light in main rigging, as a signal of distress to the lifesaving station. I certainly feared the vessel would be lost, and that our lives were in great danger, if assistance was not rendered. The vessel would strike bottom between every heavy sea. At daybreak I displayed my ensign at half-mast, union down, and about 7:30 AM observed the answering signal from the station. About eight o'clock saw the surfboat coming out. We were about three miles southeast from the station. Lost sight of surfboat in a few moments; thought the sea was too heavy for her, and that she had gone back, but in about 1.5 hours (9:30) saw her again about one mile north of us, pulling to the eastward, to get out of the breakers on the reef. In a short time, I saw her go down in the troughs of a heavy sea, and when she came up, we saw she had capsized. We saw them right her and bail out, when she again started to pull for us. In about twenty minutes she again capsized. Saw several men clinging to her, for some time, but finally saw only one. Our boat was in good condition. She is 16 feet long. Did not think of launching her. No ordinary yawl-boat could live in such a sea. I thought the life-saving crew used good judgment in crossing the reef where they did. I then commenced throwing my deck-load overboard, and at noon, the wind shifting to the northeast, we made all sail and started, cleared the reef, and arrived in Sand Beach all safe, but leaking badly. The weather was piercing cold, and all that day the spray would freeze as it came aboard of us."

Captain Kiah, after he recovered sufficiently, provided his statement describing the tragedy.

"A little before sunrise on the morning of the 23rd, James Nantau, on watch on the lookout, reported a vessel showing signal. I got up, and saw a small vessel about three miles from the station, bearing about east and by south. She was flying signal-of-distress flag at half-mast. I saw that she was at anchor close outside the reef. All hands were immediately called; ran the boat out on the dock; and, when ready to launch, Surfman Deegan, on patrol north, came running to the station, having discovered the vessel from McGuire's Point, 1.5 miles north from the station. At this time a warm cup of coffee was ready, of which we all hastily partook, and a little after sunrise (5:15 by our time) we launched the boat. Wind east, fresh, sea running northeast, surf moderately heavy. We pulled out northeast until clear of the shore surf, and then I headed to cross the reef where I knew there was sufficient water on it to cross without striking bottom.

"We crossed the reef handsomely, and found the sea outside heavier than we had expected, but still not so heavy as we had experienced on other occasions. After getting clear from the breakers of the reef, the boys were in excellent spirits, and we were all congratulating ourselves how nicely we got over. I then bore down toward the vessel, heading her up whenever I saw a heavy sea coming. When heading direct for the vessel, the sea was about two points of the compass forward of our port beam, and for the heaviest seas I had frequently to head the boat directly for, or dodge them. When about a quarter of a mile from the vessel, and half a mile outside the reef, and very nearly one mile from the nearest point of land, I saw a tremendous breaker coming for us. I had barely time to head her for it, when it broke over our stern and filled us. I ordered the boys to bail her out before the sea had got clear of her stern, but it became apparent at once that we could not free her from water, as the gunwales were considerably under water amidships, and two or three minutes after she was capsized.

"We then righted her, and again were as quickly capsized. We righted her a second time, but with the same result. I believe she several times capsized and righted herself after that, but I cannot distinctly remember. As near as I can judge, we filled about one hour after leaving the station. For about three-quarters of an hour we all clung to the boat, the seas occasionally washing us away, but having our cork jackets on, we easily got back again

"At this time Pottenger gave out, perished from cold, dropped his face in the water, let go his hold, and we drifted slowly away from him. We were all either holding on the lifelines or upon the bottom of the boat, the latter position difficult to maintain owing to the seas washing us off.

"Had it been possible for us to remain on the bottom of the boat, we would all have been saved, for in this position she was buoyant enough to float us all clear from the water. My hope was that we would all hold out until we got inside the reef where the water was still.

"I encouraged the men all I could, reminded them that there were others, their wives and children, that they should think of, and to strive for their sakes to keep up, but the cold was too much for them, and one after another each gave out as did the first. Very little was said by any of the men; it was very hard for any of us to speak at all. I attribute my own safety to the fact that I was not heated up when we filled. The men had been rowing hard and were very warm, and the sudden chill seemed to strike them to the heart. In corroboration of this theory, I would say that Deegan, who did the least rowing, was the last to give out. All six perished before we had drifted to the reef

"I have a faint recollection of the boat grating or striking the reef as she passed over it, and from that time until I was taken to the station, I have but little recollection of what transpired. I was conscious only at brief intervals. I was not suffering, had no pain, had no sense of feeling in my hands, felt tired, sleepy, and numb.

"At times I could scarcely see. I remember screeching several times, not to attract attention, but thought it would help the circulation of the blood. I would pound my hands and feet on the boat whenever I was conscious. I have a faint recollection of when I got on the bottom of the boat, which must have been after she crossed the reef. I remember too in the same dreamy way of when I reached shore; remember of falling down twice, and it seems as if I walked a long distance between the two falls, but I could not have done so, as I was found within thirty feet of the boat.

"I must have reached the shore about 9:30 AM, so that I was about 3.5 hours in the water. I was helped to the station by Mr. Shaw, lightkeeper, and Mr. McFarland; was given restoratives, dry clothes were put on, my limbs were dressed, and I was put to bed.

"I slept till noon (two hours), when my wife called me, saying that Deegan and Nantau, had drifted ashore, and were in the boatroom. My memory from this time is clear. I thought possibly these two men might be brought to life, and, under my instructions, had Mr. Shaw and Mr.

Pethers work at Deegan for over an hour, while I worked over Nantau for the same time, but without success.

"I then telegraphed to the superintendent and the friends of the crew. The four other men were picked up between 1 and 2 PM, all having come ashore within a quarter of a mile from the station. The surfboat and myself came ashore about one mile south of the station, the bodies drifting in the direction of the wind, and the boat more with the sea. I ordered coffins for all."

Captain Kiah resigned his position. The history of Pointe aux Barques lighthouse is suited for the spirits of the restless dead. Many lighthouses reportedly have ghosts. The stories usually revolve around a ship that crashes because of some misfeasance or malfeasance on the part of the lighthouse keeper. While there was no hint of malfeasance in the death of the six crewmen who went to the aid of the *Magruder*, they may be among the spirits who haunt the Pointe aux Barques Lifesaving Station. Their deaths, lives violently cut short, could provide motive to haunt the place of their earthly demise.

<<>>

The Heroic Spirit of Pointe aux Barques. Another suspected ghost in the area of Pointe aux Barques lighthouse is that of Captain Henry Cleary who died of pneumonia on April 10, 1916, at age fifty-four. Cleary had been a crew member of the old Pointe aux Barques Lifesaving Station. There are at least two stories that suggest he played a hero in many rescue operations during his lifetime. In death he allegedly was unwilling to abandon his good deeds.

The first story: In 1966 the *D.J. Morrell* went down near Port Austin and all but one member of the crew perished. (See related story under Port Austin Shipwrecks in this book.) The sole survivor, Dennis Hale, told the story of an apparition that appeared to him as he lay near freezing in his life raft.

The ghost had long hair and loomed rather unkempt. Hale's beard was heavy and white with ice. Twice he started to eat the ice from his beard, and twice the figure appeared and warned him that if he did so he would die of pneumonia. Hale heeded the advice and was later rescued.

The second story involves a sixteen-year-old girl, who in her later years, came to believe that the ghost both she and Hale witnessed was that of Captain Cleary.

The young woman was home alone for a weekend while her parents visited Sault Ste. Marie. They mistakenly believed she had invited three friends to stay with her. The keeper's cottage for the Pointe aux Barques Lighthouse was fewer than 200 feet from the young woman's family home.

During the middle of the night, the girl was startled awake to find a milky, translucent image standing at the foot of her bed. She tried to scream, but no sound came out. She observed the intruder's dark, neat, almost military style of clothing. She noted his handlebar mustache. But it was his piercing eyes that transfixed her. As he stood there, she heard a man's deep voice, whether from him or inside her head, telling her she needed to get up and quickly go downstairs and lock the door. After his warning, the solitary specter vanished.

With his departure, her body was released from whatever immobilizing force had paralyzed her. She scurried downstairs where she found the front door unlocked. She slid the bolt and then lay down on the couch and tried to go back to sleep. She was too frightened to climb back upstairs to her bedroom. About 3:00 a.m., she heard someone or something turn the handle of the front door. There was a thudding against it. The sound was not a knock intended to awaken anyone, but more like a hard push by a strong shoulder.

Scared out of her wits, she forced her trembling legs to carry her to a side window which offered a view of the enclosed front porch on the other side of the door. There stood a stranger she later described as appearing to be the embodiment of pure evil. This was no ghost. She screamed at him, "Get out of here!"

He returned her look, and after a few long moments of obvious deliberation, he turned and walked out the porch door. The young girl never saw him or the ghost again. Upon hearing the story of Dennis Hale and coupling it with some research of the lighthouse and the life-saving crew, she believed she could identify their ghost as that of Captain Cleary.

22. HURON CITY

In the late 1800s, Huron City employed several hundred people and boasted more than one-hundred buildings including a blacksmith shop, general store, icehouse, roller rink, and hotel.

The city was founded by wealthy lumber magnate Langdon Hubbard in 1854. Today, Hubbard's descendants keep his memory alive through preservation of the Huron City Museum under the auspices of the Lyon Phelps Foundation. (See Museums and The Famous and Infamous with Ties to Port Austin.)

The two catastrophic forest fires that raged through Michigan's Thumb in 1871 and 1881 each destroyed Huron City, causing it to lose its dream of becoming a prosperous lumber center. Although reconstructed after these disasters, the trees were gone, and the local wells dried up causing residents to abandon the area. The city no longer exists as a separate village, and the geographic area it once occupied is now technically part of Port Austin. It is, however, still the site of one of the more interesting museums and historic villages in the Thumb. It is worth making time in your travels to stop here. Ten of the remaining buildings are open to the public, and the museum is a historical site.

● MUSEUM

Huron City Museum, 7995 Pioneer Drive (Off M-25) between Port Hope and Port Austin. The museum and grounds are the legacy of Huron City, and the reason the small town has not been erased from memory. The restored village includes a log cabin, church, carriage shed, U.S. Lifesaving Station, barns, inn, and a general store. The information center contains a variety of artifacts.

- The **House of Seven Gables** is a restored 1881 Victorian mansion fully furnished with original pieces.

- **Pointe aux Barques Lifesaving Station** at Huron City Museum. Completed in 1876, the lifesaving station was scheduled for demolition, but was preserved thanks to an Evans Graham Preservation Award to members of the Pointe aux Barques Lighthouse Society (PABLS) and Huron County Road Commission (HCRC). The lifesaving station currently houses a remarkably complete collection of lifesaving equipment and artifacts. It also stages a reenactment of the training drills of the courageous surfmen. The surfmen had a saying, "You have to go out, but you don't have to come back." They recognized the dangers involved with manning lifesaving equipment in these treacherous waters. (See additional history and Ghost Stories under Port Hope.)

23. GRINDSTONE CITY

Grindstone City is unincorporated and part of Port Austin Township with no separate population statistics. In its heyday, Grindstone City had a population of 600, which dwindled to only ten year-round residents before seesawing up again to about sixty year-rounders.

The city was named by its founder, Captain Aaron Peer. As the name suggests, the city was known for the grindstones it produced. Grindstones are round sharpening stones, usually made from sandstone, used for grinding or sharpening ferrous tools. During the late 1800s and early 1900s, these grindstones were shipped all over the world.

By 1875 the city had two churches and two hotels. The latter were the Huron House and the Grindstone Hotel. The major industry, and the one that employed most of its populace, was the quarry.

Today, Grindstone City appeals to anglers who come from all over the state, and it is considered one of the better fishing spots in Michigan. If fishing is your vacation goal, you might want to stop here. If you are looking for wonderful beaches, shopping, and fine dining, this will not be your vacation destination. It is a place you will drive through on your way to Port Austin traveling the shoreline around Michigan's Upper Thumb. As you make your way, check out the grindstones, pieces of history in many front yards. If you are a diver, you can also find grindstones in the Underwater Preserve (See Shipwrecks under Lexington in this book for more details about Underwater Preserves.)

Grindstones mark the driveways to many homes and businesses.
Courtesy of Bob Royce.

24. PORT AUSTIN

At the top of Michigan's Thumb, less than three hours from Detroit, sits a little town with a population of 712 residents in 2020. It is sometimes called the other "up north." The history of Port Austin traces back to 1837 when Jonathon Bird became its first settler. In 1839 it was named for P. C. Austin who was part owner of a sawmill built there that year. Austin constructed a dock for himself and then enlarged it so others could use it as well. He put a street light on a pole for a lighthouse, and it became known as Austin's Dock, later Austin Port, and finally Port Austin.

At one time, the Port Austin Harbor could accommodate steamships and sailing vessels, a fact that encouraged merchants, lumbermen, and bankers to set up business. By 1865 Port Austin was the county seat and boasted a new courthouse.

In the late 1860s, the Port Austin Hotel was built to provide lodging to stagecoach passengers from Port Huron and Bay City. Because of its unique location, this picturesque lakeside community enjoys both beautiful sunrises and sunsets. During the summer, the town is bustling with activities including boating, charter fishing, golfing, horseback riding, putt-putt golfing, birdwatching, go-karting, canoeing, swimming, restaurants, festivals, and nearby museums.

● MUSEUMS

Lighthouse Park Museum, nine miles east of Port Austin. (See Museum listing under Port Hope.)

<<>>

Huron City Museum. (See Museum listing under Huron City.)

Bird Creek County Park, M-25 in the heart of Port Austin. This county park has fishing, playground, pavilion, picnic tables, large sandy swimming beach, bathhouse, pit toilets, flush toilets, running water, and electricity. No camping.

<<>>

Gallup Park, M-25 in Port Austin. Hiking trails, tennis, fishing, playground, and picnic area. No camping.

<<>>

Huron County Nature Center Wilderness Arboretum, nine miles east of Caseville or nine miles west of Port Austin, just off M-25, turn south on Oak Beach Road to Loosemore Road, east to the nature center entrance. This 280-acre nature center was founded in 1990 on property that had been owned by the county since 1941. There are a 120-acre wilderness arboretum, accessible trails, pavilion, restrooms, and many wilderness walking trails. You can expect to see red pine, white pine, white oak, and birch trees in the wooded areas. You may also spot (in season) pink lady's slipper, white trillium, gaywings (fringed polygala), Clintonia (corn-lily), and other species. Birdwatchers catch sight of the eastern bluebird, wood thrush, great-crested flycatcher, American redstart, scarlet tanager, and rose-breasted grosbeak. Educational programs are offered at the nature center.

<<>>

McGraw County Park, M-25 between Port Austin and Caseville (day-use only). County park with hiking trails, fishing, playground, picnic grounds, swimming beach, bathhouse, flush toilets, and running water. Lake views.

<<>>

Oak Beach County Park, M-25, eight miles north of Caseville. This county park has 55 sites, fishing, playground, picnic grounds, boat launch, swimming beach, park store, sanitation, shower, bathhouse, pit toilets, running water, electricity, group camping, RV camping, and tent camping.

<<>>

Port Crescent State Park, located on M-25 near the tip of the Thumb. Port Crescent has nearly three miles of white sand beach making it a favorite summer stop. At one time Port Crescent was a little town in the Thumb. Now it is primarily a park and recreation area. In earlier days, the sand of this area was mined for manufacturing uses, but that practice stopped when it became cost-prohibitive. In 1975, 335-acres were acquired from Sand Products Corporation of Detroit and are now the day park.

The total park size is nearly 600 acres of varied terrain and woods of jack pine and oak. It is a place to spot deer and explore hidden ponds. Facilities include a modern beach house, restrooms, picnic pavilion, and arguably the best swimming beach in the Thumb—complete with small dunes, playground areas, horseshoe courts, and hiking trails. There are paved roads, parking lots, stoves, and a water supply. A canoe slide is located in the first parking area. Small cartop boats can be launched. A birdwatching platform is popular, and the Annual Hawk Watch takes place on the fourth weekend in April. Many trails are groomed for cross-country skiing in the winter. Some campsites are available along the beach and old river channel. Each site has an electric outlet, fire circle, and picnic table. Campers, motor homes, and trailers may use the sanitation station to take on water and dump sewage. Plant life is abundant in the park, and you can find berries and wildflowers in the spring and summer. Birds and other wildlife are seen in their natural habitat. Fishing is allowed in the park with a valid Michigan fishing license. Legal hunting and trapping are allowed from September through March.

<<>>

Thompson Scenic Turnout, between Port Austin and Caseville, is worth a stop. Michigan's Thumb has numerous turnouts that provide the driver with a break and a awesome view.

<<>>

Waterfront Park, Spring Street, a block west of the traffic signal. Pier, sandy beach, tables, and playground.

• OTHER STOPS TO CONSIDER

Garfield Inn, 8544 Lake Street. Built in the 1830s in French-architectural style, the Inn is located two blocks from Lake Huron. Although lodgings and restaurants aren't listed in this guide, this inn is included for its historical significance and the story connected to it. Yes, President James Garfield stayed there, but that's not the whole story.

Garfield Inn.
Courtesy of Pixabay Free Images.

Charles G. Learned, a financial genius involved in the construction of the Erie Canal, bought the house in 1857. By age eighteen, he had earned his first $10,000, an astronomical amount of money in the mid-1800s. He set about remodeling and enlarging the house.

Learned was friends with James Garfield who would later become the twentieth president of the United States. Garfield may have carried on an even closer, possibly intimate, relationship with the mistress of the house, Maria Learned. Although both she and the future president were married, they are rumored to have enjoyed an affair that lasted for many years, as evidenced by rather risqué letters exchanged between them. Local legend says that when

Garfield was mortally wounded by an assassin's bullet in September 1881, he requested to travel to Port Austin to recover in this house imbued with many fond memories. Because of the gravity of his condition, his request was denied. The circumstances of Garfield's injury and death were quite gruesome,[3] and Port Austin would not have had the medical staff to provide his care and treatment. Since he died of malpractice, that might not have mattered as much as the fact that Maria had died from tuberculosis six months earlier.

Is there any truth to this story? Garfield's biographers reference his affair with Lucia Calhoun and note he had an eye for younger women, but there is no mention of Maria Learned. The rumor remains unsubstantiated.

The Inn was designated a National Historic Site in May 1990. Six families have owned the Garfield Inn.

● LIGHTHOUSE

Port Austin Reef Lighthouse, 2½ miles north of Port Austin in Lake Huron. The reef lighthouse marks the tip of Michigan's Thumb. Ships headed northbound used it as a guide to turn into the Saginaw Bay. The lighthouse was built in 1878 and abandoned in 1953. It originally rested on an octagonal pier. It began to deteriorate rapidly after

---

[3] Garfield was shot twice. The first bullet glanced off his arm. The second passed through the second lumbar vertebrae and lodged in his abdomen. He remained conscious and in horrific pain. Several doctors rushed to the scene, and with bare fingers—without the aid of painkillers or sterilization—probed the wound to remove the bullet. After Garfield was returned to the Whitehouse, doctors resumed their efforts. Over the next weeks and months, they continued to search for the bullet, increasing the incision from three inches to a 20-inch gash that extended from the ribs to the groin. The wound became inflamed, infected, and septic. In the last two months of his life, Garfield's weight decreased from 210 to 130 pounds. The assassin, Charles Guiteau quipped at trial, "I didn't kill the president. I just shot him. Doctors killed him." It was technically true, but Guiteau was tried, convicted, and hung.

construction. It is now under lease to the Port Austin Lighthouse Association. The group managed to evict the resident flock of more than 500 pigeons that were wreaking havoc with its interior. They have reroofed and bird-proofed the structure to save and preserve its heritage.

The Port Austin Reef Lighthouse. Courtesy of Pixabay Free Images.

The shape of the pier was modified in 1899, and the station was rebuilt to its present configuration. It stands 60 feet tall. It was decommissioned in 1984. Since 1953 the station has been automated, its fourth-order Fresnel lens replaced by a plastic optic which requires less maintenance. The light is not open for tours. It is difficult to reach by boat because of the reef, and often the fog presents a problem. On a sunny day, with a good zoom camera, you can take photos from the shore. The light was listed on the National Register of Historic Places in September 2011.

● SHIPWRECKS

The Underwater Preserve. (See Shipwrecks under Lexington in this book for details about Michigan's Underwater Preserves.) Located in the preserve at Port Austin are several noteworthy wrecks.

▪ The *Eugene*, a sailing vessel, was stranded on the south side of Port Austin during a storm in 1867.

▪ The *Jacob Bertschy*, a steamer, sank in 1879 when it wrecked on the Port Austin Reef.

▪ The *Osceola*, a steamer, foundered in 1888, 1½ miles, 35 degrees, off Port Austin.

▪ The **Water Witch**, a steamship, was believed to be one of the fastest steamers on the lakes, but its speed was no contest for one of the raging storms of November that came calling in 1863. Twenty-eight men lost their lives when the ship slipped below the waves. Some of the *Witch*'s wreckage washed ashore at Pointe aux Barques.

Divers might be interested in the caves located near the edge of the reef near Port Austin Lighthouse. The caves were created by eroding limestone.

● The Famous or Infamous with Ties to Port Austin

Port Austin brags no truly famous people who started life or spent a goodly portion of their existence in the area. A couple of notable individuals are worth a mention.

V. Floyd Campbell. An illustrator and caricaturist, Campbell was born in Port Austin in 1873. He was the son of a blacksmith. He studied under Joseph Giles at the Detroit Art Academy. He was a regular contributor to Detroit and Grand Rapids newspapers.

<<>>

Napoleon Chagnon, an American anthropologist, was born on August 27, 1938, in Port Austin. He is remembered for his reproductive theory of violence and hailed as a pioneer of scientific anthropology. His ethnography *Yanomamö: The Fierce People* was written in 1967 and became a bestseller. It is often assigned as an introductory anthropology course.

<<>>

William Lyon Phelps. Born on January 2, 1865, in New Haven, Connecticut, Phelps taught the first American university course on the modern novel. He was childhood friends with Frank Hubbard, the son of Langdon Hubbard, who founded Huron City, Michigan. In 1882 Hubbard built a family estate at Port Austin on a bluff overlooking beautiful Lake Huron.

Phelps was engaged to marry Frank Hubbard's sister Annabel when Langdon Hubbard died. Annabel inherited the family estate in Port Austin, and Phelps christened it *The House of the Seven Gables* after the Nathanial Hawthorne novel. The couple married on the estate, which then became their summer home.

Phelps studied the Russian novelists Leo Tolstoy and Ivan Turgenev. His course in modern novels brought Yale unfavorable attention, but his students loved his class, so he taught it outside the official curriculum. His courses were the most popular and well-attended of any on the Ivy League campus. Phelps continued to teach at Yale for 41 years until he retired permanently to Port Austin. During his tenure as a professor, the following story was told about Phelps: A student handed in his exam whereupon he had written, "Only God knows the answer to your question. Merry Christmas." Professor Phelps returned the paper after Christmas with the note, "Happy New Year. God gets an A—you get an F."

The Seven Gables home is part of the Huron City Museum.

• BOOK WITH A TIE TO PORT AUSTIN

Elmore Leonard's **The Big Bounce** is set in the fictional town of Geneva Beach at the tip of Michigan's Thumb which is geographically Port Austin. Jack Ryan wants to be a professional baseball player. His backup plan is less respectable but easier to attain. Jack becomes a slippery con man managing illegal immigrant farmworkers and stealing from local cottages along the lakeshore. He meets Nancy, and together they cook up capers that will make you happy you don't own a second home on Michigan's waters—or if you do, will make you reconsider how secure it is. In the end, Jack's biggest challenge will be to survive Nancy's scheme which doesn't include a happy ending for him. Elmore Leonard has won more awards than you can count. He spent most of his writing years in the Detroit area where many of his books are set. He is remembered best for his crime thrillers and suspense novels.

25. CASEVILLE

Caseville's 2020 population of 726 swells with the summer months, and during the Cheeseburger Festival, the place is positively crowded. The village has been called by many names—The Mouth, Pigeon River Settlement, and then Port Elizabeth. It was settled in 1836 by Ruben Dodge. The first sawmill was constructed in 1852 to further the important lumbering industry. Shipbuilding and salt manufacturing played key roles in the economy of Caseville. Today, tourism seems to be the area's economic mainstay. When the summer ends, the village transforms back into a tiny, quiet hamlet. The view remains equally spectacular in all seasons, and sunsets are unparalleled.

Caseville has one of the most popular beaches in the Thumb. The town exudes a beach-party character all summer. The drive to Caseville, along M-25, is filled with lovely views of the Saginaw Bay, its islands, and several parks and turnouts.

The Cheeseburger Festival is probably the rowdiest, craziest, and longest festival in the Thumb. It runs more than a week and has a Margaritaville flavor—literally and figuratively. By the time it is over, the townspeople are happy to reclaim their small village. It sure is fun while it lasts!

● MUSEUM

Caseville Museum, 6733 Prospect Street, a historical landmark, contains a history of Caseville and Huron County with over 300 history books, military and nautical artifacts, tools, and other interesting exhibits. The *Good Night Moon* display will delight children and grandchildren. This little museum isn't a destination site. No one drives from Detroit, Toledo, or Chicago to visit, but if you happen to be in Caseville with a bit of time to fill, give it a shot. Open seasonally.

• BEACHES, PARKS, AND TRAILS

Caseville County Park, M-25, at the northern limits of Caseville, offers fishing, playground, picnic tables, swimming beach, sanitation, shower, bathhouse, flush toilets, running water, electricity, group camping, RV camping, and tent camping. It is located on the lake and provides picturesque views.

<<>>

Rush Lake State Game Area, two miles north of Caseville, near Sleeper Park (see next entry) with 2,000 acres for hunting. You will have the best success hunting waterfowl, but there is also some deer hunting. You will need a local license.

<<>>

Albert E. Sleeper State Park, 6573 State Park Road, is located on the shores of Lake Huron with more than 700 acres of forest, wetlands, sandy beach and dunes, hiking trails, and a secluded campground. Spectacular sunrises and sunsets. The four miles of hiking trails are groomed in the winter for cross-country skiing (assuming sufficient snowfall). Hikers also have access to more than 2,000 acres of adjacent Rush Lake State Game Area, an area of forests and wetlands populated by many types of wildlife. Several rustic and primitive trails wind through the game area presenting a challenge for the more adventurous hiker.

The park hosts many special events including the Harvest Festival in the fall and a Civil War Reenactment during the summer. The campground has two modern toilet/shower facilities both of which are accessible. Campsites are available from mid-April through late October. Sanitation stations and a fish cleaning station are available. The day-use visitor will find beautiful sandy beaches, a public restroom (accessible), picnic tables, and grills. There is a pavilion for rent. This state park has 226 sites and allows both RV and tent camping.

<<>>

Philp's County Park, M-25, six miles north of Caseville (day-use only). This county park has a picnic ground and a swimming beach.

<<>>

● OTHER STOPS TO CONSIDER

Civil War Monument, downtown Caseville. A tribute to those who served their country in time of war.

<<>>

The Crawford House, 6249 Main Street. This mansion was built in the 1860s by Francis Crawford on the bank of the Pigeon River. It has heavy walnut front doors with frosted glass from France. There is a square belvedere on top of the house. The home was moved from its original site to its current place on Main Street where it serves as the Champagne Funeral Home. Worth looking at as you go by.

<<>>

Fishing. Caseville is nicknamed the Perch Capital of Michigan and not without reason. It has 300,000 shallow, sandy acres of water which are favored by Lake Perch. Farther from shore, the water depths can reach nearly one hundred feet and offer great opportunities to snag walleye, lake trout, and salmon. The Charity Islands have a reputation for providing fishermen with a place to catch their limit.

<<>>

All things water related. Boating, water skiing, jet-skiing, swimming. You'll find places to rent any equipment you need. You'll also see lots of cute shops, golf, and putt-putt golf.

<<>>

The Annual Cheeseburger in Caseville Festival. August brings the biggest and craziest of all small-town festivals. It lasts more than a week as Caseville transforms into Key North. The celebration includes a two-hour-long Parade of Fools. It seems every organization and business from all the villages and towns within a fifty-mile radius decorate a pickup, flatbed truck, wagon, bus, scooter, car, or golf cart and enter the parade. Many walk the parade route, and everyone throws candy and bead necklaces to children along the sidelines.

Parade of Fools. Courtesy of Joe Jurkiewicz.

One memorable float had a giant crane on the back of the flatbed. In its real life, it may have moved drywall or other construction materials. The crane was disguised as a flamingo, and a live man in scuba diving gear dangled from its bill. Parade watchers did a doubletake and must have wondered if the diver got motion sickness after the first hour. The parade is estimated to draw up to 50,000 onlookers.

Many restaurants and tents offer cheeseburgers, and you can grab elephant ears, cotton candy, kettle corn, funnel cakes, or cheese dogs from local vendors. Margaritas are the drink of choice, Jimmy Buffet music fills the air, and you can catch a great concert in the park. Wander the crowded street for a peek at the most outrageous costumes you will see in the Thumb.

● LIGHTHOUSE

Charity Island Lighthouse. It's a short boat cruise from Caseville to Big Charity Island. Michigan has several well-known islands including the most famous of all—Mackinac Island. Mackinac is lovely and a destination trip, either for a day, a weekend, or longer. However, Charity Island, the largest island in the Saginaw Bay, is lesser known and largely untouched. It may prove the island dream escape of your summer with its 11-acre, spring-fed pond—a mini-lake within the greater lake.

The island was named by the lake mariners for its location midway between the city of Au Gres and the Thumb at the entrance to the Saginaw Bay. During a trip through this dangerous channel, sailors were said to exclaim that they made it through to safety "only by the charity of God."

The lighthouse was built to help ships avoid a number of shoals extending from the northern and southern shores of the island. The island is 322-acres of stone and mixed hardwood forest. The many rare and protected species of plants include trillium, Jack in the pulpit, pink lady slippers, and pitcher's thistle.

The lighthouse first beamed onto Lake Huron waters on May 26, 1857, the date the lighthouse keeper arrived. The lighthouse is a 39-foot-tall brick tower located on a slight rise. It provided a 13-mile range of visibility.

The Charity Island light was a difficult lighthouse to maintain because its location in the middle of a rocky, forested island left it vulnerable to the elements. Of all of the lighthouses in the Thumb, it may have been in the worst condition when the Charity Island Preservation Committee began attempts to stabilize and preserve it.

A note of interest: The lighthouse and the keeper's house were built on different parcels of land. The house was owned by individuals who finally had it demolished because it attracted too many curious visitors and could be restored to accommodate safety. The preservation attempts are only for the lighthouse.

A few words about Lighthouse Preservation. Michigan has more lighthouses than any other state in the country, and it is the only state that currently supports lighthouse preservation. Most lighthouses receive assistance from volunteers who are interested in saving, restoring, and maintaining these historical treasures. It is worth visiting the lighthouses that are open to the public and taking a peek from the outside at the

Charity Island Light.
Courtesy of Pixabay Free Images.

ones that are not. Along the way, if you meet any of the dedicated volunteers, let them know you appreciate their effort.

● SHIPWRECKS

The Saginaw Bay is a prominent indentation on Lake Huron. It runs from Pointe aux Barques across to just north of Tawas. With an average depth fewer than 50 feet, the shallowness contributes to steeper waves than a sailor might encounter on the open lake. When warmer bay water meets the colder water of the deeper lake, it often creates fog. As upbound ships sail from the lee side of the Thumb, they may also experience extreme wind conditions, especially during westerly storms. It is a difficult task to control ships when storms swoop down, so it is not surprising that the bay is the final resting place for the unfortunate who tangled with fickle weather witches.

Michigan author James Oliver Curwood claims the Saginaw Bay is the resting place of more lost ships than any other Michigan bay. He included in his count the many tugs and schooners that went to the bottom carrying lumber camp payrolls. Curwood dubbed them the treasure shipwrecks. He explained that currents sweep in from the open lake and deposit sand in random fashion leaving ankle-deep shallows. This hazard is exacerbated by rocks, pinnacles, and boulders.

Marine historian David Swayze declares the Saginaw Bay the most dangerous spot on the lakes. Swayze recounts 80 ships that have sunk within 20 miles of Pointe aux Barques.

<<>>

The **Erie Board of Trade**. The coal ship *Erie Board of Trade* tells a fascinating story. *The Board of Trade* sank in Saginaw Bay more than one hundred years ago, and there are claims she haunts Lake Huron to this day. The ship was taken down by a ghost and became a ghost ship herself. It is a story best told in the words of one who was there. The following account was carried in the Saginaw

Courier in 1883, written by an unknown author. This is the exact, unedited story told by the mystery writer as he described it from the words of a sailor who was there.

"Down in the lower part of South Street the other day, an old sailor sat on an anchor stock in front of a ship chandler's store. He was an intelligent-looking man and was fairly well-dressed for one of his calling. Other sailors were seated on a bale of oakum, on a wide-mouth pump without a plunger, and on the single stone step of the store. The ship chandler and a young friend sat in chairs just inside the door. The group was talking about ghosts. One of the men had just told his experience.

"You're a sorry dog," said the ship chandler to him. "You were drunk, and the spirits you'd taken within made you see the spirits without. It's always that way."

The old sailor threw one leg over the anchor stock, faced the ship chandler, and said: "You know I never take no grog, don't you, captain?"

The ship chandler nodded. "Well, I saw a ghost once. I saw it as plain as ever I saw anything. The captain of the schooner I was on and the man in the waist both saw it, too. There wasn't a drop of liquor on board. It happened up on the Lakes, and I reckon you know the captain. It was the talk of the docks the whole season."

"I know a Captain Jack Custer of Milan. He's the only fresh-water captain I'm acquainted with," said the ship chandler.

"He's the man. I heard him speak of you once. It was a little over ten years ago. I was before the mast then. It was at the opening of the season, and I was in Chicago. I'd been through the canal from Toronto on one of these little canallers. What with tramping through mud with a line over my shoulder and taking turns around snubbing posts everytime the schooner took a notion to run her nose into the bank, I'd got enough of canal schooners.

"I heard at the boarding house that some men were wanted on a three-masted schooner called the *Erie Board of Trade*. The boys gave her a pretty hard name, but they said the grub was good, and that the old man paid the top wages every time, so I went down and asked him if he'd got all hands aboard. He looked at me a minute, and then asked me where my dunnage was. When I told him, he said I should get it on board right away.

"The *Board of Trade* was as handsome a craft as ever floated on the Lakes. She'd carry about 45,000 bushels of corn. Her model has as clean lines as a yacht. As I came down the dock with my bag under my arm, I had to stop and have a look at her. The old man saw me at it. He was proud of her, and I thought afterward that he rather took a fancy to me because I couldn't help showing I liked her looks.

"The first trip around to Chicago every man but me got his dunnage onto dock as soon as he was paid off. I'd seen worse times than what we'd had, and when I got my money, I asked the old man if he'd want anyone to help with the lines when the schooner was towed from the coal-yard to the elevator. He said he reckoned he could keep me by if I wanted to stay, so I signed articles for the next trip there.

"When we were getting the wheat into her at the elevator, we got the crew aboard. One of them was a red-haired Scotchman. The captain took a dislike to him from the first. It was a tough time for 'Scotty' all the way down. We were in Buffalo just twelve hours and then we cleared for Cleveland to take on soft coal for Milwaukee. The tug gave us a short pull outside the breakwater, and we had no more than got the canvas onto the schooner before the wind died out. Nothing would do but we must drop anchor, for the current, settling to the Niagara River, was carrying us down to Black Rock at three knots an hour.

"When we'd got things shipshape about decks, the old man called Scotty and two others aft and told them to scrape down the topmasts. Then he handed the boatswain's chair to them. Scotty gave his chair a look and then turned around, and touching his forehead respectfully, said, 'If you please, sir, the rope's about chafed off, and I'll bend on a bit of ratlin' stuff.'

"The captain was mighty touchy because the jug had left him so, and he just jumped up and down and swore. Scotty climbed the main rigging pretty quick. He got the halliards bent onto the chair and sung out to hoist away. I, and a youngster, the captain's nephew, were standing by. We handled that rope carefully, for I'd seen how tender the chair was. When we'd got him up chock-a-block, the young fellow took a turn around the pin, and I looked aloft to see what Scotty was doing. As I did so he reached for his knife with one hand and put out the other for the backstay.

"Just then the chair gave way. He fell all bunched up 'til he struck the crosstrees, and then he spread out like and fell flat on the deck, just forward of the cabin on the starboard side. I was kneeling beside him in a minute, and so was the old man, too, for he'd no idea that the man would fall. I was feeling pretty well choked up to see a shipmate killed so, and I said to the captain: 'This is pretty bad business, sir. This man's been murdered,' says I.

"When I said that, Scotty opened his eyes and looked at us. Then, in a whisper, he cursed the captain and his wife and children, and the ship and her owners. It was awful. While he was still talking the blood bubbled over his lips, and his head lurched over to one side. He was dead.

"It was three days before the schooner got to Cleveland. Some of the boys were for leaving her there, but most of us stayed by, because wages were down again. Going through the rivers there were four other schooners in tow. We were next to the tug, and some lubber cast off the towline without singing out first. We dropped our bower as quick as we could, but it was not before we'd drifted astern, carrying away the head gear of the schooner next to us and smashing in our own boat under the stern.

"There was a fair easterly wind on the Lake, and as we had got out of the river in the morning we were standing across Saginaw Bay during the first watch that night. I had the second trick at the wheel. The stars were shining bright and clear and not a cloud was in sight. In the northwest, a low, dark streak showed where the land was. Every stitch of canvas was set and drawing, though the booms sagged and creaked as the vessel rolled lazily in the varying breeze.

"I had just sung out to the mate to strike eight bells when the captain climbed up the companionway and out on deck. He stepped over to the starboard rail and had a look around, and then the lookout began striking the bell. The last stroke of the bell seemed to die away with a swish. A bit of spray or something struck me in the face. I wiped it away, and then I saw something rise up slowly across the mainsail from the starboard side of the deck forward of the cabin. It was white and all bunched up. I glanced at the captain, and saw he was staring at it too.

"When it reached the gaff near the throat halliards, it hovered over an instant, and then struck the cross-trees. There it spread out and rolled over toward us. It was Scotty. His lips were working just as they were when he cursed the captain. As he straightened out, he seemed to stretch himself until he grasped the maintop mast with one hand and the mizzen with the other. Both were carried away like pipe-stems. The next I knew the ship was all in the wind. The square-sail yard was hanging in two pieces, the top hamper was swinging, and the booms were jibing over.

"The old man fell in a dead faint on the quarter deck, and the man in the waist dove down the forecastle so fast that he knocked over the last man of the other watch. If it hadn't been for the watch coming on deck just then, she'd rolled the sticks out of her altogether. They got the headsails over, and I put the wheel up without knowing what I was doing. In a minute it seemed we were laying our course again. The second mate was just beginning to curse me for going to sleep at the wheel, when the mate came along and glanced at the binnacle.

"'What the heck is this?' he said. 'Laying our course and on the other tack?'

"The young man by the ship chandler had listened with intense interest. 'Here,' he said. 'That story is true. I was there. I'm the captain's nephew you spoke about. I was reading in the cabin that night. As the bell began to strike, I felt a sudden draft through the cabin, and my paper was taken out of my hands and out of the window before I could stop it. I hurried out of the cabin after it, but as I got my head up through the companionway, I heard the crash of the falling masts. When the schooner began to go off on the other tack, I saw a bit of waterspout two miles away to the leeward, and . . .

"The ship chandler laughed.

"Did you find your paper?" he asked.

"'No!' said the young man.

"'I thought not,' said the ship chandler. "'Well,' said the old sailor, 'the main facts in this story can be easily verified. The next voyage the schooner was sunk. The insurance company resisted payment on the grounds that she had been scuttled by her captain. During the trial of the case, the story of the death of Scotty and the loss of her topmasts under a clear sky was all told under oath.

Anybody who doesn't believe it can see a copy of the printed testimony by applying to Roseburg & Barker, the ship chandlers at 1789 Central Wharf, Buffalo.'"

<<>>

Other Ships that went down in the Saginaw Bay.

- The **City of Detroit**, a propeller steamship, sank in the Saginaw Bay in 1863 with all on board lost.

- The **E.P. Dorr**, a tug, went down in Saginaw Bay in 1856 and rests at a depth of 180 feet. This ship's wreckage is a favorite with divers.

- The **Governor Smith**, a steamer, sank in a collision in Saginaw Bay in 1906.

- The **Troy**, a steamer, foundered in the Saginaw Bay in 1860 with 23 lives lost.

● BOOKS AND MOVIES WITH TIES TO CASEVILLE

Murder in the Wind, set in Sand Point, is Dave Vizard's third in a series of mysteries set in Michigan. Vizard lives in and writes in Caseville. His protagonist, Nick Steele, is a newspaper reporter for the *Blade* in Bay City. Steele is called upon to investigate the murder of an ice fisherman who drowned during a storm on the Saginaw Bay. The prime suspect is the deceased's son. Steele uncovers secrets in a community torn apart by the money and politics of the area's wind turbines. Family secrets, shrouded in power, money, and lust, shatter the beauty and tranquility of the area.

26. BAY PORT

Along the primitive western shore of the Thumb beyond Caseville, it is difficult to find great places to eat and stay, and few tourists venture there looking for a beach and relaxation. The west side of the Thumb appeals to anglers and hunters. Its marshy wetlands are full of wildlife. Bay Port has a Fish Festival and refers to itself as the place where the fish caught the man. Locals believe you will love it so much you will be caught. If your vacation plans include fishing, watching wildlife, and exploring natural areas or wetlands, and if you are not averse to more rustic accommodations, then push on down the west coast of the Thumb. If you are following Michigan's lakeshores, it seems appropriate to continue this route, but do not expect quaint B&Bs, cute shops, or fine restaurants. They are scarce as grass around a cattle watering trough.

Bay Port is an unincorporated village with a 2020 population of 490. The first state maps referenced this area as Geneva. The little town was also known as Wild Fowl Bay before it became Bay Port. Commercial fishing was first established off Bay Port Island in 1868 by R.J. Gillingham, who expanded it that same year to mainland Bay Port. W.J. Orr and W. H. Wallace established the Bay Port Fish Company in 1895. The Bay Port Fish Company runs a year-round fishing operation. The factory is open to visitors and offers a family-friendly tour.

In the early years, fishermen used sailboats to make their runs for placing and tending nets. In the winter they chopped holes through the ice so they could continue fishing. Much of the catch would be salted and packed in kegs for preservation.

At the peak of the fishing industry in the 1920s and 1930s, refrigerated rail cars carried tons of fresh herring, perch, walleye, and whitefish to Chicago and New York.

The historical marker at the foot of Promenade Street near the entrance to the harbor notes the significance of Bay Port's contribution to the commercial fishing industry.

In its infancy, Bay Port was home to a luxury hotel where wealthy families from the city swarmed to its restful and inviting rooms to enjoy a welcome respite at this lakeside retreat. The Bay Port Hotel is gone; the marker a remembrance of its early glory days.

According to local village lore, the German settlers who came here were part of the religious village of Ora Labore in Germany. (See Ghost Stories in this section.) Research failed to reveal a village in Germany by that name, but the history of one village may shed light on the connection. Hirsau, Germany, was known mainly for its Benedictine Monastery. The old mythological legend of the Phoenix is a familiar one at the Abbey, where more than 300 years ago the motto was *Ora et Labore*, which translates "to pray and work." One thing is clear: the German settlers who came to this area were hardworking, industrious, folks with a deep attachment to their religious faith.

The local quarry, the Wallace Stone Plant, was the company store and a mainstay of the local economy. It provided jobs and homes for hundreds of people. It still operates in Bay Port.

Public access to the bay provides entrance to the lake for fishing. There are opportunities for sailing, water skiing, and other water sports. Winter does not close down activity in Bay Port. Hunters of small game and the whitetail deer find this a perfect area to track their quarry. Winter also brings the opportunity for cross-country skiing and ice fishing.

• OTHER STOPS TO CONSIDER

The **Bay Port Fish Company** is located on the dock in Bay Port. A sign out front proclaims, "Flopping Fresh Fish Caught by Our Own Boats Daily." You are invited to bring your children for the unique experience of seeing the live fish at a functioning fishery. Call first because they have live fish only at certain times. This is a great place to buy fresh fish to cook up for a special dinner.

<<>>

The **Bay Port Fish Sandwich Festival** is usually held the first full weekend in August. Confirm with the Chamber of

Commerce. This three-day festival includes raffles, helicopter rides, bake sales, fireworks, arts and crafts, a Rising Star talent contest, parade, and live entertainment. It wouldn't be right to leave Bay Port without trying the famous fish sandwich and fries.

The festival is a tradition started one summer when Mr. Henry Englehard and his wife decided they needed a way to help raise money for their three daughters' college expenses. They came up with the unusual idea of selling fish sandwiches from a stand in their front yard. They had a secret recipe from their friend, a local restaurant owner, and their ingenious idea caught on. The fish sandwich requires two hands to eat. More than 12,000 are sold at the annual festival. It is about the only thing on the menu. Originally the sandwich was mullet, but starting in 2013, perch also was offered.

<<>>

Fishing. Bay Port with its protected harbor is all about fishing. Sand Point stretches several miles into the Saginaw Bay to North Island off the mainland. The reefs of the local islands offer excellent walleye fishing. The islands are revered for their bass fishing. The shallow areas along the shoreline provide a preferred place to haul in perch. Public access provides the way to the deeper waters.

<<>>

● SHIPWRECKS

(See Shipwrecks in the Saginaw Bay under Port Austin.)

● GHOST STORIES

The Old Bay Port Cemetery. In the early 1860s, a group of Germans left their homeland, sailed to Michigan, and started a Methodist religious colony called Ora Labora close to the shores of Wild Fowl Bay near what is current-day Bay Port. The tiny community had all but disappeared by 1867 when there was no longer mention of it on maps. During Ora Labora's first year, 140 settlers came to this wilderness hamlet. They were plagued by illness. Within months of their arrival, the community suffered its first death. It was doubly tragic since the deceased was a child. To provide a proper burial for the little girl, Ora Labora established a cemetery on the extreme southern edge of the colony. This was the first of many burials they witnessed there.

Headstone from Old Bay Port Cemetery.
Courtesy of Pixabay Free Images.

The cemetery still exists, located at the end of Sand Road off M-25. It is a remaining vestige of the now lost community. With the demise of Ora Labora, the cemetery became the final resting place for many of the early pioneers and citizens of Bay Port. Nestled among the hills and wild trees and foliage are 241 marked graves. The last burial was almost two decades ago. In this rustic setting, mystery and unsettled souls walk the grounds. No grave markers are found for the residents of the famous historical colony of Ora Labora.

The ravages of time may account for the sparsity of markers for these German Methodists, but the absence of a single grave is curious. Perhaps with the lack of a recognized final resting place, these lost spirits are responsible for the many ghostly sightings in the area. In 2009 amateur ghost hunters visited the Old Bay Port Cemetery. While they made no pronouncements of real significance, they declared this the scariest cemetery in Michigan.

<<>>

The Ghosts of the William H. Wallace Family. Wallace was a well-off and highly-regarded early citizen of Bay Port. He practically owned the entire village. He was president of the Michigan Sugar Company and the Bay Port State Bank. He owned the Wallace Stone Quarry south of town. He built a family mansion overlooking Lake Michigan.

In later days, the home became the Sweet Dreams B&B. Sweet Dreams claimed it was haunted by Wallace, his wife Elizabeth, and at least one of their five children—a child referred to as Grace in some accounts.

William's first wife, Elizabeth, died four decades before her husband. Her death occurred in the home, and she wanders the upstairs, caught in a time warp, trying to get into the bedrooms to check on her babies. Locals report seeing little Grace in an upstairs window overlooking the Wallace property. She leaves her window perch to lurk about the upper floor, moving furniture, and having parties. Guests reported Grace touching them and speaking to them. She didn't seem malevolent, merely curious.

The Wallace House. Courtesy of Pixabay Free Images.

Besides talking to guests, the live-in spirits cried, giggled, laughed, and ran up and down the stairs. They opened and closed the doors, threw objects about, broke china, flipped lights on and off, and floated between the first and second levels. The ghosts were rumored to have their run of the place. They were described as friendly spirits that wanted company, or so the owners of the old Victorian claimed. Of course, to do otherwise would have dampened guests' willingness to stay there. Now that the B&B no longer rents rooms, it's hard to say if the ghosts have mellowed, left, or merely mourn the loss of companionship.

William Wallace. Courtesy of Pixabay Free Images.

The family patriarch, William, died in 1933 in an automobile accident. Despite his local prominence, there is no record found for his or his son's grave sites.

In addition to his above-mentioned businesses, William Wallace built and owned the Bay Port Inn. His ghost still roams the inn, disturbing guests with his heavy footsteps. He whispers in their ear, "Get out."

27. SEBEWAING

Sebewaing, population 1,713 in 2020, is located on the Saginaw Bay at the mouth of the Sebewaing River. It was originally named Auchville in honor of the Lutheran Missionary who brought settlers with him to this area during the first half of the nineteenth century. Later it was renamed Sebewaing which means crooked river in the Ojibwe language. The Ojibwe were the early inhabitants along the Sebewaing River that meanders through Sebewaing Township and empties into Saginaw Bay.

The city's industries include fishing and farming. Sugar beets are a notable local crop, and they provide the basis, or reason, for the annual Sugar Festival.

• MUSEUMS AND GALLERIES

Burns Gallery (Previously the Heidelberg Center Gallery), 27 Center Street. Features Community Art and offers free shows. Limited hours.

<<>>

Luckhard Museum and Indian Mission, 590 East Bay

Luckhard Museum and Indian Mission.
Courtesy of Wikipedia.

Street. In the mid-1800s, this was a Native American mission building. The museum displays original furniture, dishes, and Native American artifacts. Limited hours.

<<>>

Sebewaing Township Hall, 92 South Center Street, located in downtown Sebewaing. In November 1998, this hall was designated a historical site. The Hall, originally built for $640, is now a museum that contains local memorabilia. Open only during the summer.

<<>>

Charles W. Liken House Museum, 325 Center Street. In 1865 John Liken came to Sebewaing where he opened a cooper business and several other commercial enterprises. Liken shipped large quantities of white oak staves to Germany. He built two sawmills and four stave mills, and between them he employed more than two-hundred workers. Six years after he arrived in Sebewaing, he built a brick building where residents could buy anything from dry goods to household items and drugs. He had branch stores in Bay Port, Kilmanagh, and Unionville. He owned 1,500 acres of land in Huron and Tuscola counties and died wealthy in 1920.

The Museum is the former Liken home. Charles built five stately homes in Sebewaing, one for each of his children (a son and three daughters) and one for himself. Three of the homes remain in existence. One is on the historical register and is now a private residence occupied by the Liken descendants. It is not open to the public.

The museum is architecturally interesting, and the interior is embellished by rich-looking wood floors including the original parquet floor in the dining room. A chandelier and lighted china cabinet with leaded glass enhance the dining room. Various collections and Victorian furniture have been donated to the museum. Dedicated historical society members are doing much of the restoration. The museum is a work in progress. Limited hours.

None of the museums in Sebewaing are destination museums. You wouldn't make the trip for the experience of wandering through their artifacts. With extremely limited hours, they may not be open if you show up on their doorsteps. But, if you are wandering around the area and are interested and persistent, you might find something interesting.

• A PARK
Sebewaing County Park, 759 Union Street, provides hiking trails, fishing, sanitation, shower, flush toilets, running water, electricity, RV camping, and tent camping.

• OTHER STOPS TO CONSIDER
Fishing. Sebewaing is known for its excellent walleye fishing in the bay's weed beds. The Sebewaing River offers the perfect place to catch perch and bass.

Fish Point Wildlife Area, 7750 Ringle Road, M-25 South to Gotham to north on Ringle Road, about seven miles from Sebewaing. Fish Point is the most popular place in the Saginaw Bay for observing the thousands of Tundra Swans and Canada Geese that stage here each spring. According to area birders, no spot guarantees sightings because the food supply in the various fields changes from

Forster's Gull or Tern.
Courtesy of Pixabay Free Images.

year to year. It is suggested that you keep an eye open for the large flocks that feed in the corn stubble left from the previous year. Another tip is to check the observation tower at the intersection of Ringle Road and Seagull Lane near Fish Point. The tower gives you a good overview of the area. You may see yellow-headed blackbirds, snow geese, raptors, red-tailed and red-shouldered hawks, northern strike, snowy owl, fox sparrow, Forster's gull, bald eagle, wood duck, hooded merganser, pied-billed grebes, mallards, willow flycatchers, American and least bitterns, northern shoveler, cattle egret, little blue heron, and American white pelican. All have been sighted in the area.

<<>>

Sebewaing Sugar Festival, June. This is Sebewaing's big festival that runs from Wednesday to Sunday. A midway opens the first day and other events include a town-wide garage sale, petting zoo, children's games, bingo, crowning the Sugar Queen, chicken barbeque, car show, tractor pull, band concert, and additional entertainment.

28. Bay City

Bay City, located near the southern shore of the Saginaw Bay on Lake Huron, reported a 2020 population of 32,661. It is the principal city of the Greater Tri-Cities consisting of Saginaw-Midland-Bay City. Saginaw was the first of the cities settled, but eventually residents moved to what they called Lower Saginaw, later renamed Bay City, because of deeper water which fostered industry and growth.

The Saginaw River divides the city. East and west are connected by four drawbridges which permit large ships to travel along the river.

In 1834 John Trudel built a log cabin near what is now Seventeenth and Broadway and became the first citizen of Bay City. The city was established in 1837 and incorporated in 1865. Bay City is the county seat.

By 1860 Lower Saginaw became a bustling community of about 2,000 people with several mills and many small businesses. Lumbering, milling, and shipbuilding created jobs and a healthy economy. The early industrialists in the area used the Saginaw River as a convenient means to float lumber to the mills and factories, and they amassed large fortunes for themselves. Many of the mansions built during this era are registered as historical landmarks by the state and federal governments.

In 1873 Bay City pioneer Charles C. Fitzhugh Jr. and his wife Jane purchased land and built a home on property bounded by Washington, Saginaw, Ninth, and Tenth Streets. Fitzhugh acted as an agent for selling over 25,000 acres of land and farms in Bay County. In 1891 the Fitzhughs sold their land to the city for $8,500 with the restriction that it be used for the erection of a City Hall and offices and no other purposes. It wasn't until 1905 that the east bank community annexed the west side of the city.

During the second half of the nineteenth century, Bay City was home to several shipbuilders. The Defoe

Shipbuilding Company, which ceased operations December 31, 1975, built destroyer escorts, guided missile destroyers, and patrol craft for the United States Navy and the Royal Australian Navy.

• MUSEUMS

The **Bay County Historical Museum**, located at 321 Washington Avenue in the former armory building adjacent to the historic City Hall, is the designated repository for the records of the Patrol Craft Sailors Association. During the past few years, the museum has expanded and also contains several displays of local and regional history.

Bay County Historical Museum. Courtesy of Pixabay Free Images.

<<>>

The **Saginaw Valley Naval Ship Museum** is home to the *U.S.S. Edson DD-946*. This Vietnam Era Forest Sherman Class destroyer, is one of two left in the United States. Guests are invited to enjoy a self-guided tour of the ship nicknamed the Grey Ghost of the Vietnam Coast and also affectionately referred to as Fast Eddie. Visitors see what life was like for the men who served aboard the Grey Ghost. The ship is said to be haunted by a former caretaker who can't bear to leave his prior duties behind. Approximately 90% of the ship is open to the public. If it is your lucky day, you may meet a guide who served aboard the *U.S.S. Edson* or a similar ship. You must wear closed-toe, comfortable shoes since you will climb up and down ladders. Due to the amount of time it takes to tour the ship, guests are not admitted within one hour of closing.

• A Park

The Bay City State Park (also called the Bay City Recreation Area), 3582 State Park Drive, just north of Bay City, provides hiking, hunting, fishing, camping, picnic shelters and tables, restrooms, a water park, playground, and a marshland area which is home to blue herons and other wildlife. Over the years, there have been accepted sightings of more than 200 bird species. A sandy beach on Lake Huron's Saginaw Bay is across the street from the recreation area.

• Other Stops to Consider

The **Delta College Planetarium Learning Center**, 100 Center Avenue, has public shows weekly. The planetarium theater features a 360-degree, 50-foot diameter dome-shaped projection screen that puts you into the heart of the journey.

<<>>

Hell's Half Mile starts at the foot of Washington Avenue, runs west through Saginaw and Water Street and north past Center Avenue. Some argue that Hell's Half Mile in its glory days made the Wild West look like a church social. After the Civil War, starting in the late 1860s and continuing to the early 1900s, Hell's Half Mile extended the welcome mat hoping to lure thousands of the

Lumber Wagon.
Courtesy of Pixabay Free Images.

toughest, meanest, and loneliest lumbermen to its panoply of bawdy pleasures. Saloons lined the streets of these six blocks. Many façades sheltered more than drinks. Prostitution was legal, and the city welcomed the money lumberjacks carried in their pockets. The men had been deprived of female companionship and social gratification for nine months. Their grueling workdays had run from sunup to sunset. During this short respite, they drank, brawled, and gambled. (See related tale under Ghost Stories.)

<<>>

Local Festivals include St. Stan's Polish Festival, a Fourth of July Fireworks Festival, history reenactments, Hell's Half Mile Film and Music Festival, Tall Ships Festival, and other events that take place along the banks of the Saginaw River. Check with the Bay City Chamber of Commerce for details.

● LIGHTHOUSES

The first **Saginaw River Lighthouse** was constructed from 1839 to 1841. By 1867 shipping commerce required a deeper passageway through the river to accommodate large ships. The United States Corps of Engineers dredged the Saginaw River, which for safety reasons, necessitated replacing the original lighthouse, which has been gone for many years, with a pair of lighthouses.

The current Saginaw River lighthouse stands about a mile from the mouth of the river. The lighthouse works in conjunction with a beacon closer to the mouth. These lights use a range technique.

According to a U.S. government publication, The American Practical Navigator, "Range lights are light pairs that indicate a specific position when they are in line. The higher rear light is placed behind the front light. When the mariner sees the lights vertically in line, he or she is on the range line. If the front light appears left of the rear light, the observer is to the right of the range line; if the front appears to the right of the rear, the observer is left of the range line."

The Saginaw rear light was constructed 2,300 feet south of the mouth of the river on a large elevated concrete base which supported its brick dwelling with kitchen, parlor, and oil storage room on the first floor, and three bedrooms and tower above. The light and lighthouse were converted to electricity in 1915. The rear range light was closed in the 1970s but was placed on the National Register of Historic Places in 1984.

In 1999 the Saginaw River Marine Historical Society (SRMHS) approached Dow Chemical, which then owned the property, with a plan to restore the lighthouse and open it to tourists. You can only reach the lighthouse by shuttle, and it is only open at specific times, so check before putting it on your vacation to-do list.

• SHIPWRECK

(See also Shipwrecks in the Saginaw Bay under Port Austin listing.)

The **MV Jupiter**, a gasoline tanker, exploded on the Saginaw River in Bay City on September 16, 1990. The *Jupiter* was unloading its cargo of 2.3 million gallons of gasoline at the Total Petroleum depot when the accident occurred. The main cause of the disaster was attributed to the excess speed of the passing cargo ship *MV Buffalo*, which caused the *Jupiter* to pull loose from its moorings and broke the ship-to-shore fuel and electrical lines. One crewman of the *Jupiter* lost his life. Nineteen others received medals of heroism for their bravery during the blaze.

Madonna Louise Ciccone, entertainer, singer, actress, member of the Rock and Roll Hall of Fame, Grammy and Golden Globe award winner.

Madonna.
Courtesy of Pixabay Free Images.

Born in Bay City, Madonna grew up in Rochester Hills and enjoyed phenomenal success for her versatility, visuals, creativity, and willingness to push boundaries.

The Guinness Book of World Records cites Madonna as the leading female recording artist of all time with more than three hundred million albums sold worldwide. She has sold more singles than any other female artist in Australia, the United Kingdom, Italy, Spain, and Canada, and she is the highest grossing solo touring artist of all time. She has generated $1.4 billion in concert tickets in the U.S. The first year she was eligible (2008), she was inducted into the Rock and Roll Hall of Fame.

<<>>

John Emil List, born on September 17, 1925, grew up in Bay City, became an accountant, and gained notoriety as one of the most unlikely candidates for a mass murderer in history.

List married his first wife, Helen, in 1951. Two decades later the family moved to New Jersey. List claims he was burdened by financial problems, and the belief his family was straying from their Lutheran faith. He concocted a story that these concerns turned him homicidal. He first shot Helen, then his mother who lived in the attic.

His account of what happened next either signified how cold and calculating he was, or evidenced that he was mentally unhinged. His stepdaughter Patricia, age 16, arrived home from school, and List shot her with his handgun and his father's Colt revolver. He dragged her body into the ballroom of the family's comfortable home and laid it on a sleeping bag. Next, he waited for Frederick, age 13, to return. Frederick met with the same fate as his sister. List later described making himself lunch, heading to the bank to close out his and his mother's accounts, and finally driving to Westfield High School to watch his oldest son John Jr., age 15, play soccer. After the game, father and son drove home, where List carried out the final murder.

List had sent letters to the children's schools indicating his children would be visiting their maternal grandmother for several weeks due to her declining health. He also authored, and left on the desk in his study, a five-page letter to his pastor. In that letter he explained that he saw too much evil in the world and had killed his family to save their souls and ensure their place in heaven, where he would later join them.

List meticulously cleaned the crime scene before he fled. In a final bizarre act before shutting the door on the family dwelling, List went through the home and cut his picture out of every family photograph before going on the lam.

Since the family did not socialize with neighbors, weeks went by before anyone noticed that all the lights in the home had been on around the clock and then began burning out, one by one. Neighbors called the police.

List changed his name, remarried, and remained free for almost eighteen years before his capture and prosecution. Ultimately, it was a story on *America's Most Wanted* that tripped up the fugitive. He was arrested in Virginia, and extradited to New Jersey. At his sentencing hearing, List denied direct responsibility for his actions. He said, "I feel that because of my mental state at the time, I was unaccountable for what happened. I ask all affected by this for their forgiveness, understanding, and prayer." The judge was unpersuaded, and as he pronounced sentence said, "John Emil List is without remorse and without honor. After eighteen years, five months and twenty-two days, it is now time for the voices of Helen, Alma, Patricia, Frederick, and John E. List Jr. to rise from the grave." He then imposed five consecutive life sentence terms, the maximum allowable at the time. In 2009 List died in prison at age 82.

John Emil List.
Courtesy of
Pixabay Free Images.

List's crimes were the basis for movies and documentaries including the 1993 film *Judgment Day: The John List Story*, in which List was portrayed by Robert Blake, the 1987 film *The Stepfather* and its 2009 remake; and the character Keyser Söze in the 1995 film *The Usual Suspects*.

<<>>

Others with Ties to Bay City
Sports figures
- **Bob Allman**, Chicago Bears.
- **Howie Auer**, Philadelphia Eagles player (1933).
- **Ruth Born**, All-American Girls Professional Baseball League player.
- **Eric Devendorf**, McDonald's All-American basketball recruit from Bay City Central High School, a former starter at Syracuse University.
- **Spoke Emery**, Major League Baseball player.
- **Eric Esch**, Super Heavyweight Champion boxer, kickboxer, wrestler, and martial artist.

- **Troy Evans**, NFL linebacker, Houston Texans, New Orleans Saints,
- **John Garrels**, silver and bronze Olympic medal winner.
- **Ernie Gust**, Major League Baseball player.
- **Alex Izykowski**, 2006 Winter Olympics bronze medalist in short track speed skating.
- **Jim Kanicki**, Cleveland Browns, and New York Giants 1960–62 (Bay City Central High School).
- **Annie Edson Taylor**, the first person to go over Niagara Falls in a barrel who lived to tell about it.
- **Dennis Wirgowski**, played professional football for the New England Patriots and Philadelphia Eages (1970-1973).

<<>>

Politicians
- **Emil Anneke**, German Forty-Eighter and U.S. politician.
- **James A. Barcia**, U.S. Representative, state representative, and state senator;
- **James G. Birney** (1792–1857), presidential candidate 1844 and 1848 Liberty Party and a founder of Bay City.
- **Nathan B. Bradley**, first mayor of Bay City, U.S. Representative, and state senator.
- **Sanford M. Green**, Michigan jurist and politician.
- **Thomas G. Kavanagh**, Michigan Supreme Court justice.
- **Isaac Marston**, Chief Justice of the Michigan Supreme Court.

<<>>

Actors/Actresses/Musicians
- **Robert Armstrong**, known for his role in *King Kong*.
- **Betsy Brandt**, actress, *Breaking Bad*, *The Michael J. Fox Show*.
- **Harriet Hammond** (1899–1991), silent film actress.
- **Bruce LaFrance**, Tantric musician.

• BOOKS AND MOVIES WITH TIES TO BAY CITY

See the listing of Infamous with Ties to Bay City for movies featuring mass murderer, John List.

<<>>

Dave Vizard, a local Michigan writer who lives near Caseville, anchors his five Nick Steele novels, ***Formula for Murder***, ***A Grand Murder***, ***Murder in the Wind***, ***A Place for Murder***, **and** ***Murder Key West Style***, in his home state. In his first novel, *Formula for Murder*, Tanya Johnson awakens to a normal Bay City day. In less than twenty-four hours, her life is shattered. Her father dies a gruesome death with her as a witness to every horrific moment before he succumbs. Nick Steele, a reporter for the *Bay City Blade*, is asked to write an obituary for the dead man. But something isn't right, and Steele becomes involved in solving the murder and exposing a larger crime.

<<>>

Haunted Bay City Michigan (Published by Haunted America). Tri-City Ghost Hunter, Nicole Beauchamp, founder of a team called Tri-City Ghost Hunters Society, claims the raucous, disreputable Bay City of the late 1800s left its imprint on the paranormal atmosphere of her hometown. Her stories include a sinister Victorian lady who terrorizes those who visit the upper level of the Bay City Antiques Center, the ghost of a disfigured little girl who roams Sage Library, and the former caretaker of the *U.S.S. Edson* who lovingly tends the ship after death as he did in life. Beauchamp's book is intended to lead you on a bone-chilling journey through Bay City's most haunted locales.

• GHOST STORIES

The **Historic Masonic Temple**, 700 North Madison Avenue, is an architectural jewel in the center of Bay City. Educational programs, cultural events, music, and theater are offered in this delightful venue. Whether the building is haunted is a difficult question. The building's secret passageways and strange rooms provide an ambiance suitable for hauntings, but if ghosts wander those corridors, as some claim, it is not well-documented. The temple's spooky potential is taken advantage of at Halloween when the building is transformed into a haunted mansion.

Constructed in 1893, the building served for over 100 years as home to the Joppa Lodge Masons. In 2005 it was purchased by the Bay Arts Council. Today, the structure is owned by the Friends of the Historic Masonic Temple who are dedicated to preserving and restoring the building while working to establish a community school for the arts within. The Temple was added to the National Register of Historic Places because of its significance to the State of Michigan.

The Historic Masonic Temple.
Courtesy of Wikipedia Commons, by Chad Johnson.

<<>>

The **Saginaw River Rear Range Light** is haunted by former occupant Peter Brown. Built in 1876 in a swampy area north of Bay City, the light was intended to guide ships into the mouth of the Saginaw River. It was deactivated in the 1960s. Afterwards, it was used by the coastguard as living quarters until the 1970s, when a new station was built across the river. A serviceman stationed in the living quarters claimed to hear footsteps inside the old lighthouse, even though all the doors were locked, and he was the only one there. Other visitors to the lighthouse have reported hearing steps on the spiral steel staircase.

The mysterious footsteps are attributed to keeper Brown who died while serving at the lighthouse. Brown was appointed keeper in 1866. Disabled and eventually bedridden, he had help from his wife Julia and his son Dewitt in maintaining the light. Peter Brown died in 1873 before the new range lights were built, but his family remained at the station, and Julia was placed in charge. The son stayed on as an assistant. Julia remarried; her second husband, George May, also died while Julia was in charge of the lighthouse. Peter Brown has stories to tell. Unfortunately, unless we meet up with Peter's ghost, we may never hear them.

The Saginaw River Rear Range Lighthouse.
Courtesy of Pixabay Free Images.

<<>>

The Ghosts of Hell's Half Mile. Beneath the streets of Hell's Half Mile, and running into more respectable areas of Bay City, a system of underground catacombs provided discreet access for patrons who preferred to keep their visits to the red-light district quiet. For others, too inebriated to care where they spent the night, the tunnels were a place to crash for the cost of a nickel when a real hotel room cost one dollar.

Most of these underground pieces of history were filled in or buried because the city decided excavation and restoration would be too costly. Evidence of the passageways' existence can be seen today under a few local shops and restaurants. Modern-day crews of building projects have dug down and encountered pieces of a fascinating past. Sometimes those individuals who manage to connect with the tunnels' graphic history find themselves face-to-face with ghosts of the area's bygone days. Three of the most notable spirits are Joe Fournier, CJ Cunnion, and Canadian Em.

Fabian "Joe" Fournier was from Quebec. At six feet, his height wouldn't get a second look today, but he was tall for the times, and burly. Strength was his forte in life. It suited him to lumbering. His love of a good fight made others stay clear—for the most part. Joe was a lumber boss who took on all challengers to prove how tough he was. He remained undefeated until a cheating ex-con took a mallet to Joe's head and silenced him forever. Joe's legend continued to grow after his death and merged into that of the more well-known Paul Bunyan. It is rumored that his ghost likes to return to Bay City now and then to relive days past.

Bay City was also home to **Thomas C. Cunnion**, TC to those who knew him well. Cunnion was certifiably loony or so some suggested. He dropped to all fours and fought dogs—biting and growling—to earn free drinks. Most folks found it in their best interest to avoid TC.

A third character in the trifecta of crazies was **Canadian Em**, one of the prostitutes selling herself in Hell's Half Mile. Prostitutes of the day were called "pretty waiter girls," and there were hundreds of them living along Water Street, ready to comfort lumbermen when they came to town.

One ghastly story alleges that the morning after Em was detained in the former basement jail of what is now the Old City Hall restaurant, she was buried alive. Evidence of the atrocity is said to be the scratch marks on the inside of her coffin. Other versions of the sad tale say Em was thrown into a cell with drunken men who abused her repeatedly until she couldn't take another violation and killed herself. Em has refused to cross over and remains in the restaurant where she has the unusual habit of leaving a chunk of coal for the diners sitting at table fourteen.

Several ghost tours are offered in Bay City. Should you decide to take one, you will hear these and many other bloodcurdling tales. Be forewarned, some of the tours may offend the faint of heart. The Bay City Historical Society bills theirs as a scandalous, sensational, violent, and graphic excursion.

<<>>

The Should-Be-Angry Ghost of Marvin Schur. This is a gruesome tale, albeit not a true ghost story, where the deceased has every right to return to haunt his tormentors. Maybe he is just biding his time, and we'll hear from him still.

January 15, 2009, Bay City was plunged into brutally cold temperatures, disturbingly frigid even by Michigan standards. The thermometer dipped to nine below zero Fahrenheit the day Marvin "Mutts" Schur died.

The prior twenty-four hours had been equally cold. That is important because Marvin didn't die a quick death. The old man may have lingered for days. Neighbors found the body of the 93-year-old World War II veteran on his bedroom floor. A nephew lived in nearby Saginaw but didn't regularly check on his uncle.

The obituary said the old man passed unexpectedly, but given the circumstances, that seems a euphemistic stretch. Marvin's corpse wore a winter jacket and four layers of clothes. The windows were frost covered, and icicles hung from a faucet. Mr. Schur froze to death.

As a young man, Marvin Schur did his duty, shipped out to Germany, made the world a safer place, survived the war, came home, married, and worked in a foundry until he retired. All that before he froze to death—alone in his bedroom. He had lived in the same house for as long as neighbors remembered. He and his wife, who had died many years earlier, were childless.

Marvin was not a memorable citizen. He kept to himself, stayed home, minded his business, paid his bills. Then, like happens to many folks of advanced age, Marvin grew a bit discombobulated. We'll never know whether that or something else was the reason, but he didn't pay his electric bill for four months.

On January 13, a power company worker placed a power limiter on Marvin's meter and stuck a note on the front door (or maybe under the doormat) warning that the power would be shut off if Schur didn't pay his thousand dollars in unpaid utility bills. In the follow-up investigation, the worker never claimed he knocked on the door or had any personal contact with Schur although the old man was certainly home. The best anyone can tell from the sketchy details, it seems that Marvin never saw the notice, although he undoubtedly felt his home growing colder and colder and colder. The neighbor who found the corpse saw the unpaid bills on the kitchen table with money paper-clipped to each.

In a final, sad irony, Schur, according to family, willed his money—nearly a half million dollars—to the Bay Regional Medical Center. So far, no one claims to have seen Marvin's ghost. Perhaps he is resting in peace in Saginaw's Forest Lawn Cemetery, and it is those who failed him who should worry his angry spirit may come back to haunt them.

29. PINCONNING

Pinconning, named after the Pinconning River which flows through the community, had a population of 1,293 in 2020. Pinconning comes from the Ojibwe word *Opinikaaning* which translates into English as the place where the potatoes grow. The city is included in the Saginaw, Midland, and Bay City metropolitan area. It's a family-friendly place that puts out the welcome mat as you journey up north.

The town was originally settled in 1872 by George Van Etten and Henry Kaiser, early lumbermen in the area. The post office opened in 1873.

• A PARK

Pinconning County Park, 3098 East Pinconning Road, provides campsites, trails, and a boat launch. The swimming beach gets mixed reviews.

• A STOP TO CONSIDER

Pinconning's claim to fame is cheese and cheese products, especially its namesake Pinconning Cheese. If you are following the lakeshore on M-13, you'll pass through Pinconning. It's a place to stop, stretch your legs, maybe order a deli sandwich, and stock up on cheese.

Cheese manufacturing got its start in the town in 1907 when William Reid moved to Pinconning and started a creamery. By 1939 customers gravitated there to buy cheese and a variety of other products including hickory sticks, jerky, sausage, smoked fish, mustard sauce, old-fashioned candy, fudge, hot sauce, and souvenirs. You can choose between Pinconning or Williams Cheese. Repeat customers swear by both. If you are driving through, stop and taste a few samples.

Williams Cheese Shop.
Courtesy of Bob Royce.

30. TAWAS CITY AND EAST TAWAS

Tawas City and East Tawas are cities in Iosco County on the north side of Tawas Bay. The population of Tawas City in 2020 was 1,780 and East Tawas was 2,749. Downtown East Tawas has specialty shops, restaurants, and bars.

In the Saginaw Treaty of 1819, the Ojibwe, the area's first inhabitants, ceded the county's land to the United States government. The first settler of European descent to the county was Louis Chevalier, a French fur trader who lived on the banks of the Au Sable River as early as 1800. In the late 1840s, Peter Hart began fishing on Tawas Bay.

In 1854 the Whittemore family gave the name Tawas City to the town they founded. It is believed the name came from Chief O-ta-was, the leader of the Saginaw band of Ojibwe who camped along the Tawas Bay shoreline.

Tawas City was the closest city north of Bay City located on the shores of Saginaw Bay and Lake Huron. It was established as the county seat of Iosco County. The first post office was established in 1856 with James Whittemore appointed postmaster.

As with most other Michigan towns, lumbering flourished in the area. Blessed with white pine forests, abundant wildlife, and protected by the Tawas Bay, life was good. The Whittemores built a mill followed a few years later by a second mill, Smith, Van Valkenburg and Company. A community sprang up around this second mill and became known as East Tawas. For many years, residents of both towns and the farming communities surrounding them, referred to Tawas City as Old Town and East Tawas as East Town.

The United States government saw the need for a lighthouse along the shore of the largest natural harbor on the Great Lakes. One was built at Tawas Point and placed in operation in 1852.

East Tawas Downtown. Courtesy of Bob Royce.

- ● MUSEUMS

The **Iosco County Museum**, 405 West Bay Street, East Tawas. Located in a beautiful 100-year-old home, this museum is filled with artifacts from all corners of Iosco County. Exhibits include local industry, family life, culture, and traditions. Limited hours.

<<>>

Tawas Point Lighthouse Museum. (See Lighthouse in this section.)

- ● A PARK

Tawas Point State Park, 686 Tawas Beach Road, East Tawas, is favored for birding. The 183-acre park is family and pet-friendly. Situated on the end of a sand spit that forms Tawas Bay along Lake Huron, the water is shallow and warm making it a favorite with swimmers. Amenities include boat launch, day-use dockage, playground, grills, restrooms, picnic tables, fishing pier, and swimming beach.

Sunrise at Tawas Point State Park.
Courtesy of Pixabay Free Images.

● LIGHTHOUSE

The **Tawas Point Lighthouse**, 686 Tawas Beach Road, East Tawas operated from 1876 to 2016. It was electrified in 1935 and automated in 1953. The lighthouse was closed in 2021, although the Friends of Tawas Point Lighthouse and State Park and volunteer lightkeepers offered some outdoor programming. If you want to see more than the outside of the lighthouse visit, do a web search for current status.

In normal times, the Michigan Department of Natural Resources managed the lighthouse and afforded visitors the opportunity to climb the 85 steps of the tower. Each room of the lighthouse museum was open and each represented a different period from the life of the lighthouse. Lighthouse tours lasted approximately 45 minutes, and you could visit the great Lighthouse Museum Store and the Lighthouse Memory Walkway. Hopefully the lighthouse and gift shop will be open again soon, but check before making it a destination trip.

Tawas Point Lighthouse.
Courtesy of Bob Royce.

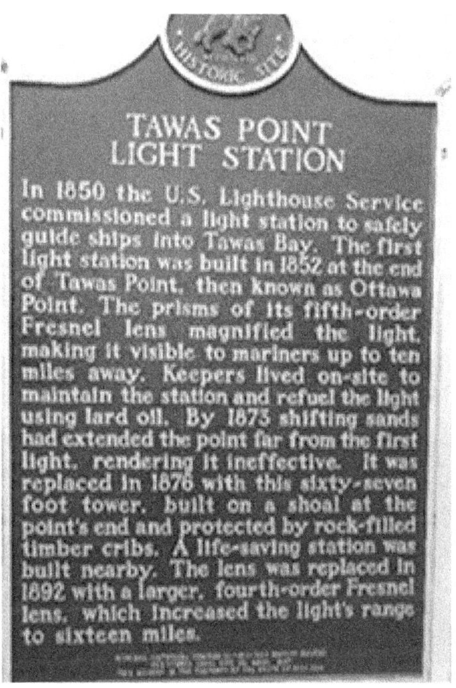

Tawas Point Light Station Historical Marker. Courtesy of Bob Royce.

• SHIPWRECKS

Four years stand out as memorable for storms and shipwrecks near Tawas Point.

1859. The **May Queen**, a 108-foot, two-masted schooner crashed in a snowstorm on November 21. Bound for Milwaukee, she carried a cargo of wheat and barley. When the storm released its full fury, the *Queen* attempted to make harbor following the Tawas Point light. Snow quickly covered the beacon's glow and without guidance, the *Queen* rounded the point too soon, ran onto a sandbar, and sprung a leak. She took on water. The crew climbed the rigging, wrapped themselves in sails, which they cut up to protect themselves from the storm, and endured the hellish night until they were rescued.

A century and a half of shifting sand has exposed a well-preserved 90-foot portion of the ship's starboard side. Swimmers near the wreckage site must remain at a distance due to the many iron fasteners that protrude from the vessel's surfaces.

<<>>

1872. The Saginaw Bay was the epicenter for a big blow in September. The brig **Globe** was forced ashore at Tawas. The barge **Table Rock** fared less favorably. She sank, and five of the six aboard lost their lives near Tawas Point. The sole survivor watched as Captain James McAuley, his wife, and the first mate drifted away on the barge's cabin.

Fifteen miles off Tawas Point, two barges, **White Squall** and **Libbie Nau**, collided in the rough sea. The *Squall*'s crew took to their yawl to save themselves. After a three-hour trip, the yawl capsized in the rough waves. A single seaman survived to tell the story.

Fifteen years later, a wooden anchor was found about seven miles off Sturgeon Point. Divers believed it was associated with the *White Squall*.

<<>>

1889. An infamous November gale rocked the region. The *Bay City Times'* November 30 edition reported that the **Wilhelm** lost both of its barges, the **Midnight** and the **Mears**, near Tawas Point. During the weather bomb, the *Midnight's* crew escaped to the *Mears* after determining that the *Mears* was in better shape to survive the gale. First Mate Elijah Powers broke his leg escaping the disaster. Seaman David Mowat was not as lucky. He stripped off his oilskin clothes and swam toward shore. He died from exposure.

Surfman from the local lifesaving station rescued the remaining survivors. The *Mears* later broke up and was a total loss.

<<>>

1920. Although not a record year for storms on Saginaw Bay, this was a year that spelled disaster for a barge named *Goshawk*. Leaving its homeport of Bay City in mid-June, it sailed down to Port Huron to pick up a load of salt for delivery to Duluth. With the steamer *P.J. Ralph* towing it north, the *Goshawk* was halfway up Lake Huron when a storm struck. *Goshawk*—at age 54, the oldest ship on the Great Lakes—sprung a leak, forcing the captain and his crew to escape to the *Ralph* in their lifeboat. The barge then settled in about 45 feet of water near Tawas Point.

The wreckage was located by A&T Recovery divers in 1990. It is one of the few Saginaw Bay wrecks that is regularly visited by divers.

● GHOST STORY

A sketchy story exists of a lighthouse keeper's wife seeing the ghost of a little girl crying as the child sat on the steps of the Tawas Point Lighthouse. As the woman approached the child, the little girl got up and ran inside the lighthouse. A two-minute YouTube video dramatizes the event, but no further detail has been established.

31. OSCODA AND AU SABLE

Au Sable on the south side of the Au Sable River and Oscoda on the north side of the river have interwoven histories. Au Sable, platted in 1849, had a 2020 population of 1,329. On September 23, 1856, it got its post office. It was incorporated as a village in 1872, became a city in 1889, was destroyed by fire in 1911, and surrendered its city charter in 1931.

In 1874 the north side of the river got a separate post office though it, too, was named Au Sable Post Office. In 1875 the name of the north side's post office was changed to Oscoda, and two villages were created from what had been one. Oscoda's 2020 population was 903, but this figure does not include the approximate 3,000 personnel stationed at the air force base.

The State of Michigan has designated Oscoda the official home of Paul Bunyan. Lumberman's Monument nearby honors the early lumberjacks of the area.

• MUSEUM

Wurtsmith Air Force Museum, 4071 East Van Ettan Street, is located on the property of the former Wurtsmith Air Force Base. The museum fills three hangers with military and aviation artifacts. Tours are available, but hours are limited.

Wurtsmith Air Force Museum.
Courtesy of Pixabay Free Images.

• ANOTHER STOP TO CONSIDER

Lumberman's Monument, 5401 Monument Road, is located in a park-like setting with a visitors center, restrooms, and vending machines. The scenery is beautiful, and you can take a relaxing hike along the trails of the Huron National Forest. From outdoor displays and materials available at the center, this is a place to learn the history of Michigan's lumbering era.

The trek to the statue involves 242 steps each way, so it may not be appropriate for some visitors. The overhang provides views of the Au Sable River. The area is stunning when the trees are dressed in their fall foliage. There is a gift shop with books about the history of the area.

- ● MOVIE WITH A TIE TO OSCODA

Bowling for Columbine. Director Michael Moore interviewed two young residents in a local pool hall for his documentary. Eric Harris, one of the shooters in the Columbine High School Massacre, spent some of his early years in Oscoda while his father was serving in the U.S. Air Force.

32. HARRISVILLE

Harrisville, 2020 population 501, is the county seat of Alcona County. The city is surrounded by Harrisville Township but is administratively autonomous. Located on Lake Huron, it is a Harbor of Refuge.

First known as Davison's Mill after Crosier Davison purchased land and water power rights here in 1854, it was later named for Benjamin Harris, who with his sons, Levi and Henry, moved to the area from West Bloomfield, New York. Harrisville got its post office in 1857. It became a village in 1887 and attained city status in 1905.

On the border of the Huron National Forest, Harrisville provides outdoor recreational opportunities that include hunting, swimming, cross-country skiing, and trout fishing. The forest contains 330 miles of hiking trails.

Harrisville is recognized for its major arts and crafts sale during Harrisville Harmony Weekend.

- ● A PARK

Harrisville State Park, 248 State Park Road, is within walking distance of the city. The park features a wooded campground with 195 sites, two mini-cabins with electricity, a fire ring and outdoor grills, and day-use facilities along the beach. There is a modern bathhouse, picnic area, pavilion, two-mile hiking trail, non-groomed cross-country ski trails, a metal detecting area, swimming beach, beach house, softball diamond, horseshoe pits, volleyball court, basketball court, children's playground, group shelter, and bicycle rental. The park was established in 1921 making it one of Michigan's oldest state parks. No fishing or boating unless you bring your canoe or kayak with you.

● LIGHTHOUSE

Sturgeon Point Lighthouse, Lakeshore Drive & US 23. A reef extends 1½ miles from Sturgeon Point making navigation dangerous, especially during Michigan's powerful storms. In 1869 the Lighthouse Service undertook construction of a lighthouse to help ships avoid the danger. The Light was put into service in 1870. Today, the grounds and lighthouse are worth a visit. You'll find a gift shop, picnic tables if you want to bring a lunch, access to the lake, and a beach known for rock collecting.

Sturgeon Point Lighthouse.
Courtesy of Pixabay Free Images.

<<>>

Baily School. This old country school was moved to the lighthouse grounds. It is authentically furnished, down to textbooks on each desk. Open hours for seeing inside the lighthouse and school should be confirmed.

33. OSSINEKE

The population of Ossineke was 926 in 2020. The name originally derived from the Anishinaabe word *zhingaabewasiniiigigaabawaad* (try saying that fast three times), which loosely translated means where the image stones stood. A more modern Anishinaabe name for Ossineke is *asiniike* which translates to quarry.

● A Stop to Consider

Dinosaur Gardens, 11160 US 23 South. An interesting stop if you are traveling with children obsessed with dinosaurs. Awaiting you in gardens that feel prehistoric are 26 handmade dinosaurs. The creations are more than 70 years old and well maintained. You can take a narrated tour along a trail that provides information about these early giants and may give you a few chuckles to accompany your walk. There is putt-putt golf and a sluice where little ones can pan for gems and fossils. There are picnic tables if you brought your lunch, and you can purchase ice cream and yogurt. Some visitors may feel the roadside attraction is overpriced, and a dinosaur-themed attraction has limited appeal, but for others, it might be a perfect way to add something unusual to the trip.

34. Alpena

Alpena is the county seat of Alpena County. It is also the only city in the county. There are unincorporated communities and one village but no other cities. The 2020 population of Alpena was 9,789 making it the second-most populous city in the 21 county Northern Michigan region. Traverse City is the largest city in that area. If you haven't visited Alpena before, it may be the favorite find of your Michigan travels. Located at Lake Huron's Thunder Bay, you'll discover unexpectedly interesting museums, wonderful water views, and an abundance of outdoor activities. The city swells during the summer months with an influx of tourists.

Originally part of Anomickee County, founded in 1840, Alpena got its own name in 1843. Henry Schoolcraft suggested Alpena meant something like good partridge country in the Ojibwe language. Since Schoolcraft's wife was Ojibwe, he may have known what he was talking about.

Initially a fishing port, the area grew to one of the most profitable lumbering regions in the state. Lumber camps dotted the landscape, and logs floated down the Thunder Bay River to the harbor where they were loaded on ships and sent to far destinations to help build the rest of the country. In its lumbering heyday, Alpena shipped out billions of board feet of lumber.

Michigan's fire of 1871 destroyed most of Alpena, and one year later, before the city completed rebuilding, a second fire wreaked havoc on the unfortunate city. The second fire started in a local barn, and in two hours had spread, killing at least four people and causing nearly four million dollars (current value) in damage as it destroyed fifteen acres and dozens of homes and businesses.

With forest depletion by fires and overcutting, the end of lumbering brought the decline of many communities that had built their economies on Michigan's trees. Alpena was

Alpena Courthouse. Courtesy of Pixabay Free Images.

an exception. It describes itself as "The Boom Town that Forgot to Bust." The city became adept at reinventing itself, initially with mining and manufacturing as its mainstays, and then adding tourism to its economic base.

Alpena has several buildings worth seeing. The county courthouse is an art deco building listed on both the National and State Registers of Historic Places. A Michigan Historical Marker was erected to honor the courthouse in 2005.

Temple Beth-El, a Reform Jewish synagogue, is located at 125 White Street. Built in 1889, it is one of the few surviving nineteenth century synagogues in the United States.

At the intersection of Ford Avenue and Wessel Road stands Huron Portland Cement Company, so-called because it resembles the color of the stone from the Isle of Portland in the British Isles.

Alpena's location in the midst of huge limestone deposits enticed the company, founded in Detroit in 1907, to move its plant to this site. Cement production began in 1908. From Thunder Bay, ships of the Huron fleet delivered cement to all parts of the Great Lakes region. The local

Alpena's Cement Company.
Courtesy of Bob Royce.

business was so well-run by the Bessers that Portland Cement became the largest cement plant in the world.

Alpena is home to the Thunder Bay National Marine World Sanctuary.

• MUSEUMS

The Besser Museum for Northeast Michigan, 491 Johnson Street, is a repository of artifacts from Alpena's past and present. You can learn about the earliest people, the European immigrant arrival, fishing, lumbering, and manufacturing in the region. There are walk-through exhibits like the 1890s Avenue of Shops, an outdoor Fossil Park, the Besser Historic Village, and a full-dome digital planetarium. A special project of the Besser is the exhibition and preservation of the ***Katherine V***, one of the last remaining large wood hull Great Lakes fishing tugs. The *Katherine V* serves as a resource for the study of such vessels, and she is a reminder of the fishermen who crewed such boats.

The Besser Museum Avenue of Shops. Courtesy of Bob Royce.

The Besser has a fine art collection that includes watercolor, oil, pastel, acrylic, and collage paintings. It also displays sculpture, pottery, and prints. The exhibits change regularly. The collection incorporates the work of local Michigan artists and world-renowned artists including Renoir, Dali, Picasso, Warhol, Rivera, Cezanne, and Chihuly—truly an amazing museum for a city the size of Alpena.

Besser Museum's Historic Village. Courtesy of Bob Royce.

<<>>

Thunder Bay National Marine Sanctuary Great Lakes Maritime Heritage Center, 500 W. Fletcher Street, is another surprising find in Alpena. The Heritage Center is the Visitor Center for the Thunder Bay National Marine Sanctuary. It has 12,000 square feet of museum space

Courtesy of Bob Royce.

where you can learn about Shipwreck Alley and explore the more than 200 ill-fated vessels that succumbed to the lakes. These are the ones that didn't make it through the murky fog banks, rocky shoals, and fierce storms. The interactive museum provides the stories of the crews and

243

wrecks of the country's only maritime sanctuary. There is a full-size wooden replica of a Great Lakes Schooner. You can walk the decks and experience a storm simulation. (See Shipwrecks in this section.)

● BEACHES, PARKS, AND TRAILS

Duck Park and Island Park.
Courtesy of Bob Royce.

Duck Park and **Island Park**, corner of US 23 and Long Rapids Road. This is the city's 500-acre wildlife sanctuary with a hand-hewn wooden covered bridge and water tower. The park offers hiking trails, fishing platforms, and five distinctive ecosystems. It's a perfect place for bird watching, and there are picnic tables and a kayak launch.

<<>>

Mich-E-Ke-Wis Park, at State Street and US 23 South, provides a swimming beach, horseshoe pits, volleyball courts, picnic facilities, bike park, and children's playground.

<<>>

Washington Avenue Park, 11th Avenue at the Thunder Bay River, offers biking trails, picnic areas, and river views.

<<>>

Starlite Beach, State Street on Lake Huron, is a swimming beach with splash park, pavilion, picnic areas, playground, indoor restrooms, and shower facilities.

<<>>

Arthur E. Sytek Park, Thunder Bay River at the bridge on Bagley Street. This roadside wildflower park has a kayak/canoe launch site, a barrier-free fishing deck, picnic facilities, and the trailhead for the bike path.

A Sandy Alpena Beach. Courtesy of Bob Royce.

• OTHER STOPS T CONSIDER

Bruski and Stevens Twin Sinkholes, M-65 North, veer left onto Leer Road as M-65 bends and drive north four miles to just before the Maple Lane Road intersection. A 31-acre parcel surrounds the two sinkholes, each about 200 feet deep, and each with trails that let you explore the unique geology and plant life at the bottom.

<<>>

Hillman Elk Preserve. If you are willing to take the 23-mile drive west of Alpena to visit an elk preserve in Hillman, you can sign up for a five-course gourmet elk dinner cooked on a 100-year-old wood cookstove and accompanied by wine tasting.

<<>>

Outdoor sports and miscellaneous. There are too many outdoor sports and other activities to list. You can bike, hike, canoe, kayak, cross-country ski in winter, swim, dive and explore sunken ships, sail, shop, wander art galleries, or take a fishing charter. And that's just to get you started.

• LIGHTHOUSE

Little Red. Courtesy of Bob Royce.

The Alpena Light or "Little Red," sits at the mouth of the Thunder Bay River. It is the only lighthouse located within the boundaries of Alpena. Locals often disparage their beloved light by insisting it's "Long on duty, short on beauty."

• SHIPWRECKS AND UNDERWATER EXPLORATION

Thunder Bay National Marine Sanctuary protects a nationally significant collection of historic shipwrecks. It is the final resting place of every type of ship known to have sailed on the Great Lakes, from canoes to wooden schooners and sidewheel steamers to modern freighters. The total number in the preserve is estimated at 116. One of the best ways to see the wrecks is to take a glass-bottom boat shipwreck tour. Scuba divers also explore the remains of these ships. There are too many to list all, but a few of the more interesting are noted here.

• The **Bay City**, a wooden schooner, went down on November 29, 1902, driven against a pier in Alpena.

• The **Benjamin Franklin**, a wooden paddle steamer, went down in 1850 when she ran aground on Thunder Bay Island.

• The **Choctaw**, a steel, semi-whaleback ship, rolled over and sank with her cargo of coal on July 11, 1915.

- The ***D.M. Wilson***, a wooden bulk freighter, went down just off Thunder Bay Island in 1894. She carried a full load of coal.

- The ***Isaac M. Scott***, a steel bulk freighter, was one of the eight ships to sink in Lake Huron during the horrific storm of 1913. All crew was lost. She met her demise as she was leaving Thunder Bay Island. (See Lake Huron, The Big Blow, the Storm of 1913.)

- The ***Marine City***, a wooden paddle steamer, sank with her cargo of roofing shingles and fish. All nine crew members were lost when she caught fire and burned near Alpena.

- The ***Monohansett***, a wooden steam barge, caught fire and sank near Thunder Bay Island on November 23, 1907. She took with her a cargo of coal.

- The ***Norman***, a steel bulk freighter, was rammed by the steamer *Jack*. The *Norman* sank with the loss of all aboard.

- The ***Pewabic,*** a wooden steamer, was bound from Houghton to Cleveland on August 9, 1865. She was loaded with copper, iron ore, and passengers when her sister ship, *Meteor,* rammed into her. She sank with the loss of all aboard.

<<>>

Middle Island Sinkhole lies a little over 1½ miles from the community of Lakewood in Alpena County. The sinkhole lies 500 feet north of the Middle Island and is about 75 feet deep. The site is available for divers to explore. The sinkhole has been studied by the NOAA Great Lakes Environmental Research Laboratory and various other scientific groups. One study, published August 2, 2021, in the journal *Nature Geoscience,* concluded that longer day length increases the amount of oxygen released by photosynthetic microbial mats. That finding suggests a link between Earth's oxygenation history and its rotation rate. While the Earth now spins on its axis once every 24 hours, day length was possibly as brief as six hours during the planet's infancy. The study's conclusion was inspired by examining present-day microbial communities growing under extreme conditions at the bottom of the submerged Middle Island Sinkhole. The water in the Middle Island Sinkhole is rich in sulfur and low in oxygen, and the brightly colored bacteria that thrive there are considered good analogs for the single-celled organisms that formed mat-like colonies billions of years ago.

• THE FAMOUS OR INFAMOUS WITH TIES TO ALPENA

Jesse Besser, inventor and benefactor of the Besser Museum for Northeast Michigan, lived in Alpena. Besser's inventions were connected to construction, and for many years the Besser block was a standard term for masonry construction blocks. The Besser Company flourished under Jesse's apt management. As a local philanthropist, he started his namesake museum and left his mark all over the city. (See Museums in this section.)

<<>>

Paul Bunker was born in Alpena. He attended the U.S. Military Academy at West Point and became the Academy's first football player selected as a first-team All-American. In 1901 he was chosen as an All-American at the tackle position, and in 1902 he was selected as a first-team halfback. Bunker served in the U.S. Army for 40 years and commanded the coastal artillery forces in the Battle of Corregidor in WWII. When Corregidor fell, Bunker was taken prisoner of war. He died of starvation and disease in a Japanese prison camp in 1943. His diary was published posthumously and became a best seller.

<<>>

William Comstock, 33rd governor of Michigan, was born in Alpena. He attended the University of Michigan before entering politics where he served as Democratic alderman for Alpena, Alpena mayor, member of the Michigan Democratic State Central Committee, member of the Democratic National Committee, and delegate to the Democratic National Convention before he ran for Michigan governor. He failed in three bids for the office but finally attained the state's highest position and served as Democratic governor from 1933 to 1935. He authorized the state's first sales tax law. He died in 1949 at age 71. His remains were interred in Alpena's Evergreen Cemetery.

<<>>

Leon Czolgosz, the son of Catholic Polish immigrants, was born in Alpena 1873. With the economic crash of 1897, he grew disillusioned and began embracing theories of anarchy. On September 6, 1901, in Buffalo, New York, he assassinated U.S. President William McKinley. Czolgosz was executed seven weeks later on October 29, 1901.

<<>>

Bob Devaney lived in Alpena where he coached high school football before leaving to coach the Michigan State Spartans as an assistant coach to Biggie Munn and continuing in that position under Duffy Daugherty. He later became head football coach for the Nebraska Cornhuskers and Wyoming Cowboys. He was inducted into the College Football Hall of Fame as a coach in 1981.

<<>>

Robert L. Emerson was born in Alpena. He was elected to the Michigan state senate where he was the Senate Minority Leader and Democratic Floor Leader. Governor Rick Snyder appointed Emerson to an eight-person committee to investigate the city of Flint's 2014 water crisis.

<<>>

The Frost, a psychedelic rock band of the 60s and 70s, originated in Alpena. The band was led by singer-guitarist

Dick Wagner who later performed with Alice Cooper. Wagner hoped to join Blood, Sweat, and Tears, but when rejected, he took disappointment in stride. He returned to Alpena and devoted his time to Frost. Several members of the original Frost band were born in Alpena. After a Meadowbrook performance before a crowd of 10,000, record companies pursued the group, and they signed with Vanguard. They recorded three albums, but with Vanguard's poor distribution and promotion, the band fared less well than other Michigan bands like Ted Nugent, Grand Funk, and Bob Seger. In 2008 Frost was voted into the Michigan Rock and Roll Legends Hall of Fame.

<<>>

Betty Mahmoody, author of *Not Without My Daughter,* was living in Alpena when she accompanied her husband on a two-week vacation to Iran. (See Books with Ties to Alpena.)

<<>>

Paul Fitzpatrick Russell was born in Massachusetts, but as a child, he moved to Alpena with his mother and siblings. He graduated from Alpena High School in 1977. A prelate of the Catholic Church since 1997, he held several positions in the diplomatic service of the Holy See. He was made an archbishop in 2016.

● Books and Movies with ties to Alpena
Books
Bunker's War: The World War II Diary of Col. Paul D. Bunker. The personal diary of Paul D. Bunker while he was held prisoner of war by the Japanese. (See Famous or Infamous with Ties to Alpena.)

<<>>

Not Without My Daughter: The Harrowing True Story of a Mother's Courage is the chilling account of Betty Mahmoody's escape from virtual enslavement by her husband. In August 1984, Mahmoody accompanied her husband Sayyed Bozorg Mahmoody to his native Iran for a two-week vacation. To her horror, she found herself and Mahtob, her four-year-old daughter, prisoners when her husband rededicated his life to his Shiite Muslim faith. Betty plotted an escape that took her through a dangerous underground that did not want to allow her child to accompany her. The book was a Literary Guild Alternative Selection.

Movie

Die Hard 2. Bruce Willis and the film crew used Alpena's airport to shoot several scenes of the film. Originally scheduled to be filmed at Denver's Stapleton Airport, the scenes were moved to Alpena because Denver lacked snow. Alpena couldn't live up to the hope of snow either, and ultimately artificial snow was used.

• GHOST STORY

The John Lau Saloon was an Alpena institution for 134 years. Its resident ghost, Agnes Lau, often whispered in customers' ears or moved their glasses around on the table.

Known locally as "The Lau," the saloon was one of the oldest buildings in Downtown Alpena. In July 2020, as this travel book was being written, a devastating fire, started by the stray spark of a workman's welding torch, lit the building's old timbers afire, and the Lau was no more.

The Lau burned to the ground one day before it was set to reopen after a COVID-19 closing. Next door, the Thunder Bay Theater, Northeast Michigan's only year-round professional theater, suffered serious smoke and water damage as firefighters battled the Lau blaze. The theater required complete renovation.

During its long life, the friendly Lau saloon shared its rich history and memories with all who dined or imbibed there. Many customers enjoyed a Michigan brew while stepping back in history to listen to local stories. The dark wood paneling, floor, and bar set the mood—the experience enhanced by Agnes' company, and the nineteenth century Alpena artifacts that vied for every inch of wall space.

The building that housed the Lau was constructed in 1885 and originally was owned and operated by Irish immigrant Peter Owens who operated a funeral parlor and furniture business within its walls. Embalming took place in the basement. When he wasn't otherwise engaged, Peter made wood furniture for his second business.

In 1892 John A. Lau bought out Owens and opened a saloon that he named after himself. He catered to thirsty lumbermen and locals alike. The new business must have suited the building's personality because it flourished for more than a century.

In June of 1900, John married Agnes, an immigrant from Germany. She helped her husband operate the business.

Local legends claim that the couple temporarily closed during Prohibition before reinventing their operation as a soda pop shop. However, as the story goes, soda pop was a mere front for selling bootleg liquor. The feds got word of the illegal speakeasy and shut down the saloon's operation until Prohibition ended.

Agnes died a young woman on June 24, 1913. For 107 years after her death, she roamed the Lau, claiming a position as its resident ghost. We can only speculate why Agnes' spirit refused to leave this world. The cause most often cited for her death is complications of childbirth, although there are also stories that she died of consumption or even in a boating accident. No matter the cause, there is no suggestion of foul play or evil.

The saloon was a lively place. She may have parked her spirit there to enjoy a bit of amusement, unencumbered by the family obligations of three small children and running a business.

Lending support to this theory is the less well-known ghost story of the Thunder Bay Theatre, also a building with historic roots. The theater played host to many productions over the years. The actors who performed on its stage insist there is a ghost named Aggie—mischievous but not malicious—who lurks in the building, hiding their costumes or otherwise toying with them. Whether this Aggie is Agnes Lau catching up on the social and cultural life she had missed, no one can say. It would be a quick step through the walls of the adjoining buildings to seat herself in the front row for the best seat at productions.

A second reason cited for Agnes' unwillingness to vanish into the spirit world suggests Agnes wanted to help keep the saloon running properly.

Validating this alternate theory, some employees of the Lau quit because Agnes tipped over their trays, perhaps a sign of her dissatisfaction with their work. Other workers have refused to go into the basement—the same basement where bodies were embalmed during the building's funeral parlor days—for fear of encountering Agnes.

Customers have reported seeing a woman dressed in old-fashioned clothes. They've also heard strange knocking noises and smelled a whiff of unexplainable odors. One patron saw Agnes sitting in a rocking chair at the top of the stairs. Ghost hunters converged on the saloon and when one hunter entered the Lau, she claimed she saw Agnes peering at the bay through a window. By that time, the window had been covered over. Sometimes a member of the waitstaff saw someone head to the upstairs dining room. They grabbed a menu and tromped after the customer to offer service—but found no one there.

The burning question—pun intended—remains. Has Agnes finally decided to go gently into that good night, or will she follow the advice of poet Dylan Thomas and continue to rave and rage against the dying light of her life?

Only the passage of time will tell if she's taken up residence elsewhere in Alpena.

35. PRESQUE ISLE HARBOR

Presque Isle Harbor's 2020 population was 572. It is an unincorporated community located about 20 miles north of Alpena. If you are fascinated by lighthouses, this is a must-stop destination for you. The 1840 light (the old lighthouse) is one of the oldest on the lakes. The 1870 light (the new lighthouse) gives you the highest lighthouse view on the lakes.

If you drive by at night, you might keep a lookout for the ghost of George Parris who makes his presence known by flashing the non-functioning lights.

• MUSEUM

The **Presque Isle Keeper's House Museum**, 4500 East Grand Lake Road, was built in 1905 and is located near the new lighthouse. It is both a visitors center and a museum. The museum does not contain original lighthouse keepers' furnishings because those were removed by each keeper when they left their service. In 1999 the Presque Isle Township Museum Society began a six-year renovation of the house. Many hundreds of hours of volunteer labor were needed and generously given to restore the building to its original appearance. It now stands as a tribute to lighthouse life and lore. The Museum Society solicited donations, borrowed, and purchased many interesting items for your viewing pleasure including china, kitchen equipment, furniture, art, books, and other artifacts from the early 1900s. The museum is open to the public. Volunteers are available to provide details and share the history.

The Old (1840) Presque Isle Lighthouse, 5295 East Grand Lake Road, one of the oldest lighthouses on the Great Lakes, is located on the Lake Huron shoreline near

1840 Light.
Courtesy of Bob Royce.

Presque Isle Harbor. The Old Light's tower rises 30 feet tall. It is 18 feet in diameter at the base. The bottom conical two-thirds is stone. Above that is a brick section with a soapstone deck. You can visit the grounds, enjoy a picnic, or relax in the tranquil lakeside setting.

The Old Light served from 1840-1870. You can access it by parking at the Presque Isle State Harbor Marina and hiking less than a third of a mile down the trail from the breakwater to the Old Lighthouse. The Presque Isle Light Station is at the north end of Presque Isle Peninsula, one mile beyond the Harbor and the Old Lighthouse. It is a 99-acre facility owned by Presque Isle Township and operated as a park and museum.

<<>>

The New (1870) Lighthouse and The Range Light Park, 4500 East Grand Lake Road, is accessible by car. The new light has served from 1870 to the present and remains an active aid to navigation. The light is 113 feet tall, the tallest accessible lighthouse on the lakes, with a diameter of 19 feet 3 inches at the base and 23 feet 4 inches at the parapet.

The 1870 Light.
Courtesy of Bob Royce.

The structure was designed by Army Engineer Orlando M. Poe. It is one of nine Poe Lights that guard the Great Lakes and the only one on Lake Huron.

View from the top.
Courtesy of Bob Royce.

The light is distinguished by four evenly spaced windows directly below the lantern room. Another signature trait is the wrought-iron bracket supporting the gallery. Its third Order Fresnel lens could be seen more than 25 miles out into Lake Huron. The restored lens is on display in the 1870 Keeper's House. The new light is open to the public and weather permitting, you can climb the tower. To do so you must be more than 42 inches tall, and children under 12 must be accompanied by an adult. Views from the tower are spectacular.

Trails near the New Lighthouse allow visitors to hike, birdwatch, and enjoy the wildflowers.

• GHOST STORY

The Ghost of George Parris. Caretakers George and Loraine Parris loved the old lighthouse and took pride in the grounds. They ran the small museum and gave tours to visitors. Loraine told anyone who listened that her husband was a trickster. His jokes only endeared him to her. George died in 1992 but wasn't ready to abandon his Old Presque Isle Lighthouse. When dusk descends, his ghost makes its presence known by flashing nonfunctioning lights across the moonlit waters.

One night shortly after her husband's death as Loraine drove toward the lighthouse grounds, she saw the tower flashing its beacon. That simply wasn't possible. She thought she had imagined it. She didn't share her story for fear of being labeled a batty old woman. The next day she climbed the tower steps to investigate. Everything was exactly as it should be. Still, in the following days, she repeatedly witnessed the same phenomenon.

Not long after Loraine's experience, others began reporting a glow coming from the tower. They thought perhaps the decommissioned lighthouse was back in operation.

It might be easy to dismiss these purported sightings as nonsense, but the Air National Guard, which flew missions over the area, and the Coast Guard, that investigated to make certain the light had not somehow been reactivated, both saw the light. Logic insisted there was no way it could be shining. Yet illogical as it was, it appeared that George couldn't tear himself away from his lighthouse, and he wanted everyone to know his spirit was still there.

36. ROGERS CITY

Rogers City, population 2,709 in 2020, is the county seat of Presque Isle County. It holds unchallenged title to being the site the world's largest open pit limestone quarry. Limestone is a raw material that formed when the region was covered by a shallow saltwater sea. Fossils have been found in the quarry from the Devonian period 325 million years ago. To put that in perspective, dinosaurs became extinct about 65 million years ago. Limestone is a component of chemicals, cement, and steel. In Michigan limestone is used in refining sugar beets, a major agricultural cash crop in the Thumb's farmland. (See Carmeuse Lime & Stone under Another Stop to Consider.)

Rogers City is one of the largest shipping ports on the Great Lakes, and the nautical theme of the city reflects its connection to the water. It was the home port of the freighter, *Carl D. Bradley* which sank in 1958. Most of the *Bradley*'s 33 victims were from Rogers City. The tragedy devastated the small city where everyone knew someone who died. (See Shipwrecks in this section.)

• MUSEUMS

Presque Isle County Historical Museum, 176 West Michigan Avenue, showcases local history. The museum is comprised of two buildings, the 1914 Bradley House and the Henry and Margaret Hoffman Annex across the street. The Annex was acquired in 2011.

The craftsman-style Bradley home was built in 1913 and 1914 by George Radke who earned his living as a local contractor He also operated the city's mill.

The Presque Isle County Historical Museum.
Courtesy of Bob Royce.

George died unexpectedly the year the house was completed. His widow sold the home to J. L. Marsters, general superintendent of the Michigan Limestone and Chemical Company, which had begun operations in 1912. It doesn't appear that Marsters moved into the house but rather sold it the next year to his boss, Carl D. Bradley. Before moving in, Bradley undertook extensive changes to the almost new structure. The renovations included a new kitchen, maids' quarters, second-floor dormers to increase the upstairs space, a two-car garage, and landscaping. With alterations completed, the three members of the Bradley family shared a seven-bedroom, four-bath home with three sun porches.

In 1920 U.S. Steel purchased a controlling interest in Michigan Lime, and made Mr. Bradley president of the company. In that capacity, he was in charge of the company's fleet, made up of three freighters—the *Calcite*, the *W. F. White*, and the *Carl D. Bradley*. The fleet operated as the Bradley Transportation Line. After Carl's death in 1928, Mrs. Bradley moved to New York. An interesting clause in her husband's employment contract required Michigan Limestone to purchase his property in Presque Isle County if he died or was fired. The clause was honored, and John G. Munson, Bradley's vice president, along with his family, occupied the home for the next decade.

In 1939 U.S. Steel transferred Munson to their headquarters in Pittsburgh, Pennsylvania. Eventually the home, still referred to as the Bradley home, had outlived its dwelling purpose. Michigan Limestone offered it to the county to use as a library. When the library outgrew the space in 1980, Michigan Limestone donated the historic building to the Presque Isle County Historical Museum which opened its doors at this location in 1981.

The museum's main house includes a General Store Room (originally a guest bedroom) that houses many items that would have been found in an early general store. There also is a Native American Room, a Millinery Room, and a room with pioneer tools.

Through its exhibit, *50 Years—Never Forgotten*, the museum pays tribute to the lives lost when the Steamer *Carl D. Bradley* went down.

The Henry and Margaret Hoffman Annex houses a number of additional exhibits, the museum's gift shop and bookstore featuring many local authors (See A Book with Ties to Rogers City), and genealogical records.

<<>>

Great Lakes Lore Maritime Museum, 367 North Third Street, tells the story of Rogers City's port activities and the seafarers of the Great Lakes. Like the County Historical Museum above, this small museum pays homage to the lives lost when the limestone carrier *Carl D. Bradley* sank in a Lake Michigan storm. The guides explain the artifacts and may share some of the personal stories of the men who perished in the greatest tragedy to ever hit Rogers City.

Great Lakes Maritime Museum. Courtesy of Bob Royce.

• BEACHES, PARKS, AND TRAILS

P.H. Hoeft State Park, 5001 US 23 North was one of 14 original Michigan state parks. The land was donated by lumber baron, Paul H. Hoeft, in 1922. The park has one mile of sandy shoreline and 301 acres on Lake Huron. Hiking trails meander through the forest and along the water. There is a campground with 142 sites, each equipped with an individual electric pole. The day-use area has picnic facilities and a new playscape with lots of room for children to frolic. There are large dunes similar to those on Lake Michigan. The camp store sells necessities and souvenirs. The park is open year-round.

<<>>

Lakeside Park on Lake Street is a smaller park with expansive water views. Amenities include a modern playground, band shell, benches for freighter watching, beach volleyball, and a pavilion with restrooms. Ice cream is available in the summer.

Lakeside Park.
Courtesy of Bob Royce.

<<>>

The Huron Sunrise Trail runs from downtown Rogers City to the 40-Mile Light. This is a paved bike path with some segments running along the Lake Huron shore and other sections snaking through the woods. A small portion of the trail is shared with vehicular traffic.

• ANOTHER STOP TO CONSIDER

Carmeuse Lime & Stone, 1035 Calcite Road. The site's stark eeriness may have you wondering if you've stepped through an invisible portal into another dimension. This is the world's largest open limestone quarry, and you can view mining and shipping operations from areas marked by viewing signs—Harbor View where you may see a freighter in the distance or Quarry View. Both are fenced and far enough from the action that you'll need binoculars.

The company's property covers 12½ square miles, is 4.1 miles long and 2½ miles wide, or a total of about 8,024 acres. Since the quarry opened, the most limestone shipped in one year was 16.6 million tons in 1953.

Charmeuse provided all of the foundation stone for the Mackinac Bridge.

The company consumes 810,000 gallons of fuel a year, fills between 200 and 275 ships with limestone, takes 10 hours per ship to fill, and has an electric bill of $225,000 a month.

• LIGHTHOUSE

40-Mile Point Lighthouse. Lake Huron is arguably the most dangerous of the five great lakes for ships. It is also the connecting link between the other lakes. In the late 1800s, hidden shoals and false bays claimed many vessels and their crews in the waters between Mackinaw City and Alpena. It was a dark area, meaning no lighthouses steered ships clear of the hazards. Recognizing the problem, the Federal Lighthouse Board approved construction plans for a new lighthouse seven miles north of Rogers City. Work began in 1896, and the light first blazed

40-Mile Point Lighthouse.
Courtesy of Bob Royce.

its beacon into the inky nighttime waters in April 1897. Its original Fresnel lens was equipped with six bullseye panels powered by a clockwork mechanism. The regulated rotation of the lens around the lamp emitted a white flash every ten seconds. Today, the tower house is automated, and its

Fourth Order Fresnel lens flashes three seconds on and three seconds off.

The total cost of the project including the lighthouse, tower, fog signal building, oil house, and barn was $25,000.

Men working on the lighthouse lived on the premises in the first building erected at the site. Known originally as the Bunkhouse, the building was repurposed twice after the lighthouse was completed. First it was used as a barn and then was converted to the current Bunkhouse Gift Shop.

Two apartments were attached to the 52-foot tower. Fireproof, metal doors gave access to the light tower from each apartment. The lighthouse keeper and his family lived in one apartment, and the assistant keeper and his family resided in the other. When the lighthouse was built, the area did not have a road to Rogers City. The keepers had to row there, but strong winds often made that impossible. Local farm families cured the problem by offering rides, picking up mail, and transporting the keepers and family members for errands, medical appointments, and shopping. In their spare time, the keepers returned the favor by helping the farmers with chores.

Every lighthouse has its story and its charm, but 40-Mile Point Lighthouse will likely become one of your favorites. It is more than a lighthouse. It is a lighthouse park and fascinating museum. It is open year-round for exterior viewing, but hopefully you'll arrive when the buildings are open. The 52-step climb up the winding iron stairs is worth the effort for the bird's-eye view of Huron's majesty.

Kitchen of the Lighthouse Dwelling. Courtesy of Bob Royce.

The keeper's quarters are furnished down to the kitchen staples, linens, and pictures. It feels almost like someone lives there—oh, wait, maybe you want to try that. If you have at least two weeks to spare, you can sign up to become a short-term keeper and park your RV on the property. You will enjoy lakeside living while you learn about lighthouses and meet interesting people.

The Pilot House of the *Calcite*, one of the first self-unloading vessels to sail the lakes, resides on the grounds and is open for your scrutiny. A volunteer is available to provide a wealth of maritime history.

Visitors can walk the beach and examine the skeletal remains of the *Joseph S. Fay*. On October 19, 1905, the *Fay* was downbound towing the schooner barge *D.P. Rhodes* when a savage storm bore down on her. The *Rhodes* survived when she was blown free of the *Fay*. The *Fay* broke up on a sandbar near the 40-Mile Point Lighthouse. All but the First Mate made it ashore. A portion of the *Fay*'s starboard side lies on the beach just west of the lighthouse. She is held steady in the sand by her rods and spikes.

Group tours are available by appointment. The one downside to this lovely lighthouse and park is that you may have to carefully pick your way through poison ivy.

● SHIPWRECK

The **Carl D. Bradley** was a self-unloading Great Lakes freighter that sank at 6:00 p.m. on November 18, 1958, during a gale-strength storm in northern Lake Michigan near Gull Island. While the ship went down in Lake Michigan, the *Bradley*'s ties were clearly to Rogers City. That dreadful night, 60-mile an hour winds and 40-foot angry waves claimed the lives of 33 of the 35 crewmen. Two men were found alive the next day.

Of the 33 lost, 23 were from Rogers City, and most of the others called nearby cities and villages home. It was said that you couldn't walk a street of Rogers City without passing the home of a widow.

The weather wasn't determined to be the single cause of the wreck. The *Bradley* was hampered by structural failure from the brittle steel used in her construction. (See Shipwrecks under Charlevoix in volume three, *Exploring Michigan's Sunset Coasts*, for additional details.)

The *Carl D. Bradley.* Courtesy of Pixabay Free Images.

• A Book with a Tie to Rogers City

In 2020 Presque Isle County Historical Museum Director and Curator, Mark Thompson, published an account of the bizarre murder of one of the county's founding fathers. ***Molitor: The Murder of a Northern Michigan King***, describes the investigation into the death of Albert Molitor, a powerful, but corrupt, political manipulater who plagued Alpena and Rogers City in their earlier years. A large number of complaints were lodged against Molitor, and he was widely despised. His murder in 1875 was not a huge surprise. Molitor's background and the circumstances of his death, however, are little short of outrageous. It was rumored that he was the illegitimate son of King Wilhelm I of the German state of Wurttemberg, and Molitor carried himself as though he were royalty. The book is available at the museum gift shop or online through the museum website.

37. Cheboygan

In 2020 the population of Cheboygan was 4,684. It is the county seat of Cheboygan County, and it sits at the point where the Cheboygan River meets Lake Huron. The precise origin of the name and its meaning is uncertain although Cheboygan was originally an Ojibwe settlement called *chabwegan*. *Chabwegan* or *Shabwegan* translates to "a place of ore."

In 1844 Jacob Sammons, a cooper from Fort Mackinac, chose the old Ojibwe campground for his cabin. Other settlers followed Sammons, and they began calling the area Duncan. In 1871 the village became known as Cheboygan. By 1876 Cheboygan looked forward to rail service coming to the village, but it took five years before the rails arrived. In 1889 Cheboygan became a city.

• Beaches, Parks, and Trails

Gordon Turner Park, at the end of Huron Street, features a large cattail marsh with a boardwalk and an observation tower for easy birdwatching. In spring and fall, you may spot a Brant or King Elder, in the fall it may be a Snowy Owl or Bald Eagle, and in the summer the gravel bars may host migrating birds. Open year-round, there are picnic facilities and restrooms in addition to hiking trails.

<<>>

Cheboygan State Park, 4490 Beach Road, provides year-round activities. There are cabins, campsites with electricity, restrooms, showers, bathing beach, and metal detection area. You can fish for largemouth bass and northern pike in Little Bill Elliot Creek which flows through the park. Rare wildflowers dot the trails.

The Cheboygan Opera House, 403 North Huron Street, is a Victorian building first constructed in 1877. It is a

Courtesy of Bob Royce.

multiple-use facility that houses the city hall, police headquarters, and a fire station as well as the theater. The acoustically-lauded theater occupies the second floor and provides seating capacity for 582. The Opera House is home to the Cheboygan Area Arts Council which promotes and encourages cultural arts and educational opportunities in the Northern Michigan Straits area.

After fire damage in 1888, the theater was rebuilt, and the layout of today's theater traces to that date. It includes an auditorium, stage, and dressing rooms—the latter on upper floors. The Opera House closed during the 60s, but like a Phoenix, rose to live again in 1984.

The Cheboygan Opera House has hosted Mary Pickford, Marie Dressler, William S. Hart, and Annie Oakley. While remaining a city treasure, the theater was at its height during the lumber boom of the late nineteenth and early twentieth centuries. It is one of the few municipally owned opera houses in the United States.

● LIGHTHOUSE

The **Cheboygan Crib Light**, Huron Street, marks the west pierhead of the mouth of the Cheboygan River as it connects with Lake Huron. This is a light, not a lighthouse. Beacons are navigational aids permanently attached to the earth's surface. They can be part of a lighthouse or a single independent structure located on land or a buoy in the water. The signal device is called a light, and it can be part of a house or a tower within the house. If connected to the house, it is a lighthouse. If there is no house, it is called a light. A light station is the light tower or lighthouse and all outbuildings. Light and lighthouse are often used interchangeably, and if you were to research the Cheboygan Crib Light, you would find it called a lighthouse although there is not now—and never has been—a keeper's house. There was for a while a sleeping space to use when needed.

The Crib Light was erected in 1884 on a timber crib in the water, just beyond the end of the pier. It first cast its beacon into the darkened waters that same year. It made ship entry into Cheboygan safer.

The light had to be manually illuminated daily by the lighthouse service that sent men rowing to the crib. When the light was automated, locals began calling the Crib Light the "Dummy" because it no longer needed human attention.

In the 1980s, the Coast Guard made plans to dynamite the light and replace it with a buoy, but the City fought to have the light relocated to the foot of the pier at Gordon Turner Park where it remains. Tours are available if you want to go inside.

- The Famous or Infamous with Ties to Cheboygan

George M. Humphrey, 55th United States Secretary of the Treasury under President Dwight D. Eisenhower, was born and raised in Cheboygan. Credited with being one of Eisenhower's most influential cabinet members, Eisenhower once quipped, "When George speaks, we all listen."

<<>>

Scott Sigler graduated from Cheboygan Area High School in 1988. He writes science fiction and horror and is well-known as a podcaster. His love of writing was encouraged by a father who favored monster films and a teacher-mother who supported his writing endeavors. Sigler wrote his first monster story, *Tentacles, Tentacles & More Tentacles*, at the age of eight. Facing difficulty getting his adult novels published, the creative author built hype and gathered an audience by podcasting.

38. Mackinaw City
39. Mackinac Island

According to state legal documents, the official name of Mackinaw City is The Village of Mackinaw City. No one seems bothered that the name includes the incongruous words city and village. The village population in 2020 was 875.

Artifacts confirm Native Americans in the Mackinaw City area at least 700 years before Europeans arrived. The Original People's presence goes back much further. Mackinac Island welcomed its first humans as early as 2,000 years ago when aboriginal inhabitants of the Woodland Period paddled canoes there to fish for trout, herring, whitefish, sturgeon, and pike. Fish were so abundant that the early inhabitants referred to the Island as "home of the fish."

The Anishinaabe-Ojibwe, believed Mackinac Island was a sacred place and the home of the Great Spirit Gitche Manitou. Its location in the center of the Great Lakes Waterway in Lake Huron, close to Lake Michigan and both the Upper and Lower Peninsulas, made the area a natural tribal gathering place. The first people believed that once the Europeans came to the area, Gitche Manitou abandoned the island to dwell in the Northern Lights.

Several questions surround the name Mackinaw/ Mackinac: Where did it come from? Does it end in a "c" or a "w?" And, how is it pronounced? The first question cannot be definitively answered, although there are at least two viable theories. The latter two questions are relatively easy.

According to one prevailing legend, Native Americans, noting the island's elliptical shape with a hump on one side, called it "place of the great turtle" which is said to translate to Michilimackinac. While visiting, you will hear references to the turtle story and see many turtle-themed books peer out from shelves at local book stores.

A second account suggests there is a different translation for the word Michilimackinac: *mish* means great, *inni* means connecting, *maki* means fault or crack, and *nong* means land or place. The Odawa and Ojibwe described it as a connecting place with a large or great fault. Over time the word Michilimackinac came to encompass the entire straits region, not just the island.

French settlers who came to the area in the late seventeenth century had at least fifty-five spellings for the name, but Michilimackinac became the accepted one. The difficult to pronounce name was shortened to the less tongue-twisting Mackinac. Later the British began spelling it Mackinaw as it was pronounced. The "c" at the end is silent, and the last syllable was always pronounced "aw" like in awe.

When the city founders named the city, they opted for the "aw" spelling to allow postal carriers to differentiate between the Island (which retained the "ac") and the occupants of the city. Both names, however, are still pronounced the same ("aw"). The bridge and the straits use the "ac" spelling.

In 1634 explorer Jean Nicolet was the first European to pass through the Straits of Mackinac, and in 1665 French Jesuit Priest, Claude Allouez, was the first missionary to travel there. It was 1671 when the second Jesuit priest, Father Jacques Marquette, established a mission for the Huron Native Americans at St. Ignace. It is believed he was the first European to settle in the area, and he is buried at his mission.

Around 1708 French soldiers constructed a strategic depot for the upper Great Lakes fur trade near present-day Mackinaw City. It became the headquarters for the fur trade and an important military post in the northwest.

Missionaries and fur traders occupy the same period in both Mackinaw City and Mackinac Island history. As the missionaries attempted to convert Native Americans, fur traders sought their assistance in trapping animals and selling lucrative furs. Ships with European goods set out for Mackinaw City and Mackinac Island where they were traded for prized beaver pelts, and the less valuable muskrat, fox, and otter furs.

The fort at Mackinaw City passed from French to British control in 1761 after the last battle of the French and Indian Wars. In 1763 the British Garrison at Old Mackinac, as the fort near Mackinaw City was called, was attacked by the Odawa and Ojibwe during Pontiac's Rebellion. These tribes chafed under British control. They staged a ball game outside the stockade to create a diversion and gain entrance to the post. They killed most of the British occupants.

During the American Revolution, the beleaguered British were threatened by American General George Rogers Clark. The British retreated to Mackinac Island where they could more easily protect their position. In 1781 the Native American chiefs in the area sold Mackinac Island to the British in an attempt to protect their interests in the Great Lakes fur trade. In 1783 the island and the straits became United States property according to the terms of the Treaty of Paris. However, they remained in British hands until 1794 when the U. S. took possession.

In the War of 1812, the British recaptured Mackinac Island and forced an American surrender after a surprise landing on the north side of the island allowed them to occupy the high ground of Fort Holmes. The island continued to be a battleground during the War of 1812, and it was the site of many casualties. The 1814 Treaty of Ghent returned the island to U.S. control.

After the war, Mackinac Island became a center of fur trade operations for John Jacob Astor's American Fur Company which merged the Mackinaw Fur Company and the Southwestern Fur Company.

The area's fur industry gave way to fishing which ushered in a new economic era. By the 1830s, fishing was the island's primary industry.

Today the tourist trade generates significant revenue for the area.

Mackinac Island was designated the country's second National Park in 1875. Yellowstone became a National Park three years earlier.

When Fort Mackinac was decommissioned in 1895, the land was given to the state, and it became Michigan's first state park, Mackinac Island State Park. Both the island and the city are places to reach out and embrace history.

In Mackinaw City you can sit in Alexander Henry Park and soak up a view of the Mighty Mac which opened to traffic on November 1, 1957. The initial idea for Mackinac Bridge construction was discussed nearly 75 years earlier in 1884. From then on, Michiganders never gave up the dream of a bridge to connect their two peninsulas. The bridge is five miles long and spans the shortest point between the Upper and Lower Peninsulas. Five men died during construction of the bridge, but contrary to myth, none are buried in the concrete supports.

• MUSEUMS AND HISTORICAL SITES

Colonial Michilimackinac, along the waterfront in downtown Mackinaw City, was built in 1715. A National Historic Landmark, the reconstructed fort and fur trading village, come alive with staff dressed in period costumes waiting to assist you and answer your questions. An audio tour describes early inhabitants of Michilimackinac. Watch the recreation of the British firing muskets and cannons or keep an eye out for French voyageurs arriving at the fort's water gate. Seasonal.

<<>>

Fort Mackinac and Mackinac Island. (See Beaches, Parks, and Trails in this section.)

<<>>

The Richard and Jane Manoogian Mackinac Art Museum, 7070 Main Street, Mackinaw City. The focus is on Mackinac related art and photography that paint a visual of the Mackinac story. You'll see everything from photographs to hand-beaded Native American garments.

The displays are presented in four long-term exhibits. The first-floor main gallery showcases works depicting views of Mackinac from the early nineteenth to the late twentieth century. Native American Art is featured in two smaller galleries on the second floor.

<<>>

Mackinac Bridge History Museum, 230 Main Street above Mama Mia's Pizzeria, Mackinaw City. This tiny museum is a special interest museum. If you have a passion for learning more about the bridge, you won't want to miss it. You can order a pizza and wander around upstairs until your food is ready. The space has the feel of a dedicated collector rather than a traditional museum, but it may be the way to spend a rainy afternoon.

<<>>

Icebreaker Mackinaw Maritime Museum, 131 South Huron, Mackinaw City. Known as the Queen of the Great Lakes, the Icebreaker *Mackinaw* was the largest icebreaker on the Great Lakes. She was built during World War II to keep shipping open into the winter months and meet war demands. The *Mackinaw* carried iron ore and copper from the Upper Peninsula to wartime factories in the lower Great Lakes. These raw materials made possible the building of tanks, airplanes, jeeps, and other machinery that helped the U.S. win the war. The icebreaker was decommissioned in 2006 and retired in her namesake village.

A self-guided tour will take you through the Mess Deck, Engine Room, Ward Room, Sick Bay, Bridge, and Captain's Quarters as you learn about the *Mackinaw*'s career. If ships are your thing, this may be your museum.

● BEACHES, PARKS, AND TRAILS

Alexander Henry Park, 518 North Huron Avenue at the foot of the Mackinac Bridge, Mackinaw City, offers wonderful views of the bridge, the Straits of Mackinac, and Mackinac Island. Named after a fur trader and entrepreneur of the late 1700s, Alexander Henry Park is located next to the historic Colonial Michilimackinac and is adjacent to Mackinaw Point Lighthouse. It provides more than 1700 feet of handicap accessible lakefront walkway.

<<>>

Historic Mill Creek Discovery Park, five minutes southeast of Mackinaw City on US 23, is a state park, nature preserve, and historic site run by Mackinac State Historic Parks. Given the importance of the lumber industry in Michigan's early development, this 1790s reconstructed sawmill is worth visiting. Woodworkers demonstrate traditional crafts. A naturalist conducts programs about the critters you are likely to encounter if you walk the 3½ mile forest trail.

The original sawmill at Mill Creek was built by Robert Campbell to supply lumber to the Straits of Mackinac and Mackinac Island and operated from about 1790 until 1839. In 1793 the mill contracted with Fort Mackinac to make repairs on the soldiers' barracks. In 1820 a millwright's house was built near the sawmill. The dwelling provided a place for the mill operator and family to live.

Both the mill and the house were abandoned and relegated to history when the fur trade in the area declined.

However, timbers cut by the mill survived in other buildings on Mackinac Island. Saw marks on these timbers provided a blueprint for reconstructing the mill's machinery to closely resemble the original. The park has nature trails, a portion of which are handicap accessible. Seasonal.

<<>>

Mackinac Island State Park. The entire island is a park, and within the park is the city of Mackinac Island with a 2020 population of 473. A smidgeon smaller than Mackinaw City, the island is a city, and the city is a village.

As a tourist destination, Mackinac Island is no stranger to accolades. *U.S. News* ranked it as Michigan's #1 tourist destination. *TravelZoo* did likewise. *Travel and Leisure* named it the World's Friendliest Island. *Trip Advisor* called it the #1 hottest U.S. Travel Destination.

To properly enjoy Mackinac Island, you need to step into the past. A local ordinance passed in 1898 prohibits the use of automobiles or other motorized vehicles on the island. Exceptions are made for golf carts (course use only), motorized wheelchairs, and in the winter, snowmobiles. For your stay on the Island, you will rely on bicycle, horseback, or your own two feet.

To set the mood, imagine that the Odawa-French fur trader, Magdelaine La Framboise's spirit greets your arrival to the island she loved.

"Welcome to 1816." The gentle breezes whisper Magdelaine's words. "I apologize that I can't spend more time with you. The Harbor is buzzing so you won't lack for company. I must paddle my son, Joseph, to Montreal for school, and I'm waist-deep in plans for my daughter Josette's wedding. It's the social event of our busy summer. Please make yourselves at home. I'm sure you'll find plenty to do. Enjoy your stay."

The Harbour View Inn, a current B&B was Magdelaine's home, its construction overseen by her son-in-law, Captain Benjamin Pierce, brother to President Franklin Pierce.

For however many days you can spare, you can hike and bike the island that was the center of the Great Lakes Fur Trade when the luxuriant beaver pelt reigned king. You will find it a perfect place to recharge. You will take home a chapter of our country's early years rather than just breathtaking mental snapshots and dirty laundry. A small duffle bag should hold everything you'll need for several days—blue jeans, T-shirts, and a light jacket that serves double duty—warmth if a chilly east wind blows in and to dress up jeans for casual dinners. Wear good walking shoes.

Turn off your iPad and cell phones unless you are using them to take pictures. Park your car and worries in Mackinaw City. A catamaran will speed you to Haldimand

Bay. For the short fifteen-minute ride, savor striking views of the Straits of Mackinac where Lake Huron and Lake Michigan kiss. There is no additional charge for the sprinkling of magic that surrounds you as you step ashore, two centuries back to a time when traders guided fur-filled birchbark canoes to the summer gathering known as *Rendezvous.*

Your illusion of time reversal is nurtured by the horse-drawn wagon that awaits you at the harbor. If you traveled light, you won't need it for luggage transport but might call on its services later for a ride past the Grand Hotel. The hotel, built in 1887, boasts the world's longest front porch for your strolling or people-watching pleasure.

Grand Hotel. Courtesy of Bob Royce.

As you saunter down the main street, the smell of fudge wafts from small shops to tempt the purchase of a sweet indulgence for later.

Main Street Mackinac Island. Courtesy of Bob Royce.

A half-block from the shops toward the east, you'll stand where Father Jacques Marquette built his humble mission on the enchanted island that the Ojibwe and Odawa called the birthplace of the world, a sacred spot where spirits danced, and tribes gathered for council meetings. Further east you come to the Harbour View Inn.

Even if you aren't staying there, you aren't likely to be chased out for stepping inside for a peek or to ask questions about its famous original owner.

Next to the check-in counter, you can run your fingers over the raw wood wall that remains from Magdelaine La Framboise's original cabin. This more lavish home, the current B&B, was erected around the original dwelling that Magdelaine's husband Joseph had built for them on the island. Wander into the sitting room and gaze out over the harbor. Imagine the wedding of Betsy Fisher, Magdelaine's grandniece, that took place there.

Reverend William Ferry boarded students with Magdelaine when he and his wife resided with her during the construction of their Protestant Mission church. Ferry noted in his journals the price he paid for rent and the fact that he was allowed to use as much of the root cellar as he wished. Magdelaine La Framboise was a devout Catholic who deeded the front corner of her property to Ste. Anne's Church in exchange for a promise that she would be buried under the altar. You can stop at Ste. Anne's and pay

Harbour View Inn. Courtesy of Bob Royce.

your respects to Magdelaine La Framboise whose final resting place is in the basement museum. Magdelaine, her daughter Josette, and infant grandson Benjamin Langdon Pierce were originally buried in the churchyard, but Magdelaine's remains were brought inside when her descendants requested that the church move her, more in keeping with the original promise. Take time to enjoy the small museum in the basement and maybe see if there's something in the gift shop that catches your attention.

Further exploration should take you along interior roads through the center of the island to Fort Holmes, built by the English when they defeated the Americans in 1814. Visit the Catholic Cemetery where the graves provide peaceful repose for many of Mackinac Island's early notables. At Point Lookout breathe in the spectacle of Lake Huron as the bright sunshine creates a diamond-studded overlay on the sapphire waters. Admire the seventy-five-foot limestone breccias rock mass called Sugar Loaf. Investigate Skull Cave, a tribal burial ground. During an attack on mainland Fort Michilimackinac in 1763, Alexander Henry was hidden there by his Ojibwe friend, Wawatum, to save the Englishman's life.

The trails of Mackinac Island are often overlooked by tourists who delight in hitting island hotspots. That's a shame since hiking may provide your most lasting memories. A number of shallow caves dot the island. No special equipment is needed to explore them. Skull Cave is located near Fort Holmes and Arch Rock. You can read its interesting story on an interpretive panel. There is an actual Crack in the Island adjacent to the Cave of the Woods. Exactly what it sounds like, there is a gouge—once thought to be bottomless—in the limestone. Its fissure is deep enough to stand in. Further meandering will take you to overlooks with views of the water. You'll pass scampering small animals, listen as songbirds serenade you, and enjoy vibrantly-colored wildflowers.

However limited your time, you must visit Fort Mackinac where history and dazzling scenery walk like lovers, hand in hand. The fort, built by the British to control the strategic Straits of Mackinac during the American Revolutionary War, perches on a steep limestone cliff above Lake Huron's vast expanse. It was in a small room at the fort that Magdelaine La Framboise' only daughter Josette died while giving birth to Magdelaine's first grandson. Within days, the infant, Benjamin Langdon Pierce, followed his mother into death.

Park staff, dressed in the period costumes of U.S. soldiers and Victorian ladies show you around Michigan's only Revolutionary War-era fort. Fourteen original buildings sit on a bluff overlooking the narrow streets of downtown. Things to see: Post Schoolhouse, North Blockhouse, Officers' Hill Quarters, West Blockhouse,

Officers' Stone Quarters, Post Hospital, Soldiers' Barracks, North Sally Port, Post Headquarters and Quartermasters' Storehouse, East Blockhouse, Commissary, Gun Platforms, South Sally Port, Guardhouse, and the Officers' Wooden Quarters.

On the Parade Ground, soldiers assemble for roll call and practice military drills. They carry out reenactments of marches, perform a cannon salute over the harbor, and offer weapons demonstrations. You can almost hear Captain Benjamin Pierce calling his men to attention.

Your tickets to Fort Mackinac provide entrance to several historic buildings along Market Street. Saunter from the McGulpin House and Beaumont Memorial at the east end of Market Street to the Benjamin Blacksmith Shop and the Biddle House at the west end. Along the way, stand on the spot where John Jacob Astor, the country's first millionaire, established the American Fur Company's northern headquarters in the 1820s. From this site millions of dollars' worth of furs, including those Magdelaine La Framboise and her engagés[4] collected during the wintering seasons, were sorted, baled, and shipped to the East Coast and Europe.

If time permits, before saying goodbye to the magical island, you can hike the 8.3-mile island perimeter on M-185, the only Michigan highway that bans motorized vehicles.

---

[4] French term for a fur trade employee who handled all aspects of canoe travel including maintaining the canoe, loading and unloading the cargo (furs), paddling, steering, portaging, setting up camp, and often acting as translator between Native Americans and English or French speaking owners of the business. The engagé was often indentured to the owner.

Maybe as you ready to depart, Madame LaFramboise' apparition will again drift close to bid you farewell. "I saved Arch Rock for last, so its beauty will travel fresh in your mind," she murmurs. "It was carved by the tears of She-who-walks-like-the-mist, when her father tied her to the rock to separate her from her lover."

Mackinac Island ties your heart to its rich history and extracts a promise that you will return.

The park is open seasonally, and you can catch ferries to its shores from either Mackinaw City or St. Ignace.

Arch Rock.
Courtesy of Bob Royce.

<<>>

Wawatam Park, 300 North Huron Avenue at East Jamet, next to Shepler's in Mackinaw City. A nice place to relax with a morning cup of coffee before setting your day's agenda. The park is equipped with restrooms, picnic tables, grills, and a playground. The park was named for Chief Wawatam, who on several occasions saved the life of Alexander Henry, a local fur trader and entrepreneur.

● OTHER STOPS TO CONSIDER

The Original Butterfly House and Insect World on Mackinac Island, 6750 McGulpin Street, behind Ste.

284

Anne's Church, a short walk from downtown. The first of its kind in Michigan, and the third oldest live butterfly exhibit in the United States, the facility has 1800 square feet of tropical garden filled with hundreds of live butterflies from four continents. In the greenhouse, butterflies flit around guests as the visitors wander along the path or relax on benches.

There is an education room where the chrysalises are displayed, and you can watch the butterflies emerge in real time. From the garden, you exit into Insect World with exotic beetles, walking sticks over a foot long, leaf insects, praying mantises, and other arthropod varieties. Insect World was added to the butterfly exhibit in 2006.

Entomologists on staff explain the life histories and biology of animals and butterflies.

• LIGHTHOUSES

McGulpin Point Lighthouse, 500 Headlands Road, Mackinaw City. The promontory known as McGulpin Point was first occupied by the Odawa. The exhibits provide today's visitors with an interesting history of the First People, as well as the French and English newcomers. You meet these early inhabitants through signage along the Discovery Trail. A self-guided cell phone tour provides additional detail about the property.

The first lighthouse in the Straits of Mackinac, McGulpin Point sits on a bluff with extraordinary views. For many years, it was a private residence, but when it was offered for sale, Emmet County purchased it, replaced the missing light, and began restoring it to a museum. The grounds are open anytime. The path to the water leads to a unique perspective of the bridge.

<<>>

Old Mackinac Point Lighthouse, 526 North Huron, Mackinaw City, located within the boundaries of

Michilimackinac State Park. The lighthouse is nicknamed the "Castle of the Straits." A climb of the 51 steps of the old metal spiral staircase affords you an extraordinary view. The beacon light has guided ships safely through the treacherous waters of the Straits of Mackinac since 1889. A self-guided tour lets you set your pace as you wander through restored quarters and exhibits including the original lens. You enter the lighthouse through the Fog Signal Building, a unique gift shop with a nautical theme.

The Straits of Mackinac Shipwreck Museum is part of the complex. Start your exploration by watching the movie, *Shipwrecks of the Straits*. The museum houses artifacts from shipwrecks, including a map of the straits with locations of wreckage sites and models of three wrecks showing what they looked like while in service, and dioramas showing how they look on the bottom of the lake.

<<>>

Spectacle Reef Light, located 11 miles east of the Straits of Mackinac at the northern end of Lake Huron. It is not open to the public but is worth mentioning because it is said to be the most spectacular engineering achievement in lighthouse construction on Lake Huron. It took four years to finish the project. The workers faced the challenges of building an underwater crib on a shoal during the short summer season.

In July 2005, the Spectacle Reef Light Station was listed on the National Register of Historic Places. It was one of five lighthouses chosen for a series of postage stamps, Lighthouses of the Great Lakes. The light and crib are closed to the public, and can only be viewed closely by a private boat. It is a long way from shore in dangerous and open water. The Great Lakes Light Keepers Association operates an annual Grand Light Tour conducted by Shepler's Mackinac Island Ferry that includes a pass-by of the Spectacle Reef Light.

• SHIPWRECKS

The **Straits of Mackinac Shipwreck Preserve** extends from Wilderness State Park to Cheboygan, including most of the South Channel, and extending to the northern edge of Mackinac Island. The preserve is a 148 square mile area divided into halves by the Mackinac Bridge. The Preserve includes the waters offshore from Mackinaw City and St. Ignace, as well as all or part of the shorelines of Bois Blanc Island, Mackinac Island, Round Island, and St. Helena Island.

Lighthouses in the area made ship travel safer but couldn't prevent all tragedies. The preserve contains 12 marked shipwrecks, with additional sites near shore, and others in nearby deeper waters. The cause of most of the wrecks can be attributed to crowded shipping lanes and natural elements such as fog, storms, and ice.

Ships known to have wrecked in the preserve are the *Cayuga, Cedarville, Eber Ward, Fred McBrier, Maitland, Minneapolis, Newell Eddy, Northwest, Rock Maze, Sandusky, M. Stalker, St. Andrew, Uganda, William H. Barnum,* and the *William Young.*

Divers also visit underwater formations of Mackinac Breccia near Mackinac Island.

• THE FAMOUS OR INFAMOUS WITH TIES TO MACKINAW CITY AND MACKINAC ISLAND

Magdelaine La Framboise, an Odawa-French fur trader who traded successfully against, and eventually worked for, John Jacob Astor, made her home on Mackinac Island. La Framboise was inducted posthumously into the Michigan Women's Hall of Fame in 1984 for her contributions to business. (See Mackinac Island Historic Park and Books with Ties to Mackinac Island.)

<<>>

Historical figures with ties to Mackinac Island and Mackinaw City are too numerous to mention. A trip to the area will acquaint you with them and their contributions to Michigan and U.S. history.

● Books and Movies with Ties to Mackinac Island

Books

Julie Royce's **Ardent Spirit** is based on the true story of Magdelaine La Framboise. The fictionalized biography provides background and historical context of the fur trade and Mackinac Island. Magdelaine Marcotte was born in 1780, the daughter of a French fur trader and granddaughter of powerful Odawa Chief Kewanoquat. She married French fur trader Joseph La Framboise. Plagued by challenges—murders, death of a young daughter and grandson, racial prejudice, sexual stereotypes, and her illiteracy—Magdelaine persevered, defied convention, and charted a bold course through the male-dominated Great Lakes fur trade.

<<>>

Dave Vizard, **A Grand Murder**. In the second book of the Nick Steele series, the body of Zeke Zimmer has crashed onto the iconic porch of the Grand Hotel on Mackinac Island. It appears that it came from the third-floor balcony of a room above. Nick Steele, a news reporter for the *Bay City Blade* had previously written an article about Zimmer's volunteerism and Steele is pulled into the search for the killer. The investigation takes the intrepid newsman around the mystical island, through Bay City neighborhoods, and even into a Flint auto assembly plant before he finds the key that unlocks the answers to the murder's questions.

<<>>

288

The Park Service publishes interesting books about the fort and the island. You can find them at the Visitors Center on Main Street.

<<>>

Movies

Somewhere in Time was filmed on the island in 1980. Its film crew had temporary dispensation of the no-auto rule. The movie starred Christopher Reeves and Jane Seymore in the story of a Chicago playwright who travels back in time to meet the actress whose portrait hangs in the Grand Hotel. Great movie to watch before visiting the Island.

• GHOST STORIES

Mackinac Island was voted *U.S. News and World Reports* #1 travel destination in Michigan. Accolades aren't unusual for the state park that provides a carless four square miles of island paradise that weren't always serene. The location is prime real estate for hauntings that would delight Stephen King should he decide to use it as the backdrop for one of his books. The island may be the most haunted place in Michigan. When the moon rises over murky waters, and you are tucked into the crisp, clean linens of your hotel bed, the sinister side of Mackinac Island gets free rein.

If you believe in ghosts, it is easy to understand why Mackinac Island lures spirits of the undead. It has endured more than its fair share of unnatural deaths. These prematurely departed include soldiers from Fort Mackinac, and where soldiers die, you can expect their ghosts to have a word or two to say. Ghosts of Native Americans haunt the local forests and trails. The Original People considered the island sacred and buried their tribal elders there. Graves of their loved ones were desecrated when newcomers took over the island. There are also graves of folks who succumbed to cholera, consumption, and smallpox, many of them children. To all of these restless spirits, you can add victims of murder, hanging, suicide, and seven women tried and drowned as witches. These are the stories.

<<>>

The Drowning Pool. Mackinac Island was a wild place in the 1700s. The French and the British fought bitterly for control of the fur trade. Native Americans were an integral part of their battles. Summer was a season when a huge influx of humanity paddled to Mackinac Island for rendezvous, the months to barter. Traders and trappers who had been holed up in the backwoods without creature comforts for several months, looked to do more than trade bundles of fur.

The island provided brothels and women peddling pleasure. Seven women were charged with enticing unsuspecting soldiers by means of witchcraft, a serious crime. To determine the women's guilt or innocence, bags of rocks were tied around their ankles, and their accusers pitched them into water. It was believed that if they sank, they were innocent. True witches could float above the water even with rocks weighing them down.

The test was carried out in a little inlet between Mission Point and downtown. The water of the chosen lagoon had a 20-foot drop-off. All seven women sank. They were declared innocent of the charges but haunt the waters to this day. Visitors report splashing, shadows, and dark figures floating above the surface where the women drowned.

<<>>

The Ghost of the Grand Hotel. The iconic, world-famous hotel opened in 1887. During construction, as the crew dug the foundation for the monstrous building, they uncovered many human skeletons. So many that at some point they couldn't—or didn't—keep track of them. It became easier to build over them . . . pretend they didn't exist. The remains were likely Native American chiefs who had been committed to this sacred spot for eternity. Not allowed to rest in peace in their hallowed graves, those chiefs have reason to be agitated.

Another example of suspicious activity connected to the hotel involved a maintenance man who awoke two days after being hospitalized. When asked what had happened to him, he said that he and another fellow were checking the stage at the Grand. He described an overwhelming presence of evil around them, and a feeling that an unnatural force watched their movements. Looking out over the stage, the man was horrorstruck to see two glowing red eyes peering at him from a dark shadow hovering above the stage floor. A black form barreled toward him and knocked him off his feet. That's the last thing he remembered until he awoke in the hospital. He swore he would never return to his job at the Grand.

Among other odd happenings at the hotel, staffers report seeing a man in a top hat frequenting the second-floor piano bar. The man disappears when people approach him, leaving only the smell of his cigar as evidence he had been there.

Another story tells of a woman clad in Victorian dress who roams the hotel's employee housing, sometimes even curling up next to workers as they lay asleep for the night.

<<>>

The Ghosts of Fort Mackinac. Battlegrounds attract unhappy spirits. No surprise there. In the 1814 Battle of Mackinac, 20 men lost their lives. Apparitions of soldiers limping to the Rifle Range have been reported. Limbs have been spotted in the hospital. Limbs that were cut from dying or injured soldiers? These extremities disappear before they can be examined. Furniture moves about the Officers' Quarters with no apparent assistance from humans.

More than a dozen children died from diseases at the fort. Their deaths were attributed to typhoid fever or smallpox. The voices of these little ones echo through the buildings. Maybe their spirits still reside in the officer's quarters. Toys are removed from shelves and scattered about as though played with by children who can't be seen.

<<>>

Mission Point's Ghost. The first building at Mission Point was constructed in the 1950s as a center for the Moral Re-Armament Movement. Moral Re-Armament (MRA) was an international moral and spiritual group that believed moral recovery must be attained before economic recovery was possible. Moral recovery created confidence and unity that favorably impacted every phase of life. The movement has been called a cult by some, but it caught on and was quite popular in the U.S. and Britain.

The MRA's first conference on the island was held at the Grand Hotel. The group had not yet constructed what became an extensive training center with a theater and a soundstage at Mission Point. The soundstage would be used for the production of motion pictures, including *The Crowning Experience*, *Voice of the Hurricane*, and *Decision at Midnight*.

In 1966 much of the Mission Point property was deeded by the MRA to Mackinac College, and a library and classrooms were added, but the college only operated for four years. The property changed hands a few times in the 80s before it became a resort late in the decade.

Of all of the hauntings on Mackinac Island, Mission Point is the most active. The resort's best-known ghost is Harvey, although that may not have been his real name. Harvey died in the late 60s, allegedly of a broken heart. He decided to end it all, made his way to the bluffs behind the resort (then leased to Mackinac College), raised the barrel of his gun to his head, and pulled the trigger. Unexplained circumstances surround this death. Harvey's body wasn't discovered for six months. We don't have the actual date of his death, so perhaps it was during the off-season when there are only a handful of locals around, and snow buries the small island.

That may be the least troublesome oddity about the death. Ruled a suicide, detractors point out that Harvey died from two bullets to the head. You've probably watched enough *Forensic File* or *CSI* episodes to know that a suicide victim can't pull the trigger twice, at least not if both wounds were inflicted to the head. Add that the gun was never found—a difficult feat for a dead man to hide a gun—and questions remain that might account for Harvey's dissatisfaction with the circumstances and investigation of his death. Harvey is often reported lingering around the Mission Point Theatre and grabbing young women in the dark.

Numerous other spirits are rumored to inhabit the resort—from ghosts of a young girl calling to her parents to Native American spirits wandering about the property to a woman heard singing old-time music near the theater. Mission Point Resort has so many stories that it captured the attention of SyFy's Ghost Hunters who filmed an episode on the property in 2010.

Note: This ends the stops included in Book One, *Exploring Michigan's Sunrise Coasts*. Book Two of this travel series, *Exploring Michigan's Upper Peninsula Coasts* picks up at this point, taking you across the Mackinac Bridge to St. Ignace and around the U.P.

Appendix One: A Taste of Michigan

Since restaurants aren't included in this guide, here is a sampling of recipes with connections to the Lakes Huron and Erie side of the state.

A HALF DOZEN DELICIOUS MICHIGAN RECIPES

<<>>

Covered buggies are common on side roads in parts of Michigan. They belong to our Amish neighbors.

Amish Potato Dinner Rolls

<u>Ingredients</u>

2 large eggs
1/3 cup sugar
2 tsp salt
6 Tbsp softened butter
1 cup unseasoned mashed potatoes, lightly packed
2½ tsp instant yeast or active dry yeast
¾ cup lukewarm water in which the potatoes were boiled
4¼ cups unbleached bread or all-purpose flour

<u>Directions</u>
1. To make the dough: Mix and knead all ingredients together by hand, mixer, or bread machine set on the dough cycle to make a smooth, soft dough.
2. Place the dough in a well-greased bowl, turn so both sides are oiled. Cover the bowl with plastic wrap or a damp towel and let the dough rise until it doubles in bulk, about 90 minutes.
3. Gently deflate the dough, and divide it into 16 large balls, or 24 smaller balls. Round each ball into a smooth roll. Place the rolls in a lightly greased 9"x13" baking dish. Cover the dish with lightly greased plastic wrap or damp towel and let the rolls rise for 1½ to 2 hours, until they're puffy. Toward the end of the rising time, preheat the oven to 350°F. Bake for 20-25 minutes until nicely browned.

Do you remember the Woolworth lunch counter's delicious baked apples with vanilla sauce? This is the original or a reasonable facsimile. A Michigander cook/baker found it in a drawer full of old recipes and shared it with the author.

Apple Dumplings with Vanilla Sauce

<u>Ingredients</u>
Cinnamon Sugar Mixture/Apples

¾ cup sugar
1½ tsp cinnamon
12 Cortland, Jonathon, or other firm baking apples, cored and peeled

Egg Wash

1 egg
2 Tbsp water
pinch of salt

Pastry

4 cups flour
2 tsp salt
2 cups shortening
2 Tbsp vinegar
2/3 cup milk

Vanilla Sauce (Can be doubled, if you want more sauce)

2 cups milk
1 cup sugar
pinch of salt
2 Tbsp cornstarch
1 egg
1 tsp vanilla extract

<u>Directions</u>
1. Core and peel apples.
Cinnamon Sugar Apple Mixture:
2. Combine cinnamon and sugar until well mixed.
Egg Wash:
3. Beat egg, water, and salt together with wire whisk until well blended.
Apple Dumpling Pastry:
4. Mix the flour and salt in a bowl. Cut in the shortening until the size of small peas. (Continued on next page.)

(Use your hands for better control). Add the vinegar to the milk and **immediately** combine with the flour mixture. Mix until the dough holds together. Roll out dough to a rectangle measuring 24 x 18 inches and cut into 12 (6 x 6) squares.

5. Put one peeled, cored apple in the center of each pastry square.

6. Pour 1/12 of cinnamon sugar mixture into the cored-out center of each apple. (About 2 Tbsp each).

7. Join the four corners of the square together and seal by pressing with your fingers. Brush with egg wash.

8. Place on a greased sheet pan with the folded corners side up.

9. Bake in a preheated 450-degree oven for 15 minutes. Reduce the heat to 400 degrees and continue to bake an additional 30 minutes or until apples are tender. (To avoid breaking the crust, use a bamboo skewer to check the apples for doneness. They should be easy to pierce.)

Vanilla Sauce:

10. While apples are baking, make sauce. Bring milk to a boil in a large saucepan. (Volume will increase during cooking so use a pan that is twice the size you think you need).

11. Combine the sugar, salt, cornstarch, and egg until well mixed.

12. Remove milk from the stove and add the sugar mixture stirring with a wire whisk until completely blended. Return to medium heat and boil for 5 minutes stirring constantly.

13. Remove from heat. Stir in vanilla. Serve warm over apple dumplings. If you want a generous amount of sauce, double the ingredients.

Apple Dumpling and Vanilla Sauce.
Courtesy of Pixabay Free Images.

Asparagus Roll-Ups

<u>Ingredients</u>
12 slices of white bread, crust removed
8 slices bacon, cooked, drained, and crumbled
24 thin fresh asparagus spears, half cooked
¼ cup butter, melted
¼ cup freshly grated parmesan cheese
8 oz tub of cream cheese with chives

<u>Directions</u>
1. Flatten bread with rolling pin.
2. Combine cream cheese and bacon. Spread on bread and cover up to the edges. Place 2 asparagus spears on each slice of bread and roll tightly. Place seam-side down on greased cookie sheet.
3. Mix parmesan cheese with butter and brush tops of asparagus rolls. Bake at 400 degrees for 12 minutes.

Note
This recipe is a bit labor intensive, but it's always a hit. You can make the asparagus roll ups and freeze them so all you have to do is brush with the butter/cheese mixture and bake. If you freeze these roll-ups, put wax paper between layers.
Don't stack the rolls too tightly together, or they'll stick when you thaw them.

Tip
To make perfect half cooked asparagus, place trimmed and cleaned asparagus spears in glass dish with a lid, such as Pyrex. Sprinkle with salt. Cover the spears with boiling water and immediately cover with the lid. Let the asparagus sit in the boiling water until the water is no longer hot. The asparagus will be perfectly cooked with the right amount of crunch.

According to the Detroit Historical Society, the first coney dogs were served by a Greek immigrant named Gust Keros in 1917.

Detroit-Style Coney Dogs

<u>Ingredients</u>

1 pound ground beef
1 cup diced white onion
2 cloves garlic, minced
1½ Tbsp chili powder
1½ tsp kosher salt or to taste
1 tsp ground cumin
¾ tsp paprika
½ tsp smoked paprika
½ tsp onion powder
½ tsp garlic powder
½ tsp freshly ground black pepper
½ tsp sugar
dash of cayenne pepper
1 (15 ounce) can tomato puree
4 Tbsp Dijon mustard
8 hot dogs, preferably Koegel
1 bottle Michigan or other beer
1 package hot dog buns
yellow mustard and finely chopped onion for serving

<u>Directions</u>

1. Place the ground beef, onion, and garlic into a medium pan. Cook over medium heat, using a wooden spoon to break the meat into very small crumbles. When the meat is cooked (do not drain the fat) add the spices, sugar, tomato puree, and Dijon mustard and stir to combine. Reduce the heat to low, cover and simmer for 30 minutes stirring occasionally.

2. Then uncover, stir, and simmer for an additional 10 minutes to thicken the chili.

3. Place hotdogs in pot and pour beer over them. Cover tightly and cook until warmed through. Serve the hot dogs in warm hotdog buns and top with desired amount of chili, yellow mustard, and minced white onion.

Any recipe with Vernors in its name has to be a Michigan recipe. This recipe is as good as it is simple. By the way, we are lucky to have Vernors. Its creation was an accident. James Vernors was experimenting with the new drink when he got called away to fight in the Civil War. He returned four years later, and the drink he'd forgotten about had aged in an oak barrel to a perfect gingery taste.

Vernors Ginger Baked Beans

<u>Ingredients</u>

6 pieces thick-sliced bacon
1 large can (52 or 55 ounce) pork & beans
1 large onion, chopped
1 medium green bell pepper, chopped
1 large tomato, finely chopped
1 cup brown sugar
1 cup Vernors

<u>Directions</u>
1. Cook, drain, and cut the bacon into ½ inch pieces. Sauté onions and green pepper in bacon grease until slightly tender.
2. In large-holed colander, drain most of the liquid from pork and beans. Pour beans into baking dish and add onion, green pepper, and tomato. Mix gently.
3. In small bowl, combine brown sugar and Vernors and stir until sugar dissolves. Pour evenly over bean mixture and bake at 350 degrees about 35 minutes. Makes 6 to 8 servings.

Vernors Baked Beans.
Courtesy of Pixabay Free Images.

James Vernors, a Detroit Pharmacist, created his spicy ginger beverage in 1866 and sold it at his soda fountain on Woodward Avenue. It is the oldest surviving ginger soda sold in the United States. It is also the oldest soft drink in the country. There were many other drinks available including what would become Coca Cola, but all of these contained alcohol. Vernors didn't. That's why it was called a soft drink.

Spicy Vernors Cake

Vernors Cake. Courtesy of Pixabay Free Images.

<u>Ingredients</u>

1 cup unsalted butter
1½ cups brown sugar, firmly packed
1 cup white sugar
4 large eggs
2 tsp pure vanilla extract
1 cup Vernors ginger ale
½ tsp kosher salt
(Recipe continued on next page.)

2½ tsp baking powder
1 tsp rum extract
½ tsp baking soda
1 Tbsp cinnamon
½ tsp ginger
½ tsp freshly grated nutmeg
½ tsp cloves
3 cups all-purpose flour
confectioners' sugar for dusting and whipped cream if desired

<u>Directions</u>

1. Preheat oven to 350 degrees. Lightly grease a 9x13 inch pan or a 10-inch tube or Bundt pan.
2. In a large bowl, cream butter and sugars. Blend in eggs, vanilla, and rum extract. Add Vernors and mix.
3. In another large bowl, mix the dry ingredients. Add to the creamed mixture and mix well.
4. Spoon batter into prepared pan. Bake until the cake springs back when lightly pressed (45 minutes for sheet pan and 60 minutes for the tube or Bundt pan).
5. Cool for 5 minutes before removing from pan. Cool thoroughly on a rack. Dust with confectioners' sugar or serve pieces with a dollop of whipped cream.

Appendix Two: Worthwhile Trips Inland

Frankenmuth. Settled by German Immigrants as a Lutheran community, the town has grown and in 2020 boasted a population of 5,777. It is one of the few small inland towns that saw a population increase after 2010.

Frankenmuth claims that Bronner's Christmas Wonderland is the largest Christmas Store in the world. Aisles display more than 6,000 ornaments and 400 nativity scenes, along with miles of Christmas trees. It's enough to make you imagine a white Christmas in the middle of a muggy July rain.

Bronner's Christmas Wonderland.
Courtesy of Pixabay Free Images.

Frankenmuth is also known for its chicken dinners and after visitors wander the small town or collect Christmas decorations, they make time for a homestyle dinner—Frankenmuth-style.

<<>>

The University of Michigan. The rivalry between Michigan State and the University of Michigan is legendary, but each university is a worthwhile destination.

Located in Ann Arbor, the University of Michigan's attractions include the Museum of Natural History, the Museum of Art, the Ann Arbor Hands-on Museum, the Kelsey Museum of Archaeology, Sindecuse Museum of Dentistry, Nichols Arboretum, the Wolverine Stadium—one of the country's most classic and recognizable football stadiums—an arboretum, and State Street for books, coffee shops, and other shopping.

<<>>

Michigan State University is located in East Lansing, Michigan State University's attractions include the Michigan State Natural History Museum, the Beaumont Tower Carrilon, the W. J. Beal Botanical Gardens, Eli and Edythe Broad Art Museum, the Dairy Complex, and the Abrams Planetarium.

Beaumont Tower.
Courtesy of Wikipedia Commons Public Domain.

305

310

Acknowledgements

My first thank you is to my grandson, Noah Elitzur, for letting his hands be my map of Michigan. (See page iv of this book.)

Next, thank you to my long-suffering husband for being my chauffeur, tech and cover guy, and sounding board.

Working on these travel books gave me a special appreciation for the generosity of strangers. Along the way, some of those strangers became friends. Gary Martin permitted me to use his incomparable photos. The cover of book one features the *Edwin H. Gott* crossing under the Mackinac Bridge. Known primarily for his lighthouse photographs, Gary's image of Big Red enhances the front cover of book three. Visit www.coastalbeacons.com to see more examples of his amazing work. Tim Trombley gave me permission to use his gorgeous photograph of Spray Falls on the front cover of book two. To see more of Tim's photos, check his website, www.greatlakesphotography.net.

For their many kindnesses, I thank the business owners, museum staff, chambers of commerce, historical societies, librarians, and residents along the Michigan Waterways. They shared their time and stories.

In no particular order, I am indebted to Susan and Joe Jurkiewicz, Linda Cutler, Margie Lampel, Vee Byrum, Neva Hodges, Lani Longshore, Julie Rosas, Gretchen Goehmann, Diane Herron, Jordan Bernal, Maureen Scully, Sheila Bali, George Cramer, and especially Violet Moore. She is the Chicago Manual of Style expert extraordinaire. She is also a walking encyclopedia of useful information for any writing endeavor.

I appreciate the kind words of Jennifer Granholm, Jessie Voigts, Julaina Kleist-Corwin, Paula Chinick, and Kathi Hyatt.

Without the patience and creative input of Nina Rosas, these books would remain coverless.

And to those who offered a kind word, encouragement, or a suggestion, if you don't see your name here, I apologize and assure you that I feel extreme gratitude to each of you.

About the Author

Julie Albrecht Royce was born in Lexington and raised in the small town of Sandusky in Michigan's Thumb. After retiring as a Michigan First Assistant Attorney General, she turned to her love of writing and authored two travel books: *Traveling Michigan's Thumb* and *Traveling Michigan's Sunset Coast*.

She has written two novels, *PILZ*, a crime thriller, and *Ardent Spirit*, the fictionalized biography of Magdelaine La Framboise, an Odawa-French fur trader born in the Michigan Territory in 1780.

Ms. Royce has written magazine articles, has been included in several anthologies, and has had stories published in the *California Writers Club Literary Review*. In her three-book travel series, (*Exploring Michigan's Sunrise Coasts*, *Exploring Michigan's Upper Peninsula Coasts*, and *Exploring Michigan's Sunset Coasts*), she comes full circle back to her love of Michigan and the Great Lakes.

www.ingramcontent.com/pod-product-compliance
Lightning Source LLC
Chambersburg PA
CBHW071451140726
47997CB00005B/1676